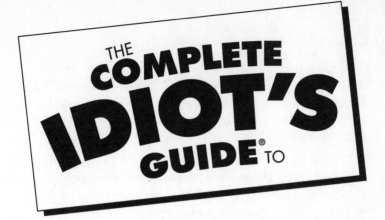

Coffee and Tea

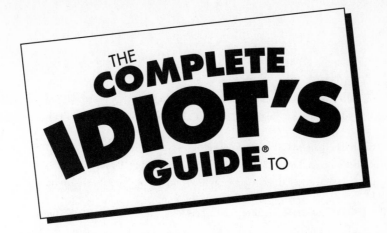

Coffee and Tea

by Travis Arndorfer and Kristine Hansen

ALPHA

A member of Penguin Group (USA) Inc.

ALPHA BOOKS

Published by the Penguin Group

Penguin Group (USA) Inc., 375 Hudson Street, New York, New York 10014, U.S.A.

Penguin Group (Canada), 10 Alcorn Avenue, Toronto, Ontario, Canada M4V 3B2 (a division of Pearson Penguin Canada Inc.)

Penguin Books Ltd., 80 Strand, London WC2R 0RL, England

Penguin Ireland, 25 St Stephen's Green, Dublin 2, Ireland (a division of Penguin Books Ltd.)

Penguin Group (Australia), 250 Camberwell Road, Camberwell, Victoria 3124, Australia (a division of Pearson Australia Group Pty. Ltd.)

Penguin Books India Pvt. Ltd., 11 Community Centre, Panchsheel Park, New Delhi—110 017, India

Penguin Group (NZ), cnr Airborne and Rosedale Roads, Albany, Auckland 1310, New Zealand (a division of Pearson New Zealand Ltd.)

Penguin Books (South Africa) (Pty.) Ltd., 24 Sturdee Avenue, Rosebank, Johannesburg 2196, South Africa

Penguin Books Ltd., Registered Offices: 80 Strand, London WC2R 0RL, England

International Standard Book Number: 1-59257-544-7
Library of Congress Catalog Card Number: 2006924290

08 07 06   8 7 6 5 4 3 2 1

Interpretation of the printing code: The rightmost number of the first series of numbers is the year of the book's printing; the rightmost number of the second series of numbers is the number of the book's printing. For example, a printing code of 06-1 shows that the first printing occurred in 2006.

Printed in the United States of America

Note: This publication contains the opinions and ideas of its authors. It is intended to provide helpful and informative material on the subject matter covered. It is sold with the understanding that the authors and publisher are not engaged in rendering professional services in the book. If the reader requires personal assistance or advice, a competent professional should be consulted.

The authors and publisher specifically disclaim any responsibility for any liability, loss, or risk, personal or otherwise, which is incurred as a consequence, directly or indirectly, of the use and application of any of the contents of this book.

Most Alpha books are available at special quantity discounts for bulk purchases for sales promotions, premiums, fundraising, or educational use. Special books, or book excerpts, can also be created to fit specific needs.

For details, write: Special Markets, Alpha Books, 375 Hudson Street, New York, NY 10014.

Publisher: *Marie Butler-Knight*
Editorial Director: *Mike Sanders*
Managing Editor: *Billy Fields*
Acquisitions Editor: *Michele Wells*
Senior Development Editor: *Christy Wagner*
Senior Production Editor: *Janette Lynn*
Copy Editor: *Amy Borrelli*

Illustrator: *Mike Davis*
Cover Designer: *Bill Thomas*
Book Designers: *Kurt Owens, Trina Wurst*
Indexer: *Heather McNeill*
Layout: *Chad Dressler, Brian Massey*
Proofreaders: *Kayla Dugger, Mary Hunt*

Contents at a Glance

Contents

Foreword

As a pastry chef and restaurateur, pairing beverages is one of the integral parts to creating a stellar meal. Coffee and tea are my brushes and paints to create the perfect experience of hot liquid with food, desserts, or bakery items—good by themselves but made more than twice as good when together.

One is a bean, one a leaf, and—depending on what happens to it from growth to harvest to making it onto your table—the flavors are varied enough for you to have a different one each day of the year. I love contemplating that idea, that one foodstuff, one single ingredient, can have so many profiles depending on how it's roasted, whether it was dried in the sun, how fine it is ground, whether it's withered and allowed to ferment, and so on. And then I want to know more. So I think this book was written for me.

Every morning, before I want to see anyone or do anything, I want a cup of tea. It's my first waking thought. It's the thing that lures me to the kitchen, ill dressed. It restores me, revives me, comforts me, and teases me to wake up, and at night it's the thing that taunts me to stay awake a little longer, if only to write this praise of it. It's one of the few things I not only want but need in life. I'm smitten with the ritual of making tea, whether it's a hand-picked first-flush loose-leaf Darjeeling or extra-strong black from a bag for my simple life-saving morning cup. A cup seems to always be next to me whether I need it or not. I even travel with my tea. And see how it's my tea, like it's a pet or a family member, something I wouldn't want to live without.

Coffee is tea's twin, having all the same attributes but from a different plant. We have an old French hand-crank coffee grinder to pulverize our beans without overgrinding them. We all take our turn leaning on the handle to push the crank around, then peeking in the drawer to see if there are enough precious grounds yet to brew that perfect cup of coffee for my husband. So yes, we have a mixed marriage where I'm a tea drinker and he has coffee … and it works, beautifully actually.

As a tea lover and a pastry chef who's intensely interested in giving the best experience possible when it comes to matters of the table, *The Complete Idiot's Guide to Coffee and Tea* is a must read to heighten awareness and enjoyment—your friends will thank you, too, for reading it. Everyone benefits!

Gale Gand
Executive pastry chef and partner of Tru, Gale's Coffee Bar, and Osteria di Tramonto
Host of Food Network's Sweet Dreams
Author of *Chocolate and Vanilla*

Introduction

You're a lover of coffee, tea, or both. It's your favorite beverage, you can't get enough of it, and maybe your friends and family chide you for being a coffee or tea geek. (No shame there!)

But maybe you want to take it up a notch, further fuel your passion, and become a well-versed consumer. That's where we can help. Armed with the knowledge in this book—and the essential beans and leaves—the cups you brew will be examples of craftsmanship, because you'll know how to ferret out all the bad information and products cluttering the marketplace and focus your sights on only the best techniques.

This book is designed to help you set up a mini-café in your kitchen, a place you can always turn to for a good cup of coffee, a comforting cup of tea, or a shot of bold espresso. Whether it's appreciating the subtle differences among white teas or discussing the impact processing has on coffee's flavor, this book helps prepare you for the exciting (and tasty) exploration of the world of coffee and tea.

So grab a cup of coffee or tea, relax, and begin the journey to being a connoisseur by turning the page. We'll be right there with you.

How to Use This Book

This book is divided into five parts:

Part 1, "Coffee: The Other Black Gold," gives you a background in coffee, including a thorough look at how coffee is grown and prepared for export. Armed with this knowledge, you'll understand how different kinds of treatment during preparation can affect coffee's flavor in the cup.

Part 2, "Capturing Coffee's Flavor," guides you through the roasting process, where coffee's flavor is developed, and then provides a detailed examination of how that flavor is best coaxed out of the beans. When you've finished this part, you'll know the ins and outs of preparing awesome coffee and probably even have an idea or two about your own special blend.

Part 3, "The Espresso Family: Cappuccino, Latte, Americano, and More," takes you through the sometimes-intimidating world of espresso, step by step. Consider this your express guide to the world of espresso, including ordering and preparing the diverse array of espresso-based drinks (lattes, cappuccinos, and mochas) on the typical coffeehouse menu. Making these drinks at home takes the right mix of equipment and know-how, so we explore just what it takes to make great espresso drinks at home.

And thanks to some of the world's best baristi (think bartenders, but behind an espresso machine), we also share some unique and delicious drink recipes.

Part 4, "Tea: From Crop to Cup," walks you through the rich world of tea. Steeped in centuries of tradition and marked by its sheer diversity, the array and variety of tea can make your head spin at times. No worries though—we explain the differences among teas, some common tea customs and, of course, how to get the most flavor from every leaf.

Part 5, "Coffee and Tea's Holistic Side," looks at the bigger picture surrounding coffee and tea. First, we discuss social and environmental movements related to coffee and tea (like certified organic and fair trade) and then we sort through some of the relevant current health information.

Extras

Along the way, we'll periodically highlight tips, terms, and other things helpful to keep in mind:

Hot Water

These notes alert to potential trouble or hazards. It might be ways to avoid overpaying for something or a risk of which you should be aware.

Buzz Words

There are a number of confusing terms in the worlds of coffee and tea. Anytime we introduce a word that's likely to be unfamiliar or is key to the industry, we'll highlight and explain it in these boxes. Consider it your jargon cheat sheet.

Cuppa Wisdom

To keep things in perspective and for a change of pace, we occasionally share a quote, proverb, or other nugget of wisdom in these boxes.

Field Notes

When we have bits of advice or time-saving tips, we spotlight them in these boxes.

Acknowledgments

We would like to thank all our friends, mentors, and industry colleagues who have shared our excitement for coffee and tea and helped us along our journey. We also appreciate all the support family and friends gave us while we worked on this project.

A special thank you goes out to Travis's parents for all their thoughtful support. As the project progressed, Travis's mother, Sharon, became the first-line proofreader, and we are both indebted to her for the insights and suggestions she offered.

Kristine's circle of writers—especially Jeanette, Lisa, and Damon—were good sounding boards for the labor that goes into a project such as this. In appreciation, I promise to make you a cup of coffee, tea, or espresso—your choice. And for my immediate family, thanks for being the cheerleaders you are and always have been.

Books are collaborative projects, and we are grateful to have worked with a patient, helpful team. As you read through the book, you'll come onto a number of original sketches done for us by Mike Davis. Mike has a knack for finding the "gag" in a situation, and his drawings bring a wonderful levity to this book.

In Chapter 13, we have the pleasure of sharing several recipes created by top baristi from around the world. We are honored and grateful that these champions (literally— check out Chapter 14 for details), some working through translators, shared their creations with us.

Trademarks

All terms mentioned in this book that are known to be or are suspected of being trademarks or service marks have been appropriately capitalized. Alpha Books and Penguin Group (USA) Inc. cannot attest to the accuracy of this information. Use of a term in this book should not be regarded as affecting the validity of any trademark or service mark.

Part 1

Coffee: The Other Black Gold

Part 1 is dedicated to the fine world of specialty coffee. We give you some background and history and then jump right in by showing you how growing and processing conditions impact the coffee in your cup. Finally, join us on a tour of the coffee-producing world as it relates to specialty beans. When you've completed Part 1, you'll understand how different processing methods affect coffee's flavor and be able to reliably predict how a coffee will taste based on its growing and processing conditions.

Bean Basics

In This Chapter

- A look at specialty coffee
- The discovery of the coffee plant
- Coffee's journey: from Arabia to Africa, then Europe and the United States
- Where and how we enjoy our brew today
- The Bean Belt

Coffee. So many of us drink it—so many of us need it to wake up in the morning and have enough go-power to get through the day. From hitting a café on the way to work to brewing a pot at the office, coffee is a staple in many people's days. But how much do you know about coffee other than where to get what you like?

You might be surprised to hear that, in many ways, coffee is as complex as wine and has more flavor compounds. Coffee grows in regions throughout the world—from Hawaii to Honduras—just like the grapes grown for wine do. Variances in soil and the microclimates of each crop—not to mention the *roasting*, grinding, and brewing processes later on—help produce each blend's different taste. Ask a coffee connoisseur why a Costa

Rican tastes unlike a Sumatra, and you're likely to get a mouthful of intelligent-sounding words. For a moment, you might think you're talking to a wine lover at a wine tasting and engaging in a conversation comparing a merlot and a cabernet sauvignon.

Over time, and throughout many centuries, coffee has evolved into a common beverage linking economic and social classes. So whether it's a coffee break for factory workers or an afternoon *café noir* in Paris, it's essentially the same thing: coffee.

> **Buzz Words**
>
> **Roasting** is a process wherein raw, green coffee beans are heated to an internal bean temperature of 375° to 450°F, which prepares them for traditional brewing. **Café noir** (pronounced *ca-fey no-our*) means "black coffee" in French. When ordered at even a midlevel restaurant or café in France, it arrives with a carafe of water, a dark-chocolate square, and a sugar cube—quite the gourmet touch!

While drinking coffee became more popular in social circles, so did the availability of whole beans or ground coffee for home consumption. Due to lower coffee prices, along with a variety of machines for brewing, grinding, and roasting, today it's possible to prepare coffee at home that suits your taste buds.

Just like wine, acquiring a good drink is as much about place of origin as it is process of preparation. For the budding coffee connoisseur, this may mean hours of tinkering with methods and coffee varieties, which can actually be great fun. Before diving into the world of coffee in the following pages—where you learn to roast, grind, brew, and pour—it's important to distinguish between specialty and nonspecialty coffee.

Oh, They're So Special(ty)!

There are 66 known species of the *Coffea* genus, but only 2 are commercially relevant: *Coffea arabica* (*ah-RAB-ica*) and *Coffea canephora*, also known as robusta (*roo-BOOsta*). Most of the specialty coffee is arabica. These beans account for 75 percent of the world's coffee production.

A lower grade of coffee, robusta beans are typically included in canned coffee blends because they're cheaper. These beans contain twice the caffeine as arabica, and the plants are just like they sound: robust. Because of their ability to create a better *crema* (the golden-red top of an espresso beverage) than arabica beans, robusta beans are often used in espresso blends.

Specialty coffee reflects quality, craftsmanship, and expertise on the part of those involved in its production. For instance, instead of mass harvesting the cherries (the red, oval-shaped berries the coffee beans grow inside of; see Chapter 2) in a coffee plant, they are handpicked and selected with care. Roughly 5 percent of coffee sold worldwide is specialty coffee, making it an $8 billion business.

Buzz Words

Coffea arabica is also *qahwa al-bon* in Arabic, or "wine of the bean." **Crema** (pronounced *cremm-a*) is the crown on an espresso. It's a bit thicker than the rest of the beverage and has a golden-red hue.

The term *specialty coffee* was coined in 1978 when Erna Knutsen, an importer with Knutsen Coffee Ltd., used it in a speech she gave in Montreuil, France, to delegates at an international coffee conference. Soon thereafter it became a part of conversations about coffee. It also set forth a clear distinction between gourmet and all other coffees.

Field Notes

Two trade associations keep tabs on legislation, consumer habits, and other coffee-related topics, as well as provide a forum for discussion within the industry. The Specialty Coffee Association of America, established in 1982, hosts an annual meeting each year for its members; in 2004, 10,000 attended, making this the largest convergence of coffee professionals to date. The Specialty Coffee Association of Europe is another trade group focused on specialty coffee. Using the term *specialty coffee* has given these groups, and the coffee industry as a whole, a marketing edge when speaking to consumers.

There's another prominent coffee-industry organization, the National Coffee Association of U.S.A. Inc., although its core interest is not specialty coffee. However, it does follow the topic closely.

This book focuses on specialty coffee, as those are the types of beans home brewers and café managers are inclined to purchase in pursuit of the best coffee.

The History of Coffee

How the practice of drinking coffee came to be a part of our culture involves more than advances in agriculture. By word of mouth, news of the beverage spread from Arabia to Africa, then to Europe, America, and Latin America. Imagine a simple, black brew and its slow travel from continent to continent until the nineteenth century, when many nations were at once familiar with it and had learned to weave a daily cup into their lifestyle.

Dancing Goats and Kaldi's Coffee Discovery

According to legend, the coffee plant was first discovered in Ethiopia. (Yes, it would be more interesting to report that it was discovered in a French bistro or a cobblestone alley in Trieste, Italy, but this is how it was.) A young goat herder named Kaldi in the horn of Africa (or perhaps Yemen or Ethiopia, as the legend's tale varies) made a quick decision one day to let his goats run a bit wild and find their own way back to base camp while he took a different route.

When Kaldi finally met up with his goats, they were kicking their little legs around—some might say they were dancing. It wasn't until later that he found the red berries they had eaten from a hillside shrub. Curious, Kaldi plucked a few berries for himself, hoping he, too, might get a sudden burst of energy. He chewed the leaves and cherries, marveling at the boost they gave him. (Too bad for him the practice of boiling water wasn't learned until after 1000 C.E.)

Cuppa Wisdom

It fortifies the members, it cleans the skin and dries up the humidities that are under it, and gives an excellent smell to all the body.

—Avicenna, an Islamic physician, referring to coffee

A leader of a nearby monastery couldn't help but notice the new vivacity in Kaldi and his goats and asked why their sluggish nature had improved. Soon he, too, was eating the cherries.

Much of Arabia quickly caught onto the coffee plants, and soon, after much toying with its preparation, coffeehouses were serving as centers of political activity—although they were later suppressed because they were primarily centers of political activity that the government did not always support. Over the next few decades, coffeehouses were banned several times. A solution was reached when it was decided that coffeehouses—as well as coffee—should be taxed. Who would have thought coffee could brew such controversy?

Coffee Spreads Throughout Africa and Arabia

After the coffee plant's discovery in Ethiopia, coffee became recognized for medicinal purposes, and also as a means of preventing illnesses such as the flu. (Ironically, in the twentieth and twenty-first centuries, the American public was preached the opposite. Concerns of high blood pressure, stillborn births, and liver swelling—all due to heavy coffee consumption—were raised, and often academic studies backed up the belief that drinking too much coffee is unhealthy.)

When holy man Sheik Gemaleddin of Aden sampled coffee in Ethiopia in 1450, he was amazed at how his health improved. His endorsement of coffee sent both locals and visitors to the region running out to get a cup of coffee at night. It is said that at least one physician began writing prescriptions for coffee for his sick patients.

The Muslim holy cities of Mecca and Medina in Islam profited from a port in Mohka, the world's busiest port at the time. However, wanting to keep a good thing under wraps, Arabs put a strict moratorium on the exportation of beans. They preferred to keep the caffeinated secret all to themselves.

Later, roasted coffee, which was likely primitive compared to today's methods, appeared in Turkey, North Africa, and Persia, southern India, the Balkan states, and Spain, thanks to pilgrims and traders who spread the word around the Muslim world. Eventually, Muslim pilgrims transported coffee seeds to the coast of India. The first coffee tree in that region was planted during the seventeenth century. And methods for roasting, although still low-tech, were constantly being improved.

Coffee became so relied upon as both a stimulant and cultural drink that it is said men made vows on their wedding day to never deprive their wives of coffee, and should they fail to provide steaming hot cups, well, then the result would be divorce. Imagine such a statement written into the wedding vows of today's married couples!

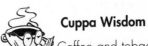

Cuppa Wisdom

Coffee and tobacco are complete repose.

—Turkish proverb

Coffee's Arrival in Europe

The first European stop for the coffee bean was in 1615 in the trade center of Venice. It seems the beans were shipped along with other goods (like Turkish rugs and silks) from the East, perhaps accidentally. When Pope Clement VIII took a sip of the coffee, he declared it "heavenly." This upset the Italian Christian leaders who were actively decrying the beverage as satanic. Despite their disapproval, however, Europe's first coffeehouse was established in Oxford in 1650 and in Italy in 1654.

Field Notes

Caffe Florian, quite famous during the seventeenth century, opened in Venice in 1720, and is still in existence today.

Sold mainly in apothecary shops, coffee was very, very expensive and, therefore, reserved for Italy's upper class. But by the mid-seventeenth century, times had changed. Now people were able to buy a cup of coffee in the streets from vendors who also sold orangeade, chocolate, and herbal infusions. At the end of that century, tiny windowless cafés were a strong part of Italian culture.

France, of course, has had its share of exposure to coffee. In 1660, merchants in Marseilles returned from a few years spent in Turkey. Because they couldn't imagine living without their daily coffee, they brought beans back with them. Lyons, France's second-largest city, got wind of the new drink and started to import beans as well.

Years of sipping the dark brew endured for much of Europe, and along the way people taught themselves how to modify the brewing techniques to their liking. Viennese coffee (which, by today's definition, includes chocolate, strong coffee, light cream, heavy cream, sugar, and dashes of cinnamon and cocoa) was one such technique invented in 1683 by Franz George Kolschitzky. In love with this method, and wanting to spread the instructions to others, the Polish man traveled behind enemy lines during the Siege of Vienna to show others how the beans could be turned into a delicious, unique drink. If you travel in Vienna today, in fact, you can still experience Viennese coffee.

Field Notes

Paris was actually a late-comer to the continent's café culture. Café Procope, the first Parisian café, opened in 1689 opposite the Comédie-Française. An expansion of the café concept quickly spread around the city, leaving nary an arrondissement without one. By the end of the 1700s, Paris boasted 800 cafés, and about 3,000 were serving coffee by the mid-1800s.

England has, throughout history, had a love-hate relationship with coffee. After three Englishmen traveled to Arabia and wrote an extensive report on their findings about coffee, the citizens wanted to try it for themselves. And so in 1650, the country's first coffeehouse opened in Oxford. It became such a favorite hang-out for students that 5 years later the Oxford Coffee Club was established. The first London coffeehouse opened 2 years later, in 1652.

Just like in Arabia and Africa, Europeans viewed their coffee as medicinal. An advertisement from 1657 promoted coffee as a "very wholesome and physical drink." It was billed as healing for the stomach; a fix for digestion; and a preventive measure toward headaches, coughs, and colds.

But over time, a coffee controversy brewed in England. Women were barred from coffeehouses—although they could, for whatever reason, own them. Charles II spoke against having coffeehouses; in 1672 he dubbed them "seminaries of sedition" and vowed to suppress them.

Notable Caffeinated Moments

Cups of coffee have long been the inspiration for building movements of philosophy, religion, and politics. So have cafés. Historical moments that are now the subject of textbooks and television documentaries were planned over coffee in a café. For instance, in 1773 the Boston Tea Party was plotted in secrecy at the Green Dragon coffeehouse, a favorite gathering place for great thinkers of the eighteenth century. Americans spoke out against England's tea tax, and the Continental Congress responded by declaring coffee the official national beverage.

> **Field Notes**
>
> Europe continues to be a hotbed for coffee talk. In 1963, the United Nations established the International Coffee Association in London, an intergovernmental body that still functions today, although under the name International Coffee Organization.

Then, in 1789, came the French Revolution, which began over discussions in a café called Café Foy. It heightened when Camille Desmoulins, a journalist and social activist, as well as an unemployed lawyer, jumped atop a table at Café Foy to speak in front of a revolutionary crowd. The Bastille was stormed 2 days later.

Also during the Enlightenment of the mid-1700s, coffeehouses in Great Britain were referred to as "penny universities." For the price of a cup of coffee (presumably 1¢), people met to talk philosophy and politics, getting to know others in their neighborhoods and also structuring their communities' laws and social attitudes.

But even before this, Lloyds of London, a London insurer, began as a coffeehouse during the 1680s. Groups of businesspeople gathered there regularly. Eventually, by the end of the eighteenth century, the collection of folks formed a company and moved into their own private office to conduct underwriting.

The New York Stock Exchange, surprisingly, had its beginnings in two coffeehouses in the area of Manhattan now called Wall Street. The Merchants' Coffee House and the Tontine Coffee House, which were across the street from one another, were important sites for business transactions. In 1817, the group formally established itself as the New York Stock and Exchange Board, later renamed the New York Stock Exchange.

> **Cuppa Wisdom**
>
> "The history of coffeehouses," wrote Isaac D'Israeli, "was that of the manners, the morals and the politics of a people."

But cafés' histories lie not only in financial landmarks. Many authors have scribed an entire novel within the confines of a favorite coffeehouse, making several visits and downing lots of coffee. Caffe Trieste in San Francisco's North Beach neighborhood was a favorite gathering place for the beat poets, including Lawrence Ferlenghetti and Jack Kerouac, during the 1960s. And American novelist Ernest Hemingway developed most of his plots while sitting in Parisian cafés.

> **Cuppa Wisdom**
>
> It was a pleasant cafe, warm and clean and friendly, and I hung up my old water-proof on the coat rack to dry and put my worn and weathered felt hat on the rack above the bench and ordered a cafe au lait. The waiter brought it and I took out a notebook from the pocket of the coat and a pencil and started to write.
>
> —Ernest Hemingway

And although his piano was not in a café, Ludvig van Beethoven had a soft spot for coffee. He was rumored to grind precisely 60 beans into his daily cup. Because he was born in Bonn, Germany, and died in Vienna, Austria, in 1827, he probably got to sample various beans and became a connoisseur in his own right. Historians report that he would travel around the city in search of specific beans, mixing up the recipe for his brew on occasion.

Les Deux Magots, a very famous café in Paris's Left Bank neighborhood, was a frequent stop for philosophers Simone de Beauvoir and Jean Paul Sartre. They first began meeting there in 1929 and continued doing so until the 1940s. A similar café, Café de Flore, attracted philosophers as well during this time period. Even today, modern-day philosophers can be found at Les Deux Magots and Café de Flore, engaged in a lively debate or in personal reflection.

Viva la Bean! Coffee's Expansion to Latin America

Latin America is such a huge coffee producer today, so it's rather interesting that the coffee plant arrived there only a few hundred years ago. After Guatemala, Costa Rica, Venezuela, Columbia, and Mexico heard about the popularity of coffeehouses in Europe, their curiosity was piqued.

Around 1727, the Brazilian emperor sent the emissary, Francisco de Mello Palheta, to French Guiana to get some coffee seeds that were under close watch. However, Palheta was able to woo the wife of the French governor, and she arranged for him to get the seeds.

By 1800, Brazil was exporting coffee and continued to do so throughout that century and into the next. The tropical agriculture proved to be a good place for growing coffee and continues to do well today.

A hundred years later, 90 percent of Brazil's wealth was in coffee, but with world coffee prices dropping, Brazil was beginning to suffer. The country struggled to find new uses for the beans (such as cattle feed, locomotive fuel, and home heating) but failed. But soon coffee rebounded, and Brazil supplied two thirds of the coffee consumed during the two world wars. A terrible frost in July 1975 presented another setback, but once again, Brazil recovered. Today you can find many beans from Brazil that are excellent.

> **Cuppa Wisdom**
>
> Strong coffee, and plenty, awakens me. It gives me warmth, an unusual force, a pain that is not without pleasure. I would rather suffer than be senseless.
>
> —Napoleon, who liked a Brazilian Santos-Mocha blend

Java's Journey to the United States

Eventually, coffee made its way to America. A mortar and pestle on the *Mayflower*—which traveled to our shores during the late seventeenth century—was the crew's "grinder" for coffee beans. This shows that by the time coffee got to the United States, many other citizens around the world had tinkered with the growing, roasting, grinding, and brewing methods, perhaps weeding out poor, unsuccessful means. In turn, they were likely to have educated Americans in how to brew a bountiful cup.

In 1832, it's said that President Andrew Jackson eliminated brandy and rum from soldiers' rations, replacing it with coffee and sugar. By the time the Civil War came around (1861–1865), coffee was considered essential to a soldier's daily life. The Confederate government adopted coffee as an official U.S. Army ration and allotted 10 pounds of unroasted green coffee beans per every 100 rations.

At the end of the Civil War, Jabez Burns invented the first efficient industrial coffee roaster. This just about wiped out all roasting tools in existence before then, which, although they did the job, were not the easiest to use.

By the 1950s, coffee was a popular beverage for many Americans. Increased use of automobiles and construction of highways enabled easier travel, so a visit to a coffee shop, diner, or restaurant for a cup of coffee became commonplace. In Europe, easier travel spurred a revival of the salons during the 1700s and 1800s.

Today three major coffee corporations drive the supply of many large institutions, such as hospitals, office buildings, and universities: Philip Morris/Atria Group (Kraft and Maxwell House), Procter & Gamble (Folgers, Millstone), and Nestlé (Hills Brothers, MJB, Chase & Sanborn, Nescafé, and Taster's Choice). After oil, coffee is the second-most traded commodity in the world.

Field Notes

In 1689, in Boston, the first coffeehouse in America opened. Not long after, in 1696, New York City got its first café, The King's Arms. Coffeehouses endured in the United States, and in the mid-twentieth century espresso carts and kiosks came to Seattle, providing another type of experience for drinking coffee. Even today these carts are staples in the local culture and icons to that city. Eventually, however, people wanted a place to sit down and relax with their espresso, maybe pair it with a pastry. Coffeehouses took off based on this new demand, building in communities where there had been nothing previously and becoming a "third place" for many people.

Starbucks, a Seattle, Washington–based roaster and retailer, had 9,500 stores worldwide in 2005, with 7,000 of those in the United States. The first opened in 1971 in Seattle (where the company remains headquartered today), and in the 1990s, the coffee shop concept snowballed into a brand name that consumers learned to recognize. Starbucks is now the world's largest coffee roaster, with the highest number of stores. They can be found in business districts, along residential streets, on universities, inside grocery stores, inside a courthouse in Arizona, and even in casinos on the Las Vegas strip.

Field Notes

Today Starbucks has stores in every state of the United States and in many different countries as well. In 2005, Starbucks opened its 9,500th store and appears to be aggressive about opening even more, not just in the United States but internationally.

The Specialty Coffee Association of America (SCAA) estimates there were only 525 coffeehouses in the United States in 1992. That figure quickly snowballed into 17,400 in 2003, with Starbucks comprising about 40 percent of the cafés. Today there are about 22,000 coffeehouses in the United States, according to the SCAA. It's estimated that 500 billion cups of coffee are consumed around the world each year. That's 1.3 billion cups every day—and a lot of caffeine!

With all that coffee consumption and coffeehouses dotting the landscape, most of us now have our own *"third place,"* a spot after our home and office that we frequent several times a week. Perhaps we run into the same customers during our visits and the *baristi* know us by name—hey, it works in bars, it can work in coffeehouses, too!

Buzz Words

A **third place** is someplace, often a coffeehouse, many people go after work and/or when they're not home. Many people visit their local coffeehouse every morning, or every night, or with some other form of regularity. **Barista** (pronounced bar-EES-tah; plural: barisiti) is like a bartender to the coffee shop, trained and skilled in mixing espresso-based beverages.

Where Coffee Grows Today

Today coffee crops are found in 53 different countries around the world, within a common area called the "Bean Belt" between the Tropic of Cancer and the Tropic of Capricorn. Tropical and subtropical latitudes between 25° north and 30° south are ideal conditions for growing coffee. The sunshine is adequate, rainfall is plentiful, and the fields are set at a high altitude, usually between 1,500 and 6,000 feet.

That said, conditions do vary from country to country. For example, in Brazil's Cerrado region, coffee grows on flat farm fields. But in Costa Rica and Ethiopia, the leafy, forest-heavy climate commands a taller tree. On Mt. Kenya, coffee grows at 5,000 to 6,500 feet. Rainfall varies dramatically between these two countries. Average annual rainfall in Ethiopia is between 31 and 86 inches. Conversely, Costa Rica gets between 48 and 216 inches per year, producing more moisture in the soil and air.

Brazil is the biggest exporter of coffee, followed by Vietnam. However, you're not likely to see bags of whole-bean coffee originating from Vietnam, as its coffee industry is largely based on robusta beans, which are not used to make specialty coffee unless it's part of an espresso blend.

Field Notes

Guatemala is home to seven defined microclimates. Each produces a different, distinct flavored coffee, showing how diversity can help produce a different bean.

The Least You Need to Know

◆ Specialty coffee is considered gourmet and artisan compared with all other coffees.

◆ Coffee has a deep, and at times dark, history.

◆ Movements for philosophy, art, literature, and finance had their beginnings in coffeehouses.

◆ Today, 53 nations produce coffee. A majority of coffee is grown in the "Bean Belt," the area between the Tropics of Cancer and Capricorn.

Field of Beans: Growing and Processing Coffee

In This Chapter

- Learn about the coffee plant and its ideal climate conditions
- Understand various coffee processing techniques and how they affect taste
- Gain knowledge of how a coffee farm operates
- Read about decaffeination techniques

While you're sipping a cup of coffee, it can be difficult to imagine the immense work involved to bring you that steaming hot beverage. Think of all the workers who handled the beans, from picking to harvesting, and the miles those beans traveled to get to you in the coffee shop you sit in.

This chapter walks you through the steps for growing and processing coffee, tracing the path from crop to cup. Much care must be put into every step to guarantee high-quality coffee. At any given stage, the process has the potential to go badly, affecting the overall quality of the coffee. That's why farmers of specialty coffee work hard to perfect their harvests, paying close attention to each stage.

Understanding the growing and processing of coffee will help you comprehend what you're tasting each time you sip coffee.

A Closer Look at the Coffee Plant and How It Grows

As you learned in Chapter 1, there are two main varieties of the coffee plant, a woody perennial evergreen catalogued in the *Rubiaceae* family: robusta (*Coffea canephora*), and arabica (*Coffea arabica*).

Arabica accounts for most of the world's coffee production and is grown primarily for the specialty-coffee industry. Robusta, with its less-than-brilliant woody, inferior taste and higher levels of caffeine, is reserved for lower-grade coffees. Grown mainly in Malaysia, India, Western and Central Africa, Vietnam, Uganda, and Brazil, and at lower altitudes than arabica plants, robusta is grown mostly for commercial use in instant and blended coffees, where the taste won't overpower the cup. In specialty coffee, however, robusta's primary appearance is in espresso blends, where it can add body and deep red créma.

Robusta and arabica plants both have canoe-shaped leaves between 3 and 6 inches long that grow along the sides of a central stem. When the plant is in bloom, it is awash with white color. Rainfall provokes the blossoms, and so during the rainy time of year (which will vary, depending on the country and its climate), the plants are dotted with white flowers.

Coffee beans grow inside a red, oval-shaped berry, referred to as a cherry, not much larger than an olive. Typically each cherry contains two coffee seeds (or beans); occasionally, however, only one will form, called a *peaberry*. Small and round, these peaberries do not have the characteristic flat side most coffee beans have. They are often sold as a special grade.

Buzz Words

A **peaberry** is a bean with a bit of a different appearance. The beans are smaller and rounder, as they were the sole coffee bean produced in a cherry (whereas two typically form). Although not limited to Tanzania, much of the Tanzanian coffee that reaches the U.S. market is peaberry. Of the cherries grown worldwide, only between 2 and 10 percent are peaberries.

Coffee plants are propagated from seed or cuttings and take about 6 years to mature. At the 2- or 3-year mark, the plant bears cherries. Coffee plants can grow in the wild to a height of 14 to 20 feet, but when cultivated and pruned, they stand to about 6 to 8 feet. Soil conditions vary depending on geography and range from rich volcanic soil in Hawaii to grassland areas of Brazil with nonvolcanic dirt—but the plants absolutely must grow in a place where there is no frost or hot-temperature extremes.

The area between the Tropic of Cancer and the Tropic of Capricorn has proven to be perfect for coffee farms. The year-round temperature is between 59°F to 75°F.

Air Is Air and Dirt Is Dirt ... Isn't It?

Have you ever witnessed a roaster take a sip of coffee and immediately identify the region where the coffee was grown? How do they do that?

Roasters don't always know specifically where the coffee beans they're roasting originated, but the level of knowledge available is improving, particularly in the specialty-coffee sector, as consumers become more educated. For coffee connoisseurs and seasoned coffee drinkers, though, even just a sip of a particular coffee served blind can allow them to identify its origin.

But how do they know, and how will you learn? Each coffee-producing nation has climate conditions that are all its own, which is a big part of why a Costa Rican coffee doesn't taste like a Konan, or a Sumatran like a Peruvian. This is what makes coffee sampling fun. Let's take a look at some identifying factors of coffee-growing areas.

Arabica plants—what specialty-coffee beans are mainly grown from—flourish in both shady and nonshady conditions. They're commonly grown at high altitudes (between 2,000 and 6,000 feet), which causes them to grow at a slower pace than if they were downhill, allowing for denser beans and a cup that's a little brighter With this slower growth, the cherries also get a chance to become more concentrated and have better acidity.

Field Notes

Don't worry if you're still a beginner taster and can't discern one coffee from another just yet. When you become familiar with various varieties, your tongue will be able to recognize different flavors in a blind tasting.

Traditionally, coffee farmers in Central America, Mexico, Colombia, and Ethiopia have planted coffee trees in the shade. In Hawaii's Kona region, however, the plants are not grown under full shade because in that area of the world, rainfall is plentiful and the surrounding vegetation could block the sun from the coffee plants. Similar weather conditions occur in the Blue Mountain region of Jamaica and the west coast district of Sumatra, where there's often more rain than sun, but the cup's character won't be precisely the same.

Other rare weather conditions affect certain coffee-growing areas, such as the cloud forests of Guatemala and mist in the Blue Mountain range of Jamaica. In the highlands of Central America, coffee plants have to contend with wind, fog, and cool temperatures, whereas in Africa, it's hot and steamy on a regular basis. Coffee farmers have had to become familiar with these conditions as they learn to massage their coffee crops to produce the best beans possible.

Field Notes

Coffee-growing communities are often comprised of two types of farms: *cooperatives* (or *co-op*) and *single estates*. Cooperatives are small, democratically organized societies of farmers who produce a crop together, often with assigned plots. A single estate is only one farm or plantation; single-estate coffee is not pooled together and sold as a region like other coffees often are.

Cooperatives are designed to give equal voice and equal profit share to all farmers involved, and to prevent a situation where only a select few are ruling and running the operation. In some countries, a cooperative of coffee farmers may rival the size of a small city.

Guatemalan Antigua coffee, grown in the Sierra Mountains in a bed of volcanic soil, has high acidity, full body, and distinct notes of chocolate. Mexican Altura is grown at 4,000 feet, which is lower than the Guatemalan Antigua and, therefore, has a different acidity and a light to medium body. And in Brazil, Brazilian Santos has an earthy taste, which some believe is due to the sun-drying of the beans.

Field Notes

Where a coffee is grown has a large impact on how it will taste, just as wine does. See Chapter 3 for more on coffee flavors by region.

The presence of coastal breezes, volcanic soil, or mountains make a difference in the plant's maturity and life. Fortunately, these climatic differences often produce nuances, causing a coffee region to be celebrated for a particular taste brought out in the beans. Processing methods also have an influence on cup character. (More on that later in this chapter.)

The Coffee Harvest: Time to Pick

Like other crops, coffee plants metamorphose through stages of growth. When the cherry is mature and has ripened, it's oval in shape and likely no fatter than the tip of one of your fingers.

When picking cherries off a coffee plant, time is of the essence. Coffee plants are unlike apple trees in that the fruit is not ripe all at once. It's important to the taste of specialty coffee that only ripe cherries are processed. This can be tricky when ripe and unripe cherries share the same plant.

If a cherry is picked too soon and sent in to processing, the resulting brewed coffee will possess an astringent, grassy, and thin taste. This won't cultivate lovers of this coffee! But if the cherry is ripe, the coffee will be sweet and filled with floral notes.

There are two methods for removing cherries from the coffee plants: either by hand or with a machine. Picking by hand is preferable because it enables more selectivity, as a person can detect a ripe cherry whereas a machine cannot. Machines attempt to take only ripe berries, which are more easily loosened, but inevitably harvest un- and under-ripe cherries. Ripe and unripe cherries might mingle during processing, tainting the overall cup character.

Field Notes

The type of picking machine used on coffee farms in Hawaii, Brazil (the Cerrado and Bahia regions), and Australia has fiberglass rods that vibrate the branches, shaking cherries free from the plants. To offset the cost of a machine like this, a farm has to be quite large and already be expecting high production yields. Hawaii, Brazil, and Australia have higher costs of living, and so even replacing a machine with a small group of workers might cause the farm owner to earn a profit. In Central American and African countries, the workers are paid much less by comparison, and so a machine might actually put the farmer into debt.

Because all the bending over can be hard on the back, workers are given burlap sacks to use when picking coffee cherries. The workers place the sacks directly under the coffee plant, loosen the berries from the plant with their fingers, and the cherries drop right in the sacks. Later, when it's time to weigh what they have picked (many times the workers are paid by the pounds of cherries they pick), the sacks are dumped into woven baskets and placed on a scale.

Coffee Processing Methods

After the harvest comes processing, in which the layer of fruit covering is removed, exposing the coffee beans underneath. Each fruit removal method brings out, or rather influences, different aspects in flavor. It's important, however, that the chosen technique is done with precision, so as not to destroy the cup character with undesirable flavors.

The Wet Method

Most specialty coffees are processed using the *wet method*, or the ferment-and-wash method. In this method, a machine slips off the cherry's outer layer (this is called pulping) and another removes the outer-most pulp layer, leaving behind a sticky residue coating the bean. Next comes fermentation, when the beans are put into a tank containing natural enzymes and bacteria that loosen the sticky residue through a digestive process.

There are two variations on the wet method's fermentation process: wet fermentation, when water is added to the tank, and dry fermentation, when the tank remains dry and the beans stew in their own juice.

After fermentation, the coffee bean is washed and dried. Drying processes vary, but ultimately there's just one thin skin covering the beans. This *parchment* is easily removed with a huller.

Buzz Words

When processing coffee using the **wet method,** the sticky fruit covering the coffee seed is removed layer by layer. A sticky residue still on the bean is removed while in a fermentation tank. **Parchment** (also called *pergamino*) is the thin skin left on the coffee bean even after it has been washed and dried. Usually the parchment is crumbly to the touch and, therefore, is quite easily removable.

With the help of machines, there are variations of the wet method. Critics say that this machine-reliant method has a tendency—although not always—to prematurely separate the fruit from the bean, which can ruin the taste of the coffee. And because fermentation is regarded as a spot in the process at which farmers can truly tweak the coffee beans for specific taste results later on, with this process removed, the possibility for bland coffee is quite high.

But one sure perk for using machines is that the reliance on water use is reduced significantly because during wet fermentation a lot of water is required.

The Dry Method

In the oldest coffee-processing method, the *dry method*, cherries are spread out in a thin layer in an open field or on a patio and left to dry under the sun. Just like pancakes or a grilled-cheese sandwich in a frying pan, each side of the bean needs to be exposed to heat, so workers are tasked with raking thin layers of beans regularly so each gets a somewhat equal amount of sunshine. This raking and drying can take anywhere from 10 days to 3 weeks, depending on the hours of sun each day. (Some farms employ a mechanical drier to speed up the technique.)

After drying in the sun, the cherry's outer flesh and parchment are removed in one step—unlike with the wet method, which requires removal in layers. This is often done using a machine, as the husk is shriveled and dry.

Although the dry method is very environmentally friendly—using few if any machines that could release gases and chemicals into the air and a natural resource (the sun)—it does have some notable drawbacks. There's a lot of room for error with this method, and it takes much longer than other methods. Because there's no reliable method for predicting weather conditions, farmers run the risk of setting out beans only to have them drenched in rainfall or dry out too much in the sun. Prolonged sun exposure might create an opportunity for mold, fermentation, or rotting to occur. Too much moisture is harmful as well. But if the beans are carefully monitored and placed in a spot where the workers are aware of the conditions, then the dry method allows for coffee with a complex, fruit-toned sweetness.

> **Buzz Words**
>
> Coffee beans processed using the **dry method** are placed in thin layers to dry under the sun, either in an open field or on a patio. They are then raked to ensure each bean gets adequate sun exposure.

> **Field Notes**
>
> When purchasing coffee, you may see a label indicating that the coffee's *dry processed, unwashed,* or *natural.* These all mean the coffee was processed using the dry method.

Pulped Natural/Semi-Dry

Many of the coffees processed as "pulped natural" (also called semi-dry) come from southern Brazil and also parts of Sumatra and Sulawesi. In this method, the outer skin is removed and the fruit residue remains, drying on the coffee seed and later removed by a machine. Consider it a hybrid of the wet and dry methods. The seed absorbs the starches from the fruit, allowing for a brighter cup of coffee with recognizable floral notes when brewed.

Proponents of pulped natural or semi-dry say the coffee is sweet and well-balanced. Also, the coffee develops a fuller body because the fruit remains on the bean much longer. Nutty flavors, a common trait in Brazil beans, occur because the fruit's natural sugars are able to soak into the bean.

Drying the Beans

As mentioned in the preceding sections, there is more than one way to dry coffee beans. The most primitive, not to mention simple, way to dry coffee beans after they've been processed is to lay them out in the sun and wait, raking the beans occasionally so all the sides are exposed. The type of rake used can range from a wooden, primitively designed rake to a rake with wheels similar to a manual lawn mower (the latter is more common with a greater land mass to cover). Larger operations typically develop more sophisticated raking machines in the interest of preserving manpower.

However, many farms are drying their coffee beans in machines and furnaces. This can take between 24 and 36 hours, and sometimes the beans are partially sun-dried beforehand.

In countries like Honduras, Costa Rica, and Nicaragua, solar dryers have been implemented to replace these traditional machine dryers to cut down on pollution. Because acres of rainforest are cut for firewood to fuel coffee dryers for commercial, large-scale farms, several nonprofit groups in the United States have assisted farmers with creating a machine that can dry the beans efficiently. Harnessing power from the sun, these coffee beans dry naturally.

Field Notes

Whatever drying method is used, it's important that the beans retain a moisture content of between 11 and 12 percent. Otherwise, they may become stale during transport.

Beans can also be dried in raised beds called "African beds" because they are commonly used in Ethiopia. (In Cerrado, Brazil, this method of raised-bed drying is called "wind dry.") The advantage of using these beds is that air can circulate around the beans and ensure they are evenly dried. And not as much raking is required with this method, which can save labor for the workers.

Cleaning, Sorting, and Grading the Beans

After the beans are picked and weighed, they need to be cleaned, sorted, and grated before they're packed into large jute or burlap bags and sent out to buyers. The cleaning, sorting, and grading are very, very important because bad coffee from dirty or otherwise contaminated beans might cause a coffee buyer to select another farm to do business with next time.

The cleaning and sorting is an indoor task. When a worker has become very skilled at scanning trays of beans for discolored or defective beans, watching this task can be dizzying. Imagine a quick scan of the tray, scuttling the beans from left and right, stopping to peer closely at a few that might need closer study, and then moving on to another tray—all in just a few moments.

Generally, the worker scans the coffee beans for the following:

- *Size.* If the beans are of varying sizes, an even roast will be difficult, if not impossible, to reach.

- *Density.* Beans of higher density produce excellent quality and flavor.

- *Defects.* Malformed, discolored, or broken beans, or sticks and stones mixed in with the beans (more common with dry-processed coffee), can also cause a cup of coffee to "go bad."

You might have come across regional grade names while browsing for specialty coffee beans. Each has an influence on cup character and quality. The Specialty Coffee Association of America has a fairly calculated green coffee classification system with five grade levels from 1 to 5. Beans are slotted into a grade based on the number of defects, the moisture content (evaluated using a moisture meter), and the screen size.

Field Notes

Screens are used to check the beans' density level. The screens contain several holes, measured in $1/64$ inches and labeled, for example, 13/14, 15/16, or 17/18. Beans are dropped on the screen and then assigned a size based on what size hole they fit into best. Most beans are between 15 and 16, but the bean size can range from 10 to 22.

With the exception of dry-processed coffees, for which the beans' parchment is removed in one step, the parchment will need to be removed with the help of a hulling machine. By vibrating and shaking the beans, the parchment eventually loosens.

After the cleaning, sorting, and grading is complete, the coffee beans are packed in jute bags. The country of origin, grade name, growing region, processing method, and, in some cases, the estate name are all printed on the bags, and then they're shipped to other nations, where coffee is, no doubt, enjoyed for its quality.

Field Notes

When the coffee beans arrive to the exporter (who is in the coffee-producing country), the beans are sorted as parchment coffee because the parchment remains. The parchment is removed, however, before exporting to the United States or other countries. To remove the parchment, the beans are run through a milling machine.

Decaffeination Methods

There continues to be a consumer demand for decaffeinated coffee, as some people report hypertension or an inability to sleep after drinking caffeinated coffee. Also, pregnant women are often advised by their doctors to not drink beverages containing caffeine.

To remove naturally occurring caffeine from a specialty coffee bean, one of three methods is typically used: solvent, water, or carbon dioxide. After the beans are graded, they are shipped from the farm to a processing plant in Canada or Europe, and the coffee bean is still raw and unroasted when they're sent to the decaf plant. When done, a decaffeinated bean contains $\frac{1}{40}$ the amount of caffeine in nontreated beans.

Solvents

As one of the oldest methods, solvent is still commonly used today. In this method, the coffee beans are steamed and the heat opens the beans' pores. Then they are soaked in a solvent (either methyl chloride or ethyl acetate—more on these in the following paragraphs) that unites with the caffeine. After the beans are removed from the solvent, a second round of steaming the solvent (along with its acquired residues) removes the caffeine entirely.

A slight variation on this is the indirect solvent method. The beans are soaked in near-boiling water for several hours to reduce the caffeine. Then, in a separate tank, the water drained from the beans is combined with a solvent. The layer of solvent-heavy liquid is skimmed out of the water, and the water is poured back in with the beans. By returning the water to the beans, the flavor-promoting oils and other materials are still present, producing a cup of coffee that's drinkable, despite the lack of caffeine. This method, as well as the direct solvent method, is also referred to as European process or traditional process.

Field Notes

When shopping for decaffeinated coffee, you may run across the term *naturally decaffeinated*. This means that either ethyl acetate, which is derived from fruit, or carbon dioxide was used to remove the caffeine.

Methyl chloride and ethyl acetate are two solvents used to decaffeinate coffee beans. Ethyl acetate is derived from fruit and also obtained from the fermentation of sugar cane, as opposed to chemical synthesis. It is considered by natural-health followers to be more benign than methyl chloride, although so far neither have been shown to have harmful health effects.

Water

Because caffeine is highly water-soluble, the water process is an effective method for stripping caffeine from coffee beans. The beans are soaked in near-boiling water until the caffeine, along with flavoring compounds, is released. The water is charcoal filtered to remove the caffeine and then returned to the beans so they may reabsorb the flavor elements.

One such water-based process is conducted at Swiss Water Decaffeinated Coffee Company, Inc., in Burnaby, British Columbia, Canada. Another water process is Mountain Water Process, done at a factory called Sanroke in Mexico. The beans, holding their coffee oils and caffeine, float in water from the glaciers of Mexico's Pico de Orizaba. Then the solution is filtered to remove caffeine, and the water-soluble oils are returned to the coffee. This technique is similar to the Swiss Water process, except the brewed coffees are not as flat flavor-wise, possibly due to using different water sources.

One drawback to water methods is the cost, which exceeds that of the solvent methods. Also, some people claim coffee decaffeinated with the Swiss Water process has a mild-enough flavor but isn't that remarkable. Improvements have been made, and now many specialty-coffee roasters use the Swiss Water process—and turn out good coffee.

Field Notes ——————————————————————

Because no chemical solvents are used, the water process received much interest soon after its introduction in the 1980s.

Caffeine recovered from the decaffeination process is the largest source of natural caffeine added to foods and drinks. In fact, much of the caffeine in soda actually comes from coffee.

Carbon Dioxide

With carbon dioxide (CO_2) decaffeination, carbon dioxide is cooled and placed under pressure in large centrifuges, where it turns into a liquid. The beans soak in containers of liquid carbon dioxide, which strips the caffeine from the beans by binding the carbon dioxide with the caffeine molecule. The caffeine is soaked out of the coffee, and the delicate flavors inside the bean are unaltered. Because cooling and centrifuge equipment is required for this method, this method is used more often on an industrial scale.

A benefit to this method is that carbon dioxide is naturally selective and, therefore, does not touch the coffee bean's carbohydrates and proteins. It's also fairly renewable in that the carbon dioxide is recycled and the caffeine is sold for other uses.

Growing and Processing Coffee with a Conscience

On coffee farms all over the world, workers have created earth-friendly practices, either to save costs or to practice consciousness—and sometimes both.

Waste from the wet-processing method, essentially the pulp, is sometimes returned to the plants for use as mulch. And parchment that has fallen off during processing might be burned as fuel for mechanical dryers. Some farms have taken it a step further by eliminating their use of mechanical dryers altogether. Because coffee dryers use diesel- and wood-fire, which creates pollution, many Central American countries have started to use solar-powered dryers. In some cases, U.S.-based researchers have created this new approach and helped set it up on native farms.

Got a Green Thumb?

Are you a do-it-yourselfer or have a pretty green thumb? Think you can grow your own coffee at home? You may be on to something. Although you shouldn't expect to yield a huge amount of success, you can grow coffee plants indoors. You won't be able to stop buying all your coffee in a store, but you might—and that's a big *might*—get enough to make one cup of coffee.

Growing coffee indoors, if you're going to try it, is your best option. Start with 20 coffee seeds and soak them in an inch of water overnight. After 12 or sometimes 24 hours you will notice the embryo begin to emerge from a handful of seeds. In a deep pot, cover the seeds with about 1 ½ inches of good soil. (Using a seed tray won't work, so be sure you have access to a deep pot.) After about 60 days, you'll see a small green gooseneck peeking out of the soil.

Hot Water

If you decide to grow your own coffee, do it indoors—unless you live in Hawaii! In most other areas, either frost or humid temperatures will mar and eventually destroy coffee plants growing outdoors.

Water the seeds daily, and pay attention not to over- or underwater. Either of these situations could harm the plant and prevent it from growing. Prepare yourself for a long wait, though, because it will take about 9 months for the coffee plant start to resemble a plant. At this stage in the process, it's okay to transplant to a new, larger pot.

Field Notes

One U.S. coffee importer suggests that to grow arabica coffee right, you need to have access to just-picked cherries. Unfortunately, you can't bring that product into the country. So unless you're growing this plant in a coffee-producing region, you will have to work with seeds.

The Least You Need to Know

◆ From crop to cup, coffee beans must be grown and processed carefully to ensure a good cup of joe.

◆ The area a coffee plant is grown affects the flavor and quality of the brewed cup.

◆ Specialty coffees are processed with either a wet method or dry method. Machines are used in some processing; others require more environmentally friendly methods.

◆ There are three types of decaffeination: solvent, water, and carbon dioxide (CO_2).

◆ Coffee beans must be cleaned and sorted according to size and density, and defective beans eliminated under a watchful eye before the beans can be packed up and sold.

Chapter 3

Geography for Your Tongue: Coffee Regions and Origins

In This Chapter

◆ Discover why knowing a coffee's origin matters when choosing and sampling coffees

◆ Learn the general differences in coffees from around the world

◆ Explore coffee flavors, from Central America's sweet and vibrant coffees to Indonesia's resonant, heavy-bodied, and earthy coffees

For many of us, our first thought on coffee was that of a rather singular "Coffee is coffee." At that point, it probably seemed reasonable to assume—if you even pondered it—that coffee was just another mass-produced, mass-marketed commodity. The only real difference between one can or bag of beans and any other was the jingle its manufacturer had associated with it, right? And it's fair to say that the notion isn't far off with regard to much of the commercial-grade "supermarket brands."

As you begin to sample specialty coffee, however, it's nearly impossible to fool your palate. There's a lot going on in a coffee cup, and not every cup is alike. Sure, they all taste like coffee, but each incorporates different nuances into the experience.

Some people might be a little skeptical that coffees grown in different regions of the world vary all that much, but indeed the contrasts can be stark—and quite delicious! Touring the world from your coffee mug can be an exciting adventure, and in this chapter, we give you the tools to be confident in your explorations.

> **Field Notes**
>
> Once, in a fit of excitement about a coffee he'd recently roasted from the Huila region in Colombia, Travis buried a patient friend with detailed descriptions of the bean's amazing, delicate complexity and how it compared with the other beans he had on hand. Finally, his friend said, "Wow. Sounds great, and I'm glad for you, but my tongue is brain-dead. There's no way I could tell a difference." Minutes later, Travis set before him mugs of the Colombian and a big-bodied Sumatran. With eyes widening and then narrowing, Travis's friend simply said, "I can't believe it."

Why Origin Matters

We talked in earlier chapters how growing conditions affect the flavors beans express in the cup, and knowing a coffee's origin gives you insight into how it tastes. Let's get a bit more specific.

Although distinctions are not set in stone, region-specific stereotypical flavor profiles exist because the coffees are often grown under similar conditions and influenced by local customs and farming practices (including processing methods and, to some degree, what cultivars are raised). Altitude, weather patterns, and soil type and makeup are primary environmental factors that impact how coffee tastes, but such things as proximity to a sea can influence cup character as well.

> **Field Notes**
>
> Generally speaking, beans grown at higher altitudes are denser and display more brightness in the cup. The cooler temperatures found at high elevations promote slower growth and denser beans, which tend to pack in more desirable nuances.

Of cultural influences, perhaps the most significant are local processing conditions and methods. Key variables here are how soon the cherries are processed after harvest, whether the beans must be transported long distances, and the specific processing method used. Typically, wet-processed coffees are cleaner and brighter than their dry-processed counterparts and tend to be lighter-bodied, less fruited, and, perhaps, a bit less complex.

While it's common to think of an entire country as a single growing region, in many cases, each nation is home to several coffee-producing areas. Often, coffees grown in the same nation will be somewhat similar, but expecting that could lead to some surprises. If, for example, you were turned on by an Ethiopian Harar's deep body and fruity, blueberry flavors and then sought out an Ethiopian Yirgacheffe looking for something similar, your palate may be shocked by the bright, lemony acidy of the Yirgy.

It can be somewhat of a grab bag when coffee is labeled strictly by country of origin rather than by the region or plantation where it was grown. This is often the result of pooling, where coffees from several lots and regions are combined. Pooled coffee can be great, but many times this blind sort of blending yields only an okay, anonymous coffee. For roasters and retailers, this can mean a lot of *cupping* to locate quality coffees.

Knowing the growing region provides general insight to how a coffee may taste, but these stereotypes, like any, won't properly apply to all coffees from a given origin. The generalizations do afford a handy reference point and language for describing and comparing coffees. And with so many coffees to explore, they can also guide you to the next

Buzz Words

The systematic process of tasting and evaluating coffee is commonly called **cupping**. For more information on cupping, see Chapter 5.

coffee you might like to sample. The following descriptions were written with this in mind and introduce you to coffee-producing regions from around the world. As you sample coffees, though, let the individual coffee speak for itself, keeping in mind that coffee production is art as well as science and is far from static.

Field Notes

As consumers have become more educated about coffee, roasters and retailers have begun supplying more information about their offerings, but you may have to inquire. For example, convention still often prevails with Colombian coffees, and these coffees are commonly seen only as Colombian supremo or excelso. Because these designations speak only to the size of beans (supremo being larger), they don't tell you anything about how the coffee might taste. It's possible, though, that the same coffee could have been billed as Colombian Popayán, for example, so just ask if you'd like more detail.

Mexico and Central America

Sandwiched between the Pacific Ocean and the Caribbean Sea just south of the Tropic of Cancer, Mexico and Central America have prime locations and geography for producing high-quality coffee. High altitudes, rich volcanic soils, and near-exclusive use of wet-processing methods help give coffees from this region their clean, bright character. These coffees are perennial favorites for their range of sweet notes, including nuts, fruits, spices, and chocolate.

Mexico

The United States' southern neighbor has made significant inroads into the specialty coffee market and is a long-time producer of organic and fair trade coffees. Coffee is grown in the southern half of the country, with the primary regions being Coatepec, Oaxaca, and Chiapas.

However, Mexican coffees, which tend to be somewhat delicate, have tended to underwhelm the tongues of specialty coffee buyers, who often seek out bold or striking coffees. For this reason, a lot of Mexican coffee is used for blending or as a base for flavored coffee. To say, though, that Mexican coffees aren't noteworthy would be missing the mark. High-grown (often marked Altura) Mexican coffees are balanced and well worth appreciating in their own right, with mild to moderate acidity and body and gentle notes of fruit and spice.

Guatemala

Guatemala is one of the most renowned coffee-growing nations in the world, producing distinct, nuanced coffees in several regions throughout the country. Perhaps the most well-known region is Antigua and its complex, smoky, and spicy coffees with pronounced, pleasant acidity and full body. Coffees from the Atitlán and Frajianes regions share characteristics with those from Antigua, but they tend to be a bit lighter-bodied and, perhaps, with a few more chocolate notes *in the cup*. The Huehuetenago and Cobán regions are known for more fruity notes in the cup, although the Cobáns often have a rounder deep profile with a gentler touch of acidity. Also displaying a little less power in the cup, although still complex while clean, are coffees from the San Marcos region near the Mexican border.

Buzz Words

"In the cup" refers to how a coffee tastes when brewed.

El Salvador

Political instability and civil strife in El Salvador took a toll on its coffee industry, earning it a spotty reputation at best. El Salvadoran coffees at one time were thought of as soft, mild, and pleasant. And while some of the country's exports still fit this profile—especially those grown at lower elevations—more are being put forward that are more on par with classic Guatemalans. These have a lot of power in the cup, with a fair amount of sweetness; good depth; and strong, snappy acidity. Some important growing regions include Santa Ana, Ahuachapan, Sonsonate, San Miguel, and La Libertad.

Field Notes

The Cup of Excellence competition, which came to El Salvador in 2003, has helped spotlight the country's ability to produce stellar, distinctive coffees. (Read more about the Cup of Excellence later in this chapter.)

Honduras

Honduras is (hopefully) another up-and-coming specialty coffee producer. Despite having good soil, climate, and altitude, coffees coming out of this country have been fairly inconsistent and not of high quality. Poor infrastructure for processing and delivering coffee seems to be the primary suspect. In recent years, there has been a push to educate farmers and put into place systems to deliver superior coffee as a way for Honduras's coffee industry to regain itself after devastating losses caused by 1998's Hurricane Mitch. The trouble thus far has been a vicious cycle of low prices that don't compensate (or motivate) farmers and mills to take the extra care necessary to produce higher-quality coffee that would command a better price.

Fortunately, the Cup of Excellence competitions have demonstrated the nation's ability to produce quality specialty coffee. Sweet and clean, fine Honduran coffees tend to express gentler acidity than other Central American coffees.

Field Notes

The Cup of Excellence is a competition that recognizes farmers who produce truly outstanding coffee. Winning coffees are then entered into an Internet auction, which has brought substantial premiums and record prices for successful farmers. The competition has been adopted in eight Central and South American countries (Bolivia, Brazil, Colombia, El Salvador, Guatemala, Honduras, and Nicaragua).

Nicaragua

If nations like Honduras and El Salvador serve as examples of Central American coffee producers struggling to make a name for themselves, Nicaragua is a model of how it can be done in spite of civil strife and environmental disasters. With the help of international aid and education after the devastation wreaked in 1998 by Hurricane Mitch, Nicaragua's growers have focused on differentiating themselves by focusing on quality. This is especially so for its fair trade cooperatives, who are serving as role models for those in other countries.

Primary growing regions you'll likely run across are Matalgalpa, Segovia, and Jinotega. These coffees express a bit rounder profile than many other Centrals but are certainly not without a pleasant acidity. Expect a balanced cup with plenty of body, depth, and clean flavors, often with a chocolaty nuttiness.

Costa Rica

Good coffees from Costa Rica often display a big, "classic" coffee flavor. In fact, this clean, refined profile is sometimes criticized for being too uniform and not idiosyncratic enough. Indeed, while some of the best "Costas" have pleasing citrus-y or light berrylike acidity, they are otherwise unnuanced coffees that challenge even refined palates for detailed descriptions.

This does not, however, mean that coffees from Costa Rica are bland or substandard. It's truly a case of what excites one's tongue may not be enough to awaken the taste buds of another. Central Costa Rica is home to the primary growing regions: Tarrazu, Tres Ríos, Herediá, and Volcán Poás.

Panama

Somehow it seems coffees from Panama are lost in the shuffle of Central Americans and often underrated. Panama's primary growing region, Boquete, is in the western part of the country, just across the border from Costa Rica. The vast majority of the premium Panamanian coffees are grown on large, family-operated estates and meticulously wet-processed at modern facilities. The result is typically a gently bright coffee with medium body and good balance. Often, Panamanian coffees are intriguing, sweet coffees with a bit of fruit in the cup.

Field Notes

Panamanian coffees are commonly a "secret" blender used in Hawaiian Kona and Jamaica Blue Mountain blends due to their great cup character and relatively inexpensive price.

South America

It's quite possible you've sipped coffee grown in South America, as it's home to two of the world's largest producers of coffee. Outside of Brazil, most of the coffee is wet processed and grown at relatively high elevations. The result is clean, vibrant coffees similar to those grown in Central America. The lower-grown Brazilians are commonly dry processed and have much less acidity, more body, and complex fruitiness in the cup.

Colombia

Thanks to the National Federation of Coffee Growers of Columbia and their marketing icon, Juan Valdez, Colombia is often the first country that comes to mind when consumers think about coffee. Not only has the organization done a great job of marketing, but it's also succeeded at coordinating the production and processing of Colombian coffees, grown primarily on a patchwork of small farms, such that the quality has consistently remained good.

Ironically, this success in the mainstream American market has held Colombia back from excelling in the specialty coffee arena. The country's reliance on a system of identifying and grading coffee not by region or farm but rather by size is at the heart of the problem. While enticing-sounding, the terms *supremo* and *excleso* refer only to the size of the beans (the former being the largest) and have little relevance to cup character. So Colombian coffees marked solely with this size designation are a hit-or-miss proposition, with the outstanding lot often being elusive.

When Colombian coffee is designated by region, those you're most likely to see are Huila, Popayán, Narinõ, Santander, Magdelena, Armenia, and Antioquia. Good Colombians have a rich balance to them, having both a fair amount of body and acidity, and often show sweet fruited notes suggesting raisins or plums.

Field Notes

Recently, more Colombian coffee is being designated by the region it was grown in or even by farm (*finca*). This labeling system doesn't ensure flavor in the cup, but it is a step in the right direction—away from pooling all sorts of coffee simply under a label of "Colombian."

Peru

Peru's coffee industry is in an interesting, though not necessarily desirable, position right now. Its coffee is reasonably unknown to coffee-consuming Americans despite the fact that it's readily available. A relative newcomer to coffee producing, Peru has seemingly focused on achieving the premium often associated with organic coffees. It appears that more focus had been placed on quantity than on quality, resulting in a glut of indistinctive coffee. In fact, if you are a fan of organic blends, you've likely had Peruvian coffee and not known it, as it's one of the cheapest organic coffees.

With an increased push now on education, more excellent Peruvian coffees are being produced today, and they stand clearly apart from their lackluster and often grassy counterparts. Many of these come from the Chanchamayo growing region, although many also originate from Cuzco and Norte regions.

Good coffees from Peru often possess a gentle, grounded sweetness with snappy brightness that's supported by a medium body.

Brazil

Brazilian coffee is another coffee you might have had and not known it. It's found in a lot of canned coffees and in a great deal of espresso blends, typically as a base. Brazil is the world's leading coffee producer in terms of quantity, cranking out more than one third of the world's total coffee. However, Brazil lacks the rich, volcanic soil and mountainous altitude that many nations producing specialty coffee enjoy.

While much of its coffee is low-grown arabica and robusta, Brazil does produce a number of fine coffees. Where Brazil differentiates its coffees, though, is by processing methods. Unlike those of many other Central and South American countries, Brazil's coffee crop is processed by several different methods and are not primarily wet processed.

Field Notes

Coffees from a single Brazilian farm (or *fazenda*) may be processed using a variety of methods and, therefore, offer a great study in how processing affects flavor.

Much of the Brazilian coffees we see on the American specialty market have been dry processed. These are influenced by the fruit left on during drying and are big-bodied, low-acidity coffees, often with a husky fruitiness and some dark chocolate notes. Wet-processed Brazils offer a cleaner, more consistent cup that's brighter and less rustic, but they often afford less fruit and chocolate in the cup and carry a lighter body as well. Pulped coffees, those having just the skins removed before drying, cup much like those processed in the traditional dry method but tend to be a bit cleaner. Semi-washed Brazils have attributes of dry- and wet-processed coffees, depending on the individual processing of that lot.

Whatever the processing methods, good Brazilian coffees have a sweet nuttiness and character that is unique among coffees from the Americas.

Bolivia

Despite having the necessary elements to produce high-quality coffee, Bolivia has not been represented much on America's specialty coffee market.

Its sky-scraping altitudes have historically been a part of the trouble. Coffee grown in rural areas was partially processed before being trucked to La Paz, the capital city and important commercial center. The result of such a journey is unpredictable cup quality and often disastrous, certainly obliterating attempts at consistency.

With the help of the U.S. Agency for International Development (USAID) program and anti-drug efforts, an extensive education effort has been put in place to help farmers understand how to better care for the crop. More coffee is now processed near farms so coffee may be stabilized before undertaking a long journey. The efforts can be seen in the increase in high-quality Bolivian coffees, oftentimes organically produced, hitting the U.S. market. These show a nice snap in the acidity with moderate body and a delicately complex flavor that often shows a caramelly sweetness and hints of berries, nuts, and spices. Regions you'll most likely see these coffee crops are Santa Cruz, Cochabamba, Tarija, and Yungas.

The Caribbean and Hawaii

Softer than Central American coffees, those coffees coming from islands in the Caribbean Sea and Hawaii are somewhat tempered by their exposure to the ocean air. Sentimental tourists and aficionados alike love these balanced treats, which often sell for several times the price of other specialty coffees.

Jamaica

While Jamaica is a small producer of specialty coffees, it is world renowned for its Blue Mountain beans. Some maintain that Jamaican coffees, like those from Hawaii, are overpriced and overrated. Others swear it is exquisite, worth the premium, and unequaled. Who's right? Well, the truth, while dependent on personal preference, is most often somewhere in between. At its best, Jamaican Blue Mountain (not to be confused with the lower-grown and less-impressive Jamaican High Mountain) is a subtly detailed and rich, smooth, and balanced mild cup.

Perhaps one of the largest factors working against Jamaica's coffees is the price they command. Obviously, the high price limits the number of consumers who will sip a cup of Blue Mountain, but that's certainly not the extent of the impact. Far more tragic is that the cost often equates to low turnover of the roasted coffee, so the chances of getting a hold of stale beans are higher. Another side effect of the steep price is a market that's awash in Jamaican Blue Mountain "style" or "blend" coffees. Often these have little Blue Mountain in them, and in the case of the former, they may not have any. If you'd like to see whether the mellowness of Jamaica's coffees is for you, be prepared to shell out upward of $25 per pound and seek out a roaster that discloses the roasting date.

Other Caribbean Island Coffees

Haiti, Dominican Republic (sometimes marketed as Santo Domingo), and Puerto Rico all produce coffee with the soft island profile, but their reputations and availability on the U.S. specialty coffee market have been spotty. While all have conditions suitable for growing coffee and long histories of doing so, they all are also in the Atlantic hurricane belt and have suffered for it.

Still, well-prepared lots with a gentle richness, nice balance, and delicate nuttiness do turn up, and you should treat yourself when you run across them.

Hawaii

While their cup characters are distinct, coffees from Hawaii and Jamaica have a lot in common. High price and strong romanticism fueled by these tropical vacation hotspots put these island coffees in a similar boat. With that come the dichotomous sentiments that many have for Hawaiian Kona (as well as Jamaican Blue Mountain). It's only natural to have an affinity for products produced from places you've been, and even more so from those you've loved. This is especially the case with Hawaii, as it's such a popular and accessible special getaway spot. And who can blame the Big Island's visitors for falling in love with the memory of a great cup of Kona, with its buttery body and clean, gentle vibrancy that's complemented by notes of milk chocolate and fruit?

What, then, is not to like? For some, especially those accustomed to powerful coffees like those from Eastern Africa, the Kona cup is underwhelming with its balanced but fairly mellow nature. Kona's high price, often upward of $30 per pound, results in some of the same cost-cutting tactics by roasters as with Jamaican Blue Mountain. It often appears in Kona "blends" in very small percentages along with Central American coffees. If you're looking for Kona, expect to pay full price—largely due to the higher cost of labor in the United States—and insist on a roasting date, as there's no sense paying a premium for stale beans.

Hot Water

Coffee is now grown on the other Hawaiian Islands, but it typically doesn't receive the careful hand picking and processing Kona does and employs different cultivars. The resulting coffee is usually less impressive than Kona—but isn't significantly cheaper. Be sure you know the backgound of the coffee you're purchasing.

Africa and Arabia

Coffee is grown throughout parts of Africa, but those reaching the U.S. specialty coffee market are primarily from Eastern Africa. Much of the rest of Africa's coffee production is of robusta.

The East African cup profile is typically complex, fragrant, heavily fruited, and has a snappy acidity. Also bold and a bit wild, the coffees of nearby Yemen join this group of powerful coffees.

Ethiopia

Not only is Ethiopia the birthplace of coffee, but it's also home to some of the most diverse-tasting beans. While there is a wild fruitiness to most Ethiopian coffees, the differences between its dry-processed and wet-processed beans are dramatic.

Two of its most popular coffees, dry-processed Ethiopian Harar and wet-processed Ethiopian Yirgacheffe, illustrate this quite well. The Yirgacheffe is a spirited, high-toned cup that carries a medium to light body marked with vibrant, citrus-y acidity and floral notes. It's a relatively clean coffee compared to its kin (due largely to the wet processing), but it still often has a pleasant, somewhat wild complexity. The Harar, on the other hand, has more rustic, dark fruitiness due to being dried inside the coffee cherry. Good Harars have a fairly deep body with blueberry and jammy-winy notes and are balanced with nice but not overpowering vibrancy.

Sidamo is another Ethiopian coffee-producing region you're likely to see, with both wet- and dry-processed lots making it to market. They often have a spiciness and darkly fruited nature, with much of the final cup character being determined by the processing method.

Although typically not soft and mild-mannered coffees, Ethiopia's coffees should be on your virtual taste tour even if you tend to prefer less-powerful coffees.

Kenya

One of the most celebrated origins in specialty coffee, Kenya is famous for its power-fully vibrant cup. Some of its coffees have a fresh, zingy citrus snap to them while others carry a lot of dark fruit flavors. Of the latter, coffees exhibiting winy character-istics are often highly prized. Mixed in with the generous acidity are often layers of spice and chocolate, and it's all supported by a fairly full body.

Kenya holds weekly auctions at which exporters can bid on individual lots of coffee; this has helped drive competition and focus on cup quality. While the most common designation seen is "AA," which refers to the size of the beans, you see the coffee marked by its auction lot number, the co-op or society that grew the coffee, or the region where it was grown. A lot of coffee is grown at high altitudes around the slopes of Mount Kenya in south-central Kenya, including the Nyeri, Embu, Meru, Muragn'a, and Kirinyaga grow-ing regions. Other producing areas are Kiambu and Machakos farther south and Nakuru to the west.

Tanzania

Although not as famous as its neighbor to the north, Tanzania produces specialty cof-fee in line with the East African profile. Good Tanzanian coffees are bright with mod-erate to full body and feature complex flavors of red fruit, citrus, and cocoa. They do tend to have a little less power in the cup than Kenyans, making them an excellent introduction to the winy vibrancy of East African coffees.

While not unique to the country, peaberries, the round beans that result when a coffee cherry produces only one seed, are most often associated with Tanzanian coffee. In fact, many U.S. consumers have only been exposed to peaberry Tanzanian coffees. This is probably due to Japanese importers historically purchasing large amounts of the flatberries (the usual, flat-sided beans), making the peaberries more available to the U.S. market; as a result, American consumers have come to expect Tanzanian peaberry coffees, which encourages U.S. importers to seek them out. Some argue that peaberries offer a more intense cup because the energy, flavor, and sweetness that usually would have gone into making two beans was instead concentrated into a single seed. And while it is true that good peaberry lots seem to have a little something special to offer, it isn't necessarily the case that they outcup flatberries.

Rwanda

Rwanda is a relatively new producer of specialty coffee but has turned a lot of heads since its recent entry. In fact, its coffee was virtually unknown to the U.S. market before 2005, and today many specialty coffee roasters carry Rwanda's coffee. The success of Rwandan coffee on the specialty market is a testament not only to the hard work of the farmers but also to assistance from USAID and the PEARL project (the Partnership for Enhancing Agriculture in Rwanda through Linkages).

The PEARL project has focused heavily on educating and preparing Rwandan farmers to produce high-quality coffee that can command premium prices. To that end, the project has worked to educate farmers about proper care and processing techniques and has built cupping labs so farmers may more easily monitor the quality of their crops. Through partnerships, the project has also helped secure financial assistance and loans in addition to building modern washing stations for processing. Perhaps the greatest accomplishment of PEARL, though, has been to educate farmers and bring them together to form cooperatives. Now, not only is Rwanda turning out excellent coffee, but the new cooperatives are earning farmers higher wages and are even helping to mend some of the civil strife.

Good Rwandan coffee is distinctive East African, yet is unique. Expect a smooth, silky, medium body with sparkling acidity and a clean but complex cup with nutty, fruity, and floral notes.

Yemen

Yemen is home to some of the oldest coffee varieties and produces some of the world's most distinct coffees. Featured in the oldest coffee blend, Yemeni coffee puts the Mocha in Mocha-Java blends. While you will sometimes find hints of dry cocoa or bittersweet chocolate in Yemeni coffees, the term *Mocha* (and its variants, *Moka, Mocca, Moca,* and *Mokha*) refers to the historical port where coffee was exported.

To further confuse matters, Ethiopian Harar is sometimes designated as Mocha, most likely to associate it with the Yemeni cup character. Yemeni beans are irregular- and rugged-looking—due partially to the traditional cultivars and partially to traditional (dry) processing methods—and often are much smaller than those from other origins. Even after roasting, they typically look a little rough.

While Yemeni coffees are highly prized by connoisseurs, they are a wild, earthy cup that's bold, pungent, and adventurous. They may not appeal to those who prefer a clean cup, but their fans revel in the firm, snappy acidity and substantial body that comes layered in notes of spices and fruit.

Hot Water

Don't fall prone to "eye-cupping" (judging the cup character by the beans) and write off Yemen coffees.

Common market designations you'll see (named for towns near the growing regions) are Mattari, Sanani, Hirazi, Dhamari, Ismaili, and Raimi. Typically, the Mattari coffees exhibit the most power in the cup, while the Sananis tend to be the tamest of Yemenis and make an excellent introduction to the complex Yemen flavor profile.

Asia and Indonesia

When you're looking for big-bodied coffees, those from regions in the Malay Archipelago are a good place to start. They typically have a reserved brightness that's secondary to a lush, thick mouthfeel and lingering finish. A bit rustic in the cup, they often present complex notes of earth, leather, husky fruitiness, and spice.

India

The majority of India's coffee is high-quality washed robusta (often showing up in espresso blends), but the country also produces arabica coffee. These tend to be somewhat unassuming, round, and full-bodied coffees with a smooth, sometimes silky mouthfeel and pleasant nutty and subtle spice notes.

Perhaps due to its uniqueness, though, you're more likely to come across India's dry-processed monsooned Malabar. This coffee stands distinctly apart from other coffees due to its unique handling, which is done to replicate the pungent tastes coffees historically picked up during long shipping voyages over which they endured extended exposure to the humid, salty air and the ships' moist wooden hulls. To accomplish this labor-intensive feat, the coffee is laid out in special open-walled warehouses to be exposed to wet monsoon winds and is periodically stirred to ensure even moisture adsorption. Over time, the coffee yellows and swells considerably, resulting in a coffee with reduced acidity; syrupy body; nutty nuances; and strong, earthy and (surprise) somewhat musty flavor notes. Good monsooned coffees don't cross the line into moldy flavors, but they do present a funky cup and are typically endeared or eschewed.

Sumatra

With classic earthiness and strong, low-toned power, coffee from Sumatra is a flagship for the Indonesian cup profile. Sumatran coffees are produced using a variety of methods, and how a particular lot is prepared tends to have more influence on the coffee's flavor profile than where within Sumatra it's grown.

Much of its coffee is grown using hybrid methods, and as a result has a degree of desirable irregularity as well as musty earthiness in the cup. The longer contact with the fruit also produces a bit more body and complexity. Fully washed coffees tend to be cleaner and brighter but with a milder body.

And although accounting for only about 1,000 pounds a year, another Sumatran coffee has become well known for its unusual processing—via an animal called the palm civet. Kopi (meaning "coffee") Luwak beans are collected from the scat of civets that graze on the coffee tree's fruits. It might sound a bit less than appealing at first, but think about it from the civet's eyes: to make this delicacy, only the most delicious-looking cherries are harvested by "hand" and then are gently but thoroughly processed in small batches using an all-natural digestive process.

Opportunities to drop a joke when talking about this coffee abound, but buying a pound is no laughing matter, with prices easily hitting $200 per pound. As with any expensive coffee, pay close attention to roasting dates when you make your selection.

Java

Since the Dutch first brought coffee to this island in the early eighteenth century, the region has been renowned for its coffee. The Javanese coffee seen on the U.S. specialty coffee market is primarily from a handful of government estates, with Blawan, Djampit (alternately seen as Jampit), Kayumas, and Pancur being the most commonly encountered. These coffees are fully and meticulously wet processed and are typically of high quality.

Good Javanese coffees are relatively clean (for the Indonesian cup profile); express a subdued vibrancy; and have luxurious, creamy, or buttery mouthfeel and body that are supported by flavors of vanilla, spice, and brown sugar. While Java's coffees are full-bodied, they do tend to be a bit lighter than semi-washed Indonesians, like those from Sumatra. Occasionally, you may run into an aged Java coffee, often referred to as Old Java Brown. The aging process, often several years, mellows the coffee's acidity while increasing its pungency and body. Although not for every palate, aged coffees have a following and are sometimes used as a special ingredient to spice up blends.

> **Field Notes**
>
> Not all of Java's specialty-grade coffee is produced by government estates, but coffees from private farms do not tend to be as well prepared and are, therefore, not seen as often.

Sulawesi

Sometimes still marketed under its colonial Dutch name of Celebes, Sulawesi produces high-quality arabica (often washed or semi-washed) coffee. Like a resonant low note, Sulawesi coffees have thick, syrupy bodies and lingering mouthfeels with deep, rich, and, often, earthy flavors. They tend to have a balancing, reserved acidity that rounds out the complex cup profile nicely.

Most Sulawesi coffees you encounter will be grown on plantations in the Toraja growing region, although it is also referred to by the colonial name of Kalossi. Other coffees of the island, usually from smaller producers, tend to be slightly more rugged in the cup than Torajas and carry a bit more body.

East Timor

The quality of East Timor's coffee has improved in recent years since its bloody fight for independence in the 1990s. With the help of USAID, new washing stations have been built that allow better, more consistent processing. Much of Timor's coffee is grown organically by smallholders and so is reliant on proper infrastructure to produce consistent, high-quality coffee. The efforts have been paying off, and the nation is regaining a reputation for its coffee.

Good Timorese coffee is full-bodied, with a smooth mouthfeel that lingers a bit less than is typical for Indonesian coffees, although nonetheless is enjoyable. They often have pleasant cocoa and woody tones that are set off by moderate to mild acidity.

Papua New Guinea

Coffees from Papua New Guinea (often seen abbreviated as PNG) are, at times, hidden in the shadows of those from nearby origins like Sulawesi and Sumatra because their cup character is not typically as heavy or earthy. But a good PNG coffee, with its medium to full body, lively acidity, and deeply fruited flavors, is worthy of praise in its own right.

One issue that heavily influences the consistency of PNG coffee is that the vast majority is grown on small farms and village gardens. Unlike larger plantations that have modern processing facilities onsite and meticulous quality control, coffee from these small growers is processed somewhat differently by each farm and with a variety of homemade equipment. The resulting character of the coffees ranges quite a bit, with a tendency to be fruitier and more rustic.

> **Field Notes**
>
> Unfortunately, the rudimentary methods small growers employ often produce coffees that cross the line of desirable wildness into an unpleasant musty or fermented nature. Although no reason to avoid smallholder's or cooperative's coffees, it can take more sampling to find special lots (precisely what good roasters do).

Regional labeling is a fairly new concept for PNG coffees, and often coffees are designated by the producing estate or cooperative.

The Least You Need to Know

- Coffee's taste is influenced by its growing conditions and by how it is processed.

- Coffees from the Americas (save Brazil) are generally wet processed and are enjoyed for their clean acidity.

- Due to their surrounding seas, the Caribbean Islands and Hawaii produce coffees that are soft and balanced.

- The coffee-growing region of Africa and Arabia is the oldest area, producing beans that are lively, fruity, and complex.

- Notoriously big-bodied and earthy coffees of Indonesia and the nearby islands (e.g., Papua New Guinea) are resonant and low in acidity.

Part 2

Capturing Coffee's Flavor

Now that you have a good background in the world of specialty coffee, it's time to really dig in to coffee's flavor equation. We begin in Part 2 by examining the roasting process, where coffee's flavor is developed. Then we take a closer look at taste perception and learn how to break down and evaluate the flavors and characteristics in coffees. Finally, join us as we thoroughly explore how to brew great coffee at home and take a look at several of the most common brewers.

When you've completed Part 2, you'll be prepared to make coffee that out-cups the coffee served at most coffeehouses. So grab a steaming mug and join us on an exciting adventure through the flavorful realm of coffee!

Chapter 4

Now We're Roastin'

In This Chapter

- Learn how roasting affects coffee's flavor

- Understand the roasting process

- Discover the advantages of roasting at home

- Get an overview of the various methods and tools you can use to roast coffee at home

It pays to understand how the roasting process affects the taste of coffee, whether you buy your beans from a specialty roaster or roast your own. The impact of roasting can hardly be overstated, as it influences flavor more than any other variable from seed to cup.

In this chapter, you learn about the various steps involved in the commercial roasting process. And with just a bit of patience and the knowledge of how to manage the process, you'll soon be roasting your own coffee beans in your kitchen. We explain how this happens and what to expect from different roast styles. Now let's get roastin'!

The Roasting Process

The roasting process is seemingly straightforward—heating green coffee beans until they're browned to a desired degree—but it can be a bit complex as well. Variables such as where the coffee was grown, the method used to prepare it (e.g., wet or dry process), and the cultivar from which it was grown all impact how it roasts. Additionally, the roasting conditions, like batch size and manner of heat transfer (e.g., convection), play a role in determining how a roast develops.

Regardless of just how the variables for a roast come together, however, all roasts progress through some major milestones along the way. The time needed to do so can vary widely, from less than 6 minutes to more than 20.

Drying Time

During the initial stage of roasting, beans are essentially dried out so they lose all their moisture. As they dry, they turn a pale yellow and then begin to brown. The steam driven off during this initial phase of roasting smells at first grassy and then somewhat bready. The drying time varies quite a bit depending on the type of roasting machine used; the hot-air roasters many home roasters use do this very efficiently, taking about half the time commercial drum roasters do.

First Crack: Where the Action Begins

As the bean is heated and the moisture is driven off, structural changes occur in the bean, causing a distinct popping noise called *first crack*. This crackling, which sounds like popping corn, marks the beginning of the transformation to roasted coffee and indicates that the beans have reached an internal temperature of approximately 380°F. If the beans continue to be roasted, another round of popping, referred to as *second crack*, occurs.

Buzz Words

First crack is the point in the roasting process at which the beans begin to pop and make a crackling noise much like popcorn. It effectively marks the light end of the roasting spectrum.

After the coffee has passed first crack, the bean is in a lighter roasting stage (typically called cinnamon) and could be removed from the machine if that's the darkest color desired. At this point, the roast begins to smoke a bit and smell more like coffee as the beans' internal sugars are caramelized.

The expanding of the bean through this process essentially loosens and allows the *chaff*, the thin

silverskin covering on the bean, to be
released and fly free. Most roasting
machines have a chaff collection device
to separate the chaff from the rest of the
coffee.

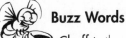 **Buzz Words**

Chaff is the paper-thin skin
that detaches from the surface of the coffee bean as the
temperature increases.

The Calm Before the Storm

Between first crack and second crack is a relatively quiet period. During this time, the
beans warm up approximately another 50°. Chaff and smoke continue to be released,
and sugars are further caramelized. By this point, the roast must be watched quite
closely, as it changes significantly in a short period of time.

Roasts stopped during this time would generally be labeled medium roasts. By this
point, the beans have expanded considerably—by approximately 50 percent; have
smooth, dry surfaces; and tend to be a bit more evenly colored than those stopped at
light roasts.

Second Crack: The Gateway to Dark Roasts

Near the end of the roast (in most cases) the drama really increases, and this is especially the case for dark roasts. The roast develops so quickly that just seconds can
mean the difference between hitting your ideal roast level and a botched batch.

Second crack, the gateway to the darker roasts, begins at approximately 440°F, with
most roasts concluding at less than 475°. Smoke intensifies and grows more pungent
as second crack begins. The cracking noise is fainter-sounding than first crack but
violent enough to shear off pieces of the beans.

The beans begin to develop spots of oil and can even be glazed in oil if darkly
roasted, as the fats in the bean are liquefied and driven to the surface. Roast tastes
become more prominent and pungent, with the bean's origin character fading more
and more into the background. Eventually, the unique character of the bean becomes
impossible to distinguish as the roast notes overwhelm the coffee's flavor.

To some palates, dark, bittersweet roasts are quite desirable. To others, however, they
serve only as a sharp reminder that the beans have lost their individuality.

Stopping the Roast

When the desired level of roast is reached, the beans must be cooled as quickly as possible. Due to built-up heat, they continue to roast even after they're removed from the roaster, so it's easy to overshoot your desired roast unless the beans are quickly cooled.

Beans are usually cooled by drawing cool air through the beans and agitating them slightly. They can also be sprayed with cool water, but we don't think it's necessary and more often, especially when not closely controlled, it can be overdone, leading to more harm than good. Most commercial drum roasters have a cooling tray into which the beans are dumped. Air is sucked over and through the beans as paddles gently churn them. At home, shaking the hot beans in a colander does a good job, and if you can do it in front of a fan, all the better.

How Roasting Affects Flavor

Roasting is a process of amazing transformation. Not only does it turn hard, dense little green beans into the dark, somewhat brittle beans we're most familiar with, it also changes the chemical makeup and brings out new flavors. In fact, if curiosity has ever gotten the better of you and you've tried a green coffee bean, you've probably been struck by just how great the change is from unroasted to roasted product.

Cuppa Wisdom

The more techniques you have absorbed, the more you are master of *la cuisine*.
—Julia Child

The degree of change is determined, generally speaking, by how fast the roast progresses and how dark the resulting roast is. The same beans can exhibit quite a range of flavors—from negative to positive, depending on how it's roasted.

Acidity

The acidity in coffee—not the kind that burns holes into things, but rather the tasty sort that brings a pleasant sparkle to your tongue—can be manipulated quite a bit by adjusting the roast.

Generally speaking, the lighter the roast, the more acidity is displayed. At very light roasts, the acidity can be somewhat sour and even overpowering, depending, of course, on the bean's varietal characteristics. With more roast, the acidity becomes tamer and is eventually muted until it folds into the bittersweet roast tastes. Roasts designed to bring out the best vibrancy from a bean tend to be at a medium level but yet on the lighter side and completed fairly quickly. Roasting more slowly and to a bit darker level subdues the coffee's brightness and is a technique often employed when roasting for espresso extraction.

Body

The body of brewed coffee, or the sense of the coffee's thickness on your tongue, is also affected by the degree of roast. To understand how roast level and body interact, imagine a bell curve. At both very light and very dark roasts, a coffee displays its thinnest body. At moderate roasts, coffee shows a fair amount of its potential for body and continues to build until it crescendos at the lighter side of dark roasts, shortly after second crack. Like acidity, the speed of the roast impacts the resulting body, and given the same end level, slower roasts tend to have more body.

Varietal Characteristics

Ah, varietal characteristics—those nuances, quirks, and unique tastes we prize in well-prepared specialty coffee. Broadly speaking, these elements are displayed at their peak in light roasts. As the roast level builds, more subtle notes are obscured—which, depending on exactly what those are (and your perspective), can either be good or bad. This is, however, the reason importers and roasters roast coffee lightly when evaluating it prior to buying. Sometimes referred to as a *sample roast*, these light roasts allow a window into what the particular beans have to offer with as little interference from roast notes as possible.

Because more roast just obscures the varietal details farmers take care to preserve, it's fair to wonder why all coffees aren't simply lightly roasted. We admit our bias is indeed toward roasts at the middle and lighter side of the spectrum, but choosing a roast for a particular coffee is a complex balancing act that demands compromises. Additionally, some palates prefer the effects for increased roast, be it reduced acidity, increased body, or the presence of roast-dependent tastes. And in some cases, the varietal characteristic that the roaster wants to highlight can be best showcased at a dark roast, like when spotlighting the syrupy body of an Indonesian bean.

Roast Tastes

As a roast develops, the taste it imparts changes. In lighter roasts, toasted cereal or grain notes can typically be found. Practically speaking, though, these very light roasts aren't usually desirable because of the sourness the acidity displays.

Roasts that are too light may also have an undesirable breadiness. As the sugars in the roasting coffee caramelize, the coffee begins to pick some corresponding sweet tones. At the same time, the acidity is transformed from a snappy vibrancy to a rich, pungent quality. Carmalized sugars eventually burn and impart deeper, sharper notes, which often have a bit of a chary taste.

How Dark Is Dark?

If you've purchased much coffee, you've probably run into a number of terms used to describe the level to which the coffee has been roasted. Unfortunately, the use of such terms is not consistently applied, which can lead to confusion and frustration when buying coffee. Not only might the same roast level be referred to by several terms, the roast level described as "full city" by one roaster may be another's "city" roast.

Field Notes

Roast style terminology has developed over the years and generally falls into two categories: those named for geographical areas and those spun out of traditional American use. The first group takes the name of regions known for a particular roast preference, like French roast denoting a darker roast akin to the traditional preference in France. The other group of roast names was born in America as a way of comparing roasts with familiar things, like the color of cinnamon. Another common term from this group is "city," which refers to coffee available in cities (as opposed to rural areas) before commercial roasts were widely available; today "city" connotes a medium roast.

All is not lost, however, as long as you keep in mind that the use of any roast-level terminology is relative. The trick, of course, is to understand how a roaster uses the terms, so once you're familiar with its system of descriptions, you're set. Don't, however, expect the Vienna roast you've fallen in love with from one roaster to match the roast level of another's Vienna roast.

Field Notes

Never be afraid to ask your roaster for more details about a specific roast you're considering. Roasters who take pride in their work tend to love to talk about their craft.

In the following table, we've given you a general guide to help you determine degree of roast.

Quick Guide to Roast Styles

Roast Level	Roast Names
Light	Cinnamon
	New England
Medium	American
	City
Dark	Full city
	Viennese
	French
	Italian
	Spanish

Note: This list is intended to give you an idea of relative degree of roast assigned to several commonly used roast identifiers. Terms listed here are subjective in nature and their use can vary.

The Perks of Home Roasting

Perhaps the most obvious way to get quality roasted coffee is to head to your nearest specialty coffee retailer, but you may not even have to leave the house. Today more than ever, roasting at home is a viable alternative to buying preroasted coffee. The last 5 or so years have brought several new home-roasting machines to the consumer market, and high-quality green coffee is readily accessible in small quantities suitable for personal use. But perhaps most important, roasting coffee at home is fairly simple and has some definite advantages.

Savings Are in the Bag

One of the first perks of roasting at home many people recognize is that it costs less. Making a direct comparison is somewhat challenging because the particular lots of coffee available roasted and green tend to vary, but it's clearly cheaper to roast your own.

At the time of this writing, high-quality green coffee runs roughly $5 to $6 per pound, depending on origin and lot specifics (Cup of Excellence lots, for example, tend to cost a little more). Roasted coffee of similar quality tends to vary more in price but is typically at least twice as expensive. It's important to remember, however, that green coffee weighs more than roasted coffee due to moisture loss during roasting; a loss of between 14 and 20 percent is fairly usual and depends on how darkly roasted the coffee is.

Field Notes

An easy (and fairly conservative) way to estimate the true cost of green coffee is to multiply the purchase price by 1.25. This accounts for the weight loss during roasting and gives you an easy number to use when comparing to roasted coffee sold by the pound. If you're comparing green coffee to roasted coffee sold in 12-ounce bags, though, just using the green purchase price will get you pretty close.

Of course, to make a true cost comparison, you'll need to factor in the cost of the equipment. The pleasant surprise here is that you may already have equipment that will work or you can secure simple roasting tools for less than $20. Granted, if you decide to roast a lot, you may want to spring for a more elaborate (and more expensive) setup. However, if you start with a simple system that requires only a small investment, it's easy to justify buying a few pounds and giving home roasting a try. Even if you later decide it's not something that works for you on a regular basis, you will have recouped your costs. What's more, you'll have gained invaluable experience and understanding from the process. We'll get into more detail on home roasting equipment and tackling the task in a minute.

Fresh Is Best

While the cost savings of roasting at home can indeed be alluring, it's the freshness factor that sinks the hook for many people. Roasting a batch of coffee (including cleanup time in most cases) doesn't take much more than about 20 minutes, so it's easy to always have freshly roasted coffee on hand. This can be especially attractive for those who don't live near a coffee roastery.

Although some roasters and retailers are starting to include roast dates on their packaging, many aren't because it usually wouldn't be to their advantage. This is especially the case for coffee distributed through third-party channels like grocers and coffee shops that don't roast their own. Even in fast-distribution scenarios, coffee is likely to be several days past the roasting date. That's still fresh, but you have missed out on much or all of the coffee's peak freshness period. More typically, distribution situations are far less freshness-friendly.

Consider a hypothetical example of a local roastery supplying a chain of grocery stores with prepackaged coffee. Large quantities are often ordered at once, which may take the roaster several days to pack. From there, the coffee likely is shipped to the grocer's centralized warehouse. Extra days are lost as the stock finds its way first to the individual stores and then from the stockroom to the shelf. If you were the first customer to buy that coffee, you'd have coffee past its prime but it would still most likely taste okay. But what if you're the last customer to buy that coffee?

Field Notes

Ordering online from roasters that package and ship their coffee shortly after roasting it does mitigate freshness concerns to some degree, but shipping costs rarely make it attractive to purchase only enough for a week or less. So consumers are forced to pay dearly for freshness or buy more coffee than can be quickly consumed to defray shipping costs; obviously, the latter "solution" is self-defeating.

In fairness, some roasters have bulk displays in stores that sell high enough volumes to ensure the coffee is never more than a few days old. And if you're buying only enough coffee to last a week, the system works pretty well. Other roasters may deliver and stock prepackaged coffees for the grocer so bags of stale coffee are routinely culled from the shelves. Often, a coded sticker tells the roaster but not the consumer about the coffee's freshness.

It's in freshness that home roasting truly shines. You can easily keep yourself supplied with very fresh beans. A small note of warning, however: don't be surprised if you become quite attached to the aroma and taste of truly fresh coffee.

Hot Water

It's only fair to question any freshness-dating system that's not totally transparent in nature. If the manufacturer isn't giving you that information, assume there's a reason. That said, look for a *roasting* date rather than a *freshness* date. The latter is merely the time the roaster is willing to accede that it's extremely likely the coffee is stone-cold stale.

Your Way Tastes Great

Another key advantage of roasting at home is the inherent flexibility it brings. Just as when you cook or bake other fine foods, you can tailor coffee to your tastes. Because you are in control at home, you can roast to your own preferences rather than being stuck with someone else's. Let's say, for example, you are particularly fond of lightly roasted Sumatran coffee but all your local roasters bring their Sumatran offerings to a much darker roast. You're stuck with the dark roasts—unless you roast your own.

It's also much easier to come up with your own blends when you roast your own. Not only can you mix together just the beans you want, but you also have the flexibility to play around with multiple roast levels for the component coffees to tweak the resulting blend to your tastes.

Getting the Green (Coffee Beans)

As we mentioned earlier, it's easier now than ever to find high-quality green beans. The trouble has been that the market just isn't set up for the home roaster. Coffee is typically exported to the United States in 60- or 70-kilogram burlaps sacks, which is way too much for the typical home roaster—that is, unless you usually consume more than 100 pounds of roasted coffee (from the same origin) every few months. Even if you did, buying a bag from an importer/broker would prove quite an undertaking. Quality varies considerably in the coffees any given broker carries, and ending up with 132 pounds of a musty, defective Sumatran, for example, would leave a fairly bad taste in your mouth.

Hot Water

Dry-processed green coffee sometimes has foreign objects mixed in with it—small sticks, stones, and even nails. Commercial roasters use de-stoners to ensure these hazards are removed so they don't wreak roasting machines and grinders, but as a home roaster, you'll have to stay alert and remove them manually.

Both issues—available quantities and quality—are solved by several intermediary businesses that have sprung up to serve home roasters. Granted, their involvement means the green coffee price you pay goes up, but it's well worth it. A good green-coffee supplier (to the consumer market) will cup a lot of green samples from each origin and only purchase those that make the grade.

The benefit of this can hardly be overstated. You want a supplier who puts cup character first and doesn't carry coffees just to fill a roster. Naturally, this can be a little challenging to assess just by looking over the shop's offerings, but you might be surprised how much you can discern by looking through the store's literature or website. The descriptions of the offerings should indicate intimate knowledge of how that particular lot of coffee (not just origin) cups.

Another possible option for getting high-quality green coffee is to buy from your favorite local roaster. This is handy because you can taste their roasts before you buy. Not only does this give you a good idea of the quality of the green they're using, but it also gives you a reference point to compare with as you evaluate your roasts. Few roasters actively promote green coffee sales, but many are open to the idea. The challenge here lies in pricing, as they may not have established prices for unroasted coffee. So prepare yourself ahead of time to make an offer or to quickly evaluate theirs. Paying more than 80 percent of their roasted price is obviously a losing situation, as the end cost of the green would be roughly equivalent to buying a pound roasted. It's a bit of a hit-or-miss proposition that depends, essentially, on how big of a markup the roaster desires. But it's worth inquiring, because you can sometimes find great values this way.

Field Notes

It's fair to be wary of those suppliers with enormous selections of coffees from nearly every growing region. It's rare to find so many truly excellent coffees at once, so it's likely some aren't so great—but which ones? Try a few selections from a dealer before you invest too much at first and until you know the green buyer has a palate that agrees with yours.

Storing Unroasted Coffee

The great thing about green coffee is that it's much more stable than roasted coffee and can keep for several months. As it ages, it slowly loses its edge and more delicate nuances. For example, over time, a Costa Rican coffee that has snappy acidity when it's fresh (recently harvested and processed) will start to show less and less vibrancy and power in the cup.

Additionally, old green coffees can pick up undesirable off-flavors, like a baggy taste from the burlap sack in which it's stored. The most common way to store green coffee is to simply leave it in a cloth bag in a place that's relatively cool and doesn't experience strong shifts in temperature or humidity. Most home environments are just fine.

Ever in pursuit of coffee quality, George Howell, the co-founder of the Cup of Excellence, has experimented with freezing green coffee. He recommends vacuum-sealing and freezing green coffee to lock in the coffee's nuances. His experiments indicate that even delicate coffees maintain their character well for at least a year when frozen. So convinced is he that his company, Terroir Select Coffee, now repackages and freezes all its green coffee.

The necessary cold storage makes such a commitment difficult for many commercial roasters but can easily be tackled by home roasters. We haven't had time to make our own long-term comparisons, but the method appears promising and we recommend giving it a try for yourself.

> **Field Notes**
>
> If you don't have a vacuum sealer, try putting your beans into airtight containers. To avoid repeated thawing and freezing, package the coffees in amounts that make sense for your roasting needs so you can remove one entire package at a time. When you remove a pack of frozen coffee, open it and allow it to come to room temperature prior to using it.

Home Roasting Machines

A renaissance of sorts has been underway for several years, bringing renewed interest in home roasting. Fortunately, with it have come many developments and improvements in the roasting tools available for home use. Several roasters, ranging from very simple models that resemble modified popcorn poppers to those that replicate commercial drum roasters, are now specifically designed for home roasting.

In addition to the variety of new machine designs available, a few tried-and-true low-tech alternatives remain viable options. Let's take a look at the most common methods and machines to roast coffee at home.

Fluid-Bed Roasters: Not Just Hot Air

The most common type of home roasters, *fluid-bed roasters*, keep the beans in constant motion as heated air is forced through the batch, much like hot-air popcorn poppers. People have been roasting with these simple machines for ages because they cost less than $20, do a decent job, and roast very quickly, often in less than 6 minutes.

> **Buzz Words**
>
> Roasters that use a constant stream of moving hot air to both agitate the beans (to ensure an even roast) as well as roast them are often referred to as **fluid-bed roasters.**

Fluid-bed roasters make good starting machines because they allow you to see and smell the roast so you can easily monitor the beans' progress. And although these roasters do have a small capacity (typically between $\frac{1}{4}$ and $\frac{1}{2}$ pound unroasted coffee—roughly the same as the manufacturer's recommended amount of popcorn), they hold enough beans for about 2 or 3 days worth of coffee and ensure you're always using beans at their peak freshness.

Be sure any popper you use has vents in the side of the roasting chamber (where the popcorn swirls and pops). Poppers that blow hot air up from the center of the roasting chamber can cause the chaff to catch fire and are not safe to use.

The rapid roast poppers yield can lead to somewhat simpler cup profiles with less body compared with the longer roasts (roughly 10 to 17 minutes) achieved in a commercial drum roaster. Also, you don't have any control over roasting temperature, which limits your ability to finesse roasts. Another drawback is that roasting smoke is not vented and chaff flies freely out the chute.

Hot Water

If you're using a popcorn popper to roast coffee, it's most practical to roast under a strong ventilated stove hood or outdoors. Point the chute over a bowl or a sink to catch the loose chaff—or risk having it shoot everywhere! Also, the smoke produced during the roast cycle will fill the room with a lingering pungency guaranteed to draw scorn from anyone who lives with you.

If you use a popcorn popper to roast your beans, you'll need to cool them down manually. (Hot-air roasters designed for coffee roasting have built-in cooling cycles.) To do this, dump the beans into a metal colander and gently shake until they're cool.

Fluid-bed machines come with built-in chaff collectors and are programmed to have cool-down cycles to stop the roast quickly. More sophisticated models allow control over the roasting temperature, and most allow easily repeatable results. Prices vary from approximately $75 to $175, depending on features.

Field Notes

Unless you want coffee-flavored popcorn, it's best to dedicate a hot-air popcorn popper to coffee roasting only, as removing the scent and flavor of coffee is nearly impossible.

Drum Roasters

Home drum roasters work just as their larger commercial cousins do, by employing a spinning cylindrical roasting chamber to ensure beans are continually moving during the roast cycle. They tend to have larger capacities (½ pound or more) than air roasters and afford more control over the roast. Their larger batch capacity means more smoke is produced, increasing your need for ventilation.

Unfortunately, drum roasters for home use tend to be very expensive—often upward of $600—making them hard to justify if you're roasting to save money. On the other hand, they're hard to beat if you want the ability to coax out great roasts at home.

Hot Water _____

If your roasting equipment allows for temperature control, be sure to experiment, as different roasting parameters affect the coffee's flavor profile. For example, starting with a lower beginning temperature helps coax the best from gentle island coffees like Jamaican Blue Mountain.

Stovetop Roasting

Whether it's using a skillet, wok, or crank-style stovetop popcorn popper, all stovetop roasting methods transfer heat directly through contact with the hot metal. Therefore, if you use these methods to roast coffee, you'll find that batches tend to be somewhat uneven, especially at lighter roasts. Most of these methods work best for dark roasts.

Field Notes _____

If you opt for a stovetop popper, be sure to first drill a hole in the lid to accommodate a 550°F thermometer. Because you won't be able to see the beans, knowing the temperature will help you monitor the roast.

If you roast coffee on your stovetop, be sure you have a vented stove hood to suck out the smoke. Strong wrists come in handy, as well, to ensure the beans stay in constant motion.

Chaff collection is more work with these methods because it's not blown loose. Using a hairdryer with a cool-air setting can help blow the chaff into a garbage can. Cool the roast by tossing or shaking it in a metal colander.

Oven Roasting

Roasting in a kitchen oven allows for larger batch sizes (½ pound or more) than do most other methods for home roasting, but this type of roasting takes longer to master. When you've figured out what combination of time and temperature work best, though, you can easily replicate the results.

A good starting temperature is roughly 500°F, but temperatures as high as 550° work as well. Just spread the beans in an even, single layer on a perforated pan, and pop it into a preheated oven. Avoid the urge to multitask, and keep an eye on the roast's progress. When the beans are done, simply cool them in a metal colander and remove the chaff.

People report widely different success with this method, as ovens vary. Be prepared to experiment.

Roasting Accessories

While not necessary to roast at home, a few accessories will make the task easier—and more repeatable:

Cuppa Wisdom _____

Coffee is a beverage that puts one to sleep when not drank.
—Alphonse Allais

+ A scale

+ A thermometer

+ A roast log or notebook

A scale helps you ensure you're roasting the same quantity of beans each time, removing another variable that can throw off your results. Measuring green beans by volume doesn't work as well because beans vary in density depending on where they were grown and from what cultivar they were raised. Additionally, hot-air roasters especially have a "sweet spot" with regard to batch size, and using a scale will help you find it easily.

Field Notes _____

We find digital gram scales especially handy and recommend one that measures to $1/10$ gram if you can find one cheaply.

Besides using a scale to measure your green coffee before roasting, you can weigh the coffee afterward to calculate how much moisture the beans lost.

A thermometer can be very useful both in helping you monitor the roast and by making your roasts more repeatable. You can use simple analog probe-style thermometers with hot-air and stovetop poppers by simply drilling a small hole in the top of the roasting chamber. Stovetop poppers shouldn't be used without a thermometer, because you can't otherwise easily monitor the roast and avoid burning. Another option is a digital thermometer with a j- or k-type thermocouple probe. In many cases, you can snake these thin wires into roasting chambers without further modification, and they are more accurate.

Whatever method you use to measure the temperature of the batch, try to position the probe so it's within as large a mass of beans as possible. The temperature reading you'll get will in many cases be closer to the overall roasting environment temperature than the actual internal bean temperature. Hot-air roasters are especially challenging to take accurate temperatures with because the current of hot air skews the reading.

While it's easy to overlook as a roast accessory, the roast log may be the most important tool. By recording the batch weight (pre- and post-roast), varietal information, duration, temperature readings, and notes about the overall roast progression, you can learn from every batch. Not only will this help you fine-tune the roast, it helps point out techniques that work especially well. Likewise, if you need to troubleshoot a roast issue, having the variables written down to study is invaluable. Be sure to leave room in your log for the most important part: your reflections on the roast over a cup of the coffee.

Putting a Roast to Rest

Just-roasted coffee is a delicious treat, especially when the coffee was roasted by your hand. But the flavor of the coffee will actually improve with at least a few hours of resting time. Most coffees will taste their best with about a day's rest, but others may take longer. During this time large amounts of carbon dioxide gas, generated during the roasting process, escape, and the flavor seems to settle out just a bit.

Store your fresh coffee in an airtight container out of direct sunlight and at room temperature. For more details on storing coffee, be sure to check out our detailed discussion in Chapter 7.

The Least You Need to Know

- Roasting causes dramatic changes within the beans, readying them for brewing.
- Coffee loses moisture during roasting and weighs approximately 14 to 20 percent less than when green.
- A coffee's varietal characteristics tend to be displayed most prominently at a relatively light roast.
- Dark roasts tend to have subdued acidity but do have a bittersweet, pungent taste.
- Roasting at home takes less than 20 minutes (often much less) and is an easy way to ensure you have fresh coffee.

Chapter 5

Cupping and Blending

In This Chapter

- ◆ Understand how we taste and perceive coffee
- ◆ Learn to critically evaluate coffees
- ◆ Build your tasting vocabulary
- ◆ Discover the keys to successful blends

Now that you understand more about the variables that influence how different coffees taste, let's turn now to the tasty task of examining how it all comes together in the cup. It's important to know how dry processing, for example, affects the flavors a given coffee will express, but what's most crucial is which tastes actually end up in the cup.

Evaluating coffees and discerning all the nuances swimming in the mug may be more challenging than it first sounds. Professionals who roast and evaluate coffee on a regular basis develop and hone their taste discrimination abilities and sensory memories. In this chapter, we dissect how it all works and how you can adapt the procedures practically to help build and develop your palate.

When you've begun to be able to distinguish the flavor notes in coffees, it's natural to favor certain ones and to desire a certain *flavor profile*, or set of tastes. By combining different coffees, you can create a blend that expresses a different set of taste characteristics than a single-origin bean alone does. Just as randomly mixing a few foods together can create drastically different results, blindly combining coffees is a hit-or-miss proposition. We cover the basics of blending here so you'll be better equipped to begin your own experiments and understand the blends you purchase from your favorite roaster.

Understanding the Taste Experience

Have you ever tried to describe how something tasted, only to come up with descriptions of things you've never even tried? For example, when describing a less-than-tasty dish, maybe you compared it with saddle leather, gym socks, or damp leaves. But have you ever actually tasted any of those things? (We hope not!)

Our perception of taste is the result a highly complex marriage of many simultaneous stimuli and processes. It's perhaps a little counterintuitive that the basis of our sense of taste is actually that of another sense: smell. This is why we sometimes resort to relating the taste of something to the smell of another and why food doesn't taste as good when you have a head cold—your sense of smell is impaired. In fact, the sense of taste is so dependent on smell that it's estimated that at least 75 percent of taste is actually regulated by smell, largely because we have _gustatory_ (_taste_) _receptors_ numbering in the thousands but are equipped with _olfactory_ (_smell_) _receptors_ in the millions.

Indeed, without our sense of smell, taste is blindsided. Except for the tactile sensation in the mouth, an apple and an onion would be indistinguishable without smell! To smell something, its scent or aroma must become airborne and drawn into the nasal cavity; it must vaporize and become gaseous. Not only do we take in odors directly through our noses by sniffing but also indirectly as they waft up the passageway in the back of the mouth that leads to the nasal cavity. Scent-filled air is pumped up this channel as we chew and when we swallow.

Although olfaction is paramount to taste, one certainly cannot overlook the tongue and its taste buds. If the nose is the keystone to taste that pulls it all together, the tongue and taste buds form the basis for the experience. We can discern five basic tastes (as opposed to thousands of smells): sweet, sour, salt, bitter, and umami (a savory taste akin to MSG; pronounced *oo-MAH-mee*). The majority of our taste buds are distributed around the sides and the tip of the tongue, though others are scattered throughout the oral cavity. As our food becomes liquid, taste buds send signals to the brain, where it is synthesized into a taste experience.

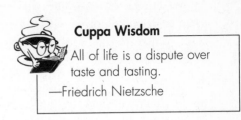

Cuppa Wisdom

All of life is a dispute over taste and tasting.

—Friedrich Nietzsche

Do You Taste What I Taste?

Because the tastes we perceive are such complex orchestrations, it's rare that we experience the same food or drink in precisely the same way every time we try it. As the complexity of what you taste increases, so, too, does the likelihood for somewhat different experiences each time you sample it. Such is the case of coffee, with its hundreds of tasty compounds. This can be both exciting and vexing. Rather than expecting a coffee to treat your taste buds the same every time, sample it several times to develop a thorough impression of its character.

What's more, taste perceptions are influenced by many factors outside the cup, including moods, environment (such as music and lighting), physical condition, genetics, age, and time of day. It's easy to assume that when we share a cup of coffee with someone that they are experiencing the same things we are, but that's not necessarily the case. As with other senses—eyesight, for example—the keenness of our abilities to perceive tastes and smells varies from person to person.

Taste scientists use the chemical 6-n-propylthiouracil, or PROP, to test taste sensitivity. PROP is a bitter compound that's handy because while some people taste it strongly, others cannot detect it at all.

During taste tests, scientists have found that roughly 25 percent find the substance horribly distasteful and bitter, while another 25 percent taste nothing at all. The remaining 50 percent taste the chemical and find it somewhat unpleasant. The primary reason for this is thought to be the concentration of clusters of taste buds on the tongue.

Field Notes

We are most able to detect bitterness, to the tune of parts per million. In contrast, we detect sweetness the least acutely, in parts per hundred.

"Super-tasters" have tongues densely loaded with the clusters, whereas "nontasters" are merely polka-dotted with the receptors. Perhaps as an evolutionary device to prevent women from ingesting poisons, which are typically bitter, women tend to be more sensitive tasters.

Because tastes are amplified for them, super-tasters tend to be picky eaters with distinct likes and dislikes. While super-tasters tend to find a few common things too strong, they don't seem to share a clear set of culinary preferences. Spicy foods are likely to seem hotter and more painful to these sensitive tongues, though, and the bitter compounds, like caffeine in coffee and tea, may be more pronounced and less pleasant.

Nontasters of PROP, on the other hand, tend to be more indifferent toward foods and, in fact, may not even sense some of the tastes others do. Obviously, both extremes have unique challenges to evaluating coffee, and the differences underscore the importance of training and believing your own tongue.

Field Notes

Getting a sense for your taste sensitivity isn't difficult and can be tested using a few household supplies. Simply paper-punch a hole in a piece of wax paper. Hold the hole to the tip of your tongue, and dab a little blue food coloring on the exposed portion of your tongue. The clusters of taste buds will remain pinkish, so you can easily count the dots you see inside the circle (you may need a magnifying glass). If they number more than about 35, consider yourself a super-taster; if you see less than 15, you're more likely to be a nontaster (of PROP). Just don't let the title of the group you fall in mislead you; everyone has the potential to refine and develop their palate.

Building Your Taste Vocabulary

For most people, the most challenging part of evaluating coffees is verbalizing what their taste buds are telling them. It's no wonder that with the hundreds of flavor compounds teeming in the cup, it's difficult to pin down the precise tastes you're tasting most prominently. Luckily, because much of the taste experience is transferable from one food or drink to another, you've been building your database of tastes for years. And if you're a connoisseur of any food or drink, whether it's cheesecake or wine, you've already been exercising your palate. For example, you're well on your way when you identify grapefruity notes in the hop character of one beer and distinguish them from piney flavors in another.

Field Notes

Communicating the nuance of taste can be intimidating enough to render some mute and resign others to the dichotomy of "I like it" or "I don't like it." The key is to toss out any worries of sounding silly and focus on describing the experience. You're already armed with the knowledge that everyone's perception is unique, so you can easily thwart any ridicule.

As you taste the coffee and move it about your mouth, think about what it brings to mind. A taste, a memory, a person, or nearly anything could form. Let's say you found your way to a defective coffee. It might remind you of your grandmother's basement or perhaps like eating a newspaper that spent a week in the rain. There's nothing wrong with that; in fact, it's good. From there, try to further break down what's driving these thoughts. Perhaps you're picking up on a damp, musty, or moldy scent.

Some people can easily associate the tastes of coffees with colors, celebrities, or models of cars. As long as you avoid oversimplification and push to bring as much meaning to your descriptions as possible, you're bound to develop an effective vocabulary for discussing coffees. And as you pay attention to taste, you'll also start to pick up nuances in other foods and drinks you consume that will further build and refine your personal dictionary of tastes.

The Art of Cupping

Given all the things that influence the taste of coffee—growing conditions, processing, shipping, storage, roasting, etc.—industry professionals needed a way to judge coffees and to help discern where flavor nuances were coming from. And so cupping was born.

Cupping refers to a routine method of tasting coffees so as to objectify as much as possible the subjective process of evaluating coffees. The process becomes a ritualistic parade of coffee for the senses and can appear a bit intimidating, but there's no reason for it. Cupping is little more than tasting coffee following a few standard procedures to ensure all the coffees judged receive a fair shake.

Field Notes

Because expectations influence our perceptions, coffee roasters and importers will sometimes perform blind cuppings, where the identity of each coffee is unknown throughout the judging process. This is an especially useful technique for ranking coffees against each other, like when comparing several from the same region.

Set the Stage

Have you ever read a roaster's description of a coffee and wondered about, for example, how they found plum flavors? It was most likely during a cupping session, which allows the most unadultered look into the flavors of coffee. You can find those same flavors, too.

The best place to cup coffee is somewhere that's free of distractions so you can concentrate on what you're sampling. Remove anything that takes your attention away from the coffee, and be sure the room is quiet and free of any rogue scents. Forgo any cologne or perfume you usually wear, and also rid the area of other foods and scented products. When you start to target and eliminate odors from your cupping area, you may be surprised at all the scents lingering around.

Hot Water

From our clothes to our cosmetics, we're a highly scented society, and stray odors can negatively impact your ability to accurately determine what you're sensing from the coffee.

When the location is prepared, the setup itself is pretty simple. You'll need to equip the area with a few things:

- ◆ Access to near-boiling water (195° to 205°F)
- ◆ Shallow, wide-mouthed cups or glasses (5- to 7-ounce capacity works well)
- ◆ A wide, shallow spoon (a soup spoon will work)
- ◆ A glass of warm water to rinse your spoon in
- ◆ A mug to spit sampled coffee into
- ◆ Bowls or plates to display unground coffee
- ◆ A scale for weighing coffee
- ◆ Paper and pencil for making notes

Place the cups on a counter or tabletop so you can easily move from cup to cup. For evaluation purposes, it's nice to be able to look at the whole, roasted beans as well as the unroasted beans as you cup, so arrange small plates or bowls of them nearby if you can. Obviously, this can demand a lot of room, especially when you're cupping several coffees at once, and it may not always be possible.

Next, set the glass of warm water within reach so you can rinse off your spoon before moving from one cup to the next.

The coffee you use can be any you want to try, but if you're roasting for the purpose of cupping, you'll want a light roast, something stopped shortly after first crack. A light roast imparts less taste and better preserves the varietal characteristics of the coffee. Later, cup the same coffee with the degree of roast you've chosen for your normal brewing. This enables you to gauge how the roast is complementing the bean and if you're harnessing its potential.

The Cupping Process

With the stage set, put on the kettle and begin preparing the coffee samples. Weigh each sample carefully to ensure uniformity, as with the relatively small amount of water used, fluctuations in coffee dose will skew your ability to make comparisons. A good place to start is by using 10 grams medium to coarsely ground coffee to 6 ounces water. Some prefer to use more coffee, feeling that using a bit extra than they would for brewing allows for a better evaluation. The most important factor to keep in mind is that you're consistent across coffee samples.

When you've finished grinding all the samples, take a moment to smell the grounds. Don't be shy; get your nose right in there. You're likely to find some delicate aromas, like a floral sweetness perhaps, that won't make it to the cup. As you begin to smell a lot of coffees, you'll note that some have "loud" and exciting dry fragrances while others are more subdued.

Field Notes

To ensure consistency among coffees when grinding, use a quality burr grinder. If you use a blade grinder, try grinding for a fixed number of seconds; you'll have to practice with your grinder to determine what duration produces the best results. Be sure to brush the grinder free of debris after each sample to reduce the possibility of cross-contamination.

Allow the just-boiled water to cool for about 30 seconds and then fill each cup. As you pour, ensure all the grounds are wetted and that no clumps of dry coffee remain. It's easiest to work with small cups and fill them completely. If the ones you're using are larger than about 7 ounces, determine in advance how full they become when 6 ounces water is added to the coffee.

As you wait for the coffee to steep for about 3 to 5 minutes, drop your spoon(s) into the warm rinse water. This prevents a cold spoon from dropping the temperature of the coffee when you first plunge it in. You'll note as you wait that the grounds form a crust on the surface of the coffee. This is desirable, as it traps within it all sorts of volatile aroma compounds. After about 4 minutes, grab your spoon, shake off the excess water, and prepare to break the crust.

Field Notes

The most reliable way to judge a coffee is to cup several samples. Because so few beans determine the flavor of the cup, you'll taste defective or lower-quality beans if there are any. A good practice is to set up at least 2 or 3 cups for each coffee you're cupping. In most cases, you'll be able to distinguish some nuances between the same-coffee samples.

This is a critical event in the process, as it amounts to a sensual tidal wave. Start by getting your nose just above the crust and use the back of your spoon to gently push the grounds from front to back and then down. As you do this, soak in the flood of aromas that's released, and continue by stirring the grounds to the bottom of the cup. Not all the grounds will sink, however, so you'll need to fish out those that float. To do this easily, hold two spoons with their bowls vertical and side by side and skim over the surface from back to front. This should trap the vast majority of the grounds and make it easy to lift them out.

Now you're ready for the main event—that is, once the coffee cools enough. Dip your spoon in a cup, lift it to your lips, but rather than sipping it gingerly, let loose with your best slurp. The idea here is twofold: to aerate the brew sufficiently so the vapors become airborne and to evenly spray the coffee all around your mouth. Then, as you swish the brew about your mouth, take note of how it tastes and feels. Does it feel thin, much like water, or is it rather viscous? What tastes come to mind?

After you've soaked in its taste, spit out the sample and immediately turn your attention back to your tongue. As the last of the vapors from the coffee evaporate off your tongue, you'll be left with yet another impression of the coffee as you savor its *finish*. Note not only what tastes you experience but also how long they linger and how the coffee makes your tongue feel. For example, does the brew tingle the sides of your tongue? Does it coat your tongue much like a thick cream sauce does?

Buzz Words

The tastes that linger after you've swallowed or spit out coffee is referred to as its **finish**. The finish of coffees is different depending on the flavor compounds left on your tongue and the rate at which they evaporate.

Naturally, if you're uncomfortable spitting and prefer to swallow the coffee, go right ahead. In fact, some will find it easier at first to rate the coffee's finish because the act of swallowing forces some of the vapors lingering on your tongue up into the nasal cavity. Experienced cuppers learn to pump their larynxes slightly after they spit to encourage the same result. However, pay attention to how much you're consuming if you swallow the coffee, as it's easy to ingest a lot of caffeine quickly while sampling coffees.

Continue the procedure, slurping samples from each cup until you feel you have a firm impression of each. Taste perception is linked to temperature, so allow the samples to cool a bit and try them again. This cooling time is a good chance for you to get a drink of water to rinse your palate before proceeding. As you cup the cooled coffees, note how things have changed. Do you notice the acidity more or less now? Has the degree of sweetness fluctuated?

As you can see, with so much to pay attention to, you'll be greatly assisted by jotting down notes about the coffees you're cupping as you experience them. Not only does it make it easier to assess the coffee's overall flavor profile, but notes also serve as a handy record to help you compare the current sample with ones you've sampled in the past. For instance, if you're roasting your own, periodically cupping a particular coffee and comparing it with your past notes helps you get a sense for how it's changing as it ages.

Make It Your Own

The cupping procedure we outlined here is how coffee professionals—roasters, importers, and growers—judge coffees and is the basis for many multimillion-dollar decisions. However, you may find the formal procedure a little cumbersome for regular practice, and you might consider adjusting this process to make it practical for you. As long as the process is consistent, it can yield useful information with which you can expand your coffee knowledge.

Perhaps the most common twist on cupping coffees at home is to brew the coffee in a French press. This makes the process somewhat simpler and is especially practical if the press is your usual brewing method; what better way to test coffees than under the circumstances you will typically brew them? You miss out on some sensory cues, but it's still a very viable method as long as you remove distractions, focus on the coffees, and engage your senses and entire palate as you make the evaluations.

Blending: The Art of Mixing It Up

People have been blending coffees since the time there were two to combine. Indeed, the Mocha-Java blend—combining the high-toned, fruity Yemeni coffee with the resonant, low-toned coffees from the estates of Java—is the oldest and most venerable of blends. Blends allow an extended flexibility that single-origin coffees do not. Blending—done well—affords a cup with characteristics that reach beyond the range one coffee affords.

Another reason to blend is to preserve a consistent flavor profile. Coffee remains a crop influenced by its growing conditions, which fluctuate to some degree from year to year. The result may be a coffee with less-expressive acidity in some crops, or perhaps the deep chocolate-cherry notes you loved a particular bean for go absent. Through careful cupping and attentive blending, one can establish a flavor profile that remains quite consistent. When a component in the blend changes due to natural variance, the blend is simply tweaked a little to make up for the difference. Naturally, this isn't always an easy task and requires a lot of tasting and effort, but nonetheless, it opens doors that would otherwise be shut.

Take a Taste Safari

Tinkering with blends can be a lot of fun, in part because it requires tasting a lot of coffees, which is enjoyable in its own right. It's also exciting to shape the overall flavor of a coffee and to see how changing the ratios of the blended components affects the outcome. Perhaps the most challenging part of blending is educating your palate to the delicious array of coffees with which you can paint your masterpiece blend. With dozens of coffee-producing regions worldwide, your palette of available blending components is immense and the combinations nearly limitless. So great are the options that it can be difficult to begin. Your first task, then, is to embark on a journey, exploring coffee. Acquaint yourself with the fragrances, aromas, textures, flavors, and overall character of as many coffees as you're able to sample.

As you try new coffees, cup them and become familiar with the coffee's dry fragrance, its brewed aroma, its tastes, and its finish. If you're lost at where to begin, try starting with a favorite or familiar coffee. What is its best characteristic? Perhaps its layers of complex, spicy flavors that vie for the center of attention as the cup cools. Or maybe it has a rich, creamy mouthfeel and long finish that wows your tongue. Likewise, note how you think the coffee could be improved. You may, for example, find the clean, bright snap of acidity in a particular coffee refreshing but its body too thin and lacking for your tastes. Continue this routine, and allow each experience to guide the next.

Field Notes

Use the general descriptions in Chapter 3 to help you find other coffees you might enjoy. For example, if you liked a Kenyan coffee for its deep fruit and winelike characteristics, next you might try an Ethiopian Harar that exhibits winy-blueberry notes. On the other hand, if the Kenyan's acidity struck a chord with you, consider trying other coffees known for their brightness, like a Guatemala Antigua.

Collect Your Thoughts

Without a concept in mind, even the most skilled artist with a broad palette will have difficulties creating successful, engaging works. So, too, is it for the blender. Without a vision of how you'd like the coffee's flavor profile, your blending efforts may lack the direction necessary to yield truly stimulating results. There are a number of ways to approach blending; let's take a look at a few tested strategies.

Build with the Power of Pyramids

One popular method of building blends is what we refer to as the pyramid method. When an overall goal for the blend is determined, a base coffee is selected. It may or may not be the most prevalent coffee in the blend by percentage, but its character provides the foundation of the blend. From there the blend is fleshed out a bit by adding one or more additional coffees. Then, to top it all off, a final coffee is added, usually in a small percentage, finishing the blend and filling out its overall flavor profile.

Let's check out an example of how this might go. We'll assume we're looking for a blend whose flavors will stand up well to rich foods and will exhibit deep, grounding body with mild to moderate acidity. We might first anchor the blend by making 40 percent of it a Java estate coffee with a huge, creamy body that coats and lingers on the tongue. The blend is then refined by adding 25 percent each of a balanced, mid-toned Papua New Guinea and a clean, relatively bright and medium-bodied Peru. The Papua New Guinea, while lighter in body than the Indonesian, brings subtle plum and spice notes and a long finish that supports the Java. Chosen for its balancing acidity and chocolatelike flavors, the Peruvian brings just enough snap to the blend to keep it exciting without taking the center stage. To add a tantalizing, spicy aroma and further hints of fruit and chocolate, the remaining 10 percent of the blend is filled out with a high-quality Yemen.

Birds of a Feather Flock Together

Another strategy to direct your blending is to focus on a quality, such as body, and then select coffees that all feature that quality. This layering technique can yield unique blends with the power to stun your taste buds with their focused energy.

Hot Water

Keep an eye out for a blend becoming too far out of balance. You want to really punctuate a certain quality; it's unlikely that a lopsided, one-dimensional coffee will be truly pleasing.

A blend using this strategy might focus on acidity by capitalizing on the zest of a sparkling, clean Costa Rican, the lemony-citrus-y brightness of an Ethiopian Yirgacheffe, and the snap of a high-toned Colombian. Make no mistake, this blend will greet your taste buds briskly and tingle the sides of your tongue, but if you're after a study in delicious acidity, you've got it.

Variety Is the Spice

If you're more of an "opposites attract" type, you may fall for the classic black-and-tan approach of combining lightly and darkly roasted coffees. The goal here is to combine the toasty or bittersweet roast flavors of a dark roast with the acidity and varietal characteristics preserved by a lighter roast.

This could be employed with either of the preceding approaches, but it's particularly interesting to explore a single coffee with this strategy. By blending two or more roast levels of the same coffee, you can coax a great deal of complexity into the cup. Obviously, some coffees lend themselves more to this sort of stretching than do others, and it's a rewarding way to learn and experiment with a single coffee.

When to Blend: Preroast or Post?

Many times when the topic of blending comes up, the debate of when to blend—before or after roasting—surfaces as well. There's merit in both approaches, and the best one for you depends on your situation and your blending goals. Obviously, if you're not roasting your own, you'll be limited to blending with what you can purchase from a roaster.

Some contend that coffees that roast together develop desirable flavor notes due to the commingling that would not otherwise occur were they roasted separately. Another key advantage to combining the chosen coffees prior to roasting is efficiency. The roasting process thoroughly mixes the components for you, and it saves time—sometimes significantly so. This is especially the case for commercial roasters with large capacities, but it ultimately depends on the batch size of your roaster, the number of coffees in the blend, and how much you want to roast.

The small batch size of most home roasting machines—usually between $\frac{1}{4}$ and $\frac{1}{2}$ pound—often renders this argument moot. For example, if you want to prepare 1 pound of your favorite four-component blend in a roaster with a $\frac{1}{4}$-pound capacity, you'll be running four batches one way or the other. On the other hand, if you have a roaster capable of handling a $\frac{1}{2}$ pound at a time, you'll cut your roasting time in half by blending prior to roasting.

The primary case against preroast blending is that the uniqueness of beans grown and processed differently reduces the effectiveness of a one-roast-fits-all approach. This somewhat depends on component coffees, and certainly cases exist in which the same roast profile works well enough for several coffees. However, there are plenty of instances where a single roast just won't bring the most out of all the coffees. You may run into this especially when mixing wet-processed and dry-processed coffees or ones grown at high altitudes with those raised at low altitudes. These situations, obviously, highlight the benefits of the postroast strategy, which, in essence, first focuses on tailoring the roast of each component coffee to bring out its best or most desired flavor profile.

In most cases, we advocate first approaching blending with a postroast strategy, at least until you have a blend developed. When you blend, you should be intimately familiar with how each component tastes and smells and use that information to guide your decisions. Preroast blending tends to encourage shortcutting this critical evaluative process, which not only leads to fewer successful blends but also diminishes the knowledge gained in the process. Once you've zeroed in on a blend by combining roasted coffees, try roasting them together. Then let your taste buds loose and cup (blindly, of course) samples from both methods.

The Case Against Blending Altogether

Combining coffees can be an exciting taste endeavor, but its appeal is not universal. Blending is a give-and-take process in which you wager that each added coffee hides or takes away something from the flavor profile that you don't mind losing while also adding desirable elements. Unfortunately, that's not always the case, and some coffee connoisseurs maintain that the bet rarely pays off in today's world of coffee.

Through the process of layering in coffees, blends often obscure the origin and unique nature of their component coffees. There's a story woven into the character of each coffee, telling its tale of preparation and journey into the cup, that can be tasted and appreciated in carefully prepared coffees. Muddying this essence and history is, to some aficionados, a disrespectful transgression against both the coffee and its preparers.

Others contend that the real ill involved in blending is that it creates a marketplace environment that does not significantly value (i.e., pay for) the extra care necessary to prepare small lots of truly fine, distinctive coffee and, rather, that it lowers the bar and encourages the production of good (though subexcellent) coffees with less remarkable characteristics that make good blenders.

Certainly, there's no doubt that we need to reward farmers for producing superior coffee, for if we don't make it worth their time, it's unlikely to happen. After which point, we leave it to your palate to determine the age-old question of whether to blend or not to blend. Appreciating a bean for its individual character—either blended carefully with others or alone—should hardly bring anything other than pride to those who prepared it.

The Least You Need to Know

- Smell plays a vital role in how we perceive tastes.

- Everyone has different tasting abilities, so it's best to refine your palate through experience and learn to trust it.

- Cupping is the process of tasting and evaluating coffees in a systematic manner.

- Careful blending enables you to control the overall flavor of a coffee and hone it to your taste.

6

Brew Tools

In This Chapter

- ◆ Meet the tools of the coffee-brewing trade, from French presses, to percolators, to ibriks—and more
- ◆ Cold brew for low-acid, low-effort coffee
- ◆ Find the right brewer(s) for you

If you've ever browsed the retail section of your favorite coffeehouse, you've undoubtedly seen a number of contraptions for brewing coffee. There are almost as many ways to prepare coffee as there are nations producing beans! And each method has its advantages, advocates, and, in many cases, its share of quirks. Some excel at bringing out the body in coffee, while others allow coffee to express its brightness a little better. Convenience commands a few, and rituals rule others.

Just as each person gravitates toward different characteristics in coffee, there's a brewer and brewing method for everyone. In this chapter, we explore a host of brew tools and ways you can use them most effectively. When you understand how each works and its benefits, you'll be able to choose ones that are compatible with your personal needs and style.

The French Press

Ah, the French press—coveted by connoisseurs as *the* way to brew—is a straightforward manual brewer. It resembles a laboratory beaker and has a tightly fitted plunger that strains and holds back the grounds as it's pressed to the bottom. Alternately called a *press pot* or *plunger pot*, the French press is an economical way to brew, with most versions starting around $30.

The cult brewer of connoisseurs, the French press is easy to use and brings coffee's nuances in a robust style.

The French press concept is pretty simple: just dump in your grounds, add water, and plunge after it has steeped to your liking. Because the grounds commingle with the water during the entire brewing cycle, more oils and solubles are released into the brew than with most other methods. This produces a cup that has a heavier body and thicker mouthfeel. The French press is commonly considered to produce stronger coffee, but you can easily adjust the strength if the standard ratio seems too stout for you.

When brewing with a press, start with coarsely ground coffee and let it steep for about 4 minutes. (Any longer than 6 minutes is likely to brew bitterness.) Some prefer the results from using more finely ground coffee—as fine as used for drip brewing—with shorter brewing times. Just be prepared for more sediment in the cup.

Hot Water

After you plunge your coffee, it will continue to steep, albeit at a slower rate. To avoid overextraction, which imparts a bitter taste to the brew, decant into a thermal carafe immediately after brewing. Better yet, make only as much as you'll drink right away and just brew another pot if you desire more later. And due to the nature of the French press's thicker, more bodied brew, you'll want to forgo the last sip or two. The chalky sediment will leave a bad taste in your mouth.

The Vacuum Pot

Adored by passionate and methodical aficionados, vacuum pot brewers produce rich, flavorful coffee in high style. Traditional vacuum brewers, which are heated by alcohol lamps or on stoves, take longer to brew coffee and have a steeper learning curve. Once mastered, though, brewing takes on a ritual-like quality and is fairly simple.

Vacuum pots offer exciting theatrics and sediment-free, delicious brew—clearly why many patient aficionados prefer brewing with them.

Sound a little too much like work? Automatic (electric) vacuum pots are simple to brew with, even for sleepy operators. They don't afford as much control as manual vacuum pots, but they are a reliable choice for those who don't want a manual brewer. Cleanup tends to be somewhat more involved than for automatic drip brewers, although the resulting brew is typically superior.

Vacuum brewers, automated or not, use physics to power the brewing process. Most vacuum brewers roughly resemble two carafes stacked one on top of the other. You begin by filling the lower chamber with the appropriate amount of water and securing

Hot Water

Not all glass can handle being set directly on a stovetop. Check the manufacturer's information for heating recommendations. You can use simple metal trivetlike devices to raise the vacuum pot up off an electric stove and prevent breaking.

the upper chamber on top. A tube extends downward from the top pot, connecting the two, and a glass, metal, plastic, or cloth filter typically sits down in this tube, preventing grounds from falling into the water below. Next, you dump the grounds in the upper chamber (on top of the filter) and you're ready for the theatrics. Turn on your heat source (start with low heat if you're using the stove), and wait for water to heat up.

As the water begins to heat up, water vapor will begin to expand and will eventually build up enough pressure to force near-boiling water up the tube and onto the coffee grounds. You may see some bubbling, but the water that's pushed onto the coffee will be at just the right temperature. If you see some bubbling in the upper chamber, there's no need to be alarmed; you're not boiling your coffee! The bubbles are from the force of the water being pushed up from below. If it seems excessive and you can control your heat, try a lower setting next time.

Field Notes

A small amount of water will remain in the lower chamber during brewing, so making less than a full pot will yield somewhat diluted coffee. Your best results, then, will be when you brew at least $2/_3$ capacity. Plan accordingly when you select the size of your vacuum brewer.

After all but a small amount of water has moved to the upper chamber, allow the brew to steep for a minute or two. Then remove the pot from the heat and allow the natural vacuum to suck the liquid through the filter and back into the bottom carafe. You can experiment with the timing to adjust the strength to your taste.

The reward for the extra bit of effort it takes to brew with a vacuum pot is in every crisp, sediment-free cup of coffee. This clarity allows nuances in some beans, especially of delicate coffees, to shine.

However, some, especially those accustomed to thick French press brew, may find coffee brewed this way a little thin.

Drip Brewers

One of the most popular ways to brew coffee is using a drip brewer. This brewing method produces a flavorful and relatively sediment-free cup that allows the coffee's natural acidity—the tasty kind—to shine through a bit better than does the French press. Filters, especially paper ones, trap flavorful oils and solubles in addition to the grounds, resulting in a lighter body and, in some cases, a slightly less nuanced cup. The drip-brewer process is easier to master than the vacuum pot and results in a cup that is nearly as clear.

Filters used in drip brewing are made of a number of materials; paper and metal are the most used. Debates are common about which is best, but any filter that strains away the grounds without imparting a taste is adequate; some papers fit this bill, while others don't. You'll find that most metal filters require a coarser grind than paper to achieve the same clarity in the cup, but they do offer the advantage of reusability; just be certain to clean them thoroughly after each use or you'll doom your brew with old oils.

As a testament to the popularity of the drip method, these brewers can be found in several varations, including manual and automatic brewers. Within the manual category, you'll find simple pour-over brewers and filter cones to more complicated models like the flip-drip brewer. Let's take a look at the drip brewers available on the market today.

The Manual-Drip

Manual-drip brewing, also known as the pour-over technique, is somewhat broad but basically refers to any method where water is poured over grounds held in a filter. Some manual-drip brewers, such as the Chemex, one of the most common pour-over brewers, look a bit like scientific equipment. The all-glass brewer, which is roughly hourglass-shaped, has a large cone-shaped upper section that provides for a very deep bed of grounds, improving extraction.

Another common brew tool in this class is the pour-over cone, a cone-shaped piece of plastic or ceramic that's placed on top of a mug or other receptacle. Key advantages here are the convenience of brewing directly into a thermos or the cup you'll be drinking out of. Plus it's easily stowed away, handy for the workplace. Pour-over cones can be found in a variety of sizes.

The process for brewing with any of the manual-drip brewers is simple: after you've ground the beans to a medium-fine consistency and placed them into the filter, thoroughly wet the grounds with near-boiling water. Wait until the grounds have soaked in a bit of water before pouring over the rest of the water to prevent the water from passing through too quickly—30 seconds should suffice. Then just continue pouring the rest of the water over the grounds. You'll get a little better extraction if you agitate the grounds a bit during the process by stirring, although it isn't necessary.

Manual drip or pour-over brewers afford the cup clarity of filtered coffee but allow you to control brewing temperature with just-boiled water, thus ensuring a great cup.

Pour-over filter cones are great portable brewers because they offer all the advantages of other manual drip brewers but are typically small enough to fit in a travel bag or desk drawer.

The Flip-Drip

The flip-drip, or Neapolitan, brewer is a self-contained, sturdy brewer that produces coffee on par with its pour-over cousins. Squat and looking like two stacked cylinders—one with a spout jutting out of it—the flip-drip brewer appears a bit more complicated than it actually is. To use, fill the spoutless chamber with water, put the grounds (a bit coarser than for other drip brewers) in the filter insert, and assemble the brewer. Now, just heat the water to a boil (on the stove), wait briefly, and then invert the brewer.

Like many all-metal brewers, the most commonly seen Neapolitan brewers are aluminum, which is unfortunate because the metal reacts with the acids in coffee. Fortunately though, stainless-steel models are available, and although they cost a bit more, we recommend these over aluminum.

The flip-drip or Neapolitan brewer is a good choice for those who like the idea of a manual drip brewer but don't want to heat the water separately.

The Auto-Drip

Nearly ubiquitous and synonymous with "coffee brewer" in mainstream America today, the automatic-drip brewer is the flagship for brewing convenience. Armed with timers and electric heating elements, this class of brewers makes it easy to brew a pot of coffee without the need to stand by with a watchful eye. As is usually the case, though, convenience comes at a price. In this instance, simplified brewing typically is at the expense of cup quality.

Automatic-drip brewers have become the flagship American brewers, sporting convenience over cup quality.

As we mentioned earlier, it is the very rare automatic-drip coffeemaker that can maintain ideal brewing temperature throughout the entire brewing cycle. All is not lost if you're attached to the idea of brewing with an automatic-drip brewer, though. When you're shopping for an auto-drip brewer, pay close attention to the size of the heating element. For a point of comparison, most have less than 900-watt heating elements, whereas the only brewer currently certified to do the job properly (by the Specialty Coffee Association of America) uses an element that draws more than 1,400 watts. Above all, taste the coffee a maker produces and let that be your guide. If you can, test it against a manual brewing method (ideally drip) using the same coffee so you can taste the differences, if they exist.

In addition to being underpowered, many automatic brewers offer another challenge to flavorful coffee: the hotplate. Touted as an advantage, these "handy" devices literally burn off the flavorful components you're after in coffee, leaving you with brew that's sub-par at best and burnt-tasting at worst. Fortunately, some models have separate switches for the hotplates. If you have a model that does not allow for turning off the hotplate, just decant or drink the coffee as soon as it's brewed.

The Automatic Single-Cup Brewer

Around 2004, a trend in coffee brewing began to reemerge: automatic-drip brewers that could whip up a single cup in about a minute. Manufacturers responded with a bevy of convenient, powerful machines. Most sport high-wattage heating elements, and some are capable of producing water hot enough for proper brewing.

Automatic single-cup brewers use preground coffee pods to prepare a cup at the touch of a button and in less than a minute.

The Achilles heel for these push-button wonders thus far has been their dependency on coffee "pods." Pods come in various configurations but all include the filter and the ground coffee in one unit, making preparation and cleanup ultra-simple. Convenience crowds out freshness with this method, though. Because you're reliant on preground coffee, you're almost guaranteed stale brew. And because fresh coffee emits a lot of carbon dioxide gas, the manufacturers must allow the grounds to de-gas before packaging to prevent the containers from rupturing. This amounts to essentially prestaling your coffee. Additionally, with this system, you have a very limited coffee selection.

Perhaps in time, manufacturers will develop good single-cup brewing systems that do not rely on pods, though we remain a bit skeptical, as this convenience is one of the single-cup brewer's primary advantages.

Field Notes _____

If you're shopping for a single-cup brewer, look for one that allows you to control the volume of water used to brew a cup.

The Percolator

Essentially a water kettle fitted with an inverted funnel on which a basket of coffee grounds rests, the percolator harnesses the raw power of boiling water to brew. As the water boils, small amounts at a time bubble up the tube, onto the grounds, and then drip back into the water. The process continues until the brew is brown enough to be called "coffee." If extracting the ground coffee with boiling water wasn't hard enough on the delicate flavor components in the first pass, the successive boiling it takes to produce coffee with a percolator certainly is.

The percolator conjures nostalgic images for many people but, unfortunately, rarely of delicious coffee.

There's something nostalgic about the percolator, and while we've had our share of coffee perc'ed over a campfire, the coffee was never the topic of conversation—unless it was to muse at how even great beans can be rendered moot.

The Moka Pot

Known for producing thick, espressolike coffee, moka pots use natural steam pressure to force near-boiling water through a loosely packed bed of coffee. The Italian-born design, inspired by laundering methods in the 1920s, was intended to bring the powerful nature of espresso into the home. Its mission was accomplished in part due to the ease of operation—something that certainly couldn't be said for espresso machines of the day—and its impact can be seen by the large percentage of Italian stovetops that are home to these brewers today. (While similar, true espresso is extracted under very high pressure through tightly packed coffee and has a unique rich and pleasant syrupy quality.)

Moka pots are the nearly ubiquitious stovetop brewers in Italy that produce thick, espressolike coffee.

Moka pots are roughly pitcher-shaped metal brewers that have narrow "waists" where the upper and lower parts screw together. To brew with a moka pot, fill the bottom unit to the pressure-release valve with water and then set in the funnel. Place finely ground coffee in the funnel and level it, but do not pack or tamp it. The grounds will expand against the bottom of the upper unit during brewing, forming them into a proper, somewhat firm "puck."

Screw the two halves together tightly, and place the moka pot on the stove. Medium-high heat is a good starting point, but be prepared to adjust on subsequent brewings until you have it fine-tuned for your stovetop. Soon, expanding water vapor pressure will force near-boiling water up the funnel, through the grounds, and into the upper chamber. From the first bubblings of the dark brew to the last should take about 3 to 5 minutes. As always, let taste be your guide.

It can be somewhat challenging at first to zero in on the best combination of grind and temperature settings due to the fact that once hot, the all-metal moka pot takes a while to cool down sufficiently enough to make a successive batch. Take good mental notes, and you'll have it figured out before long.

Field Notes

In the summer of 2005, Bialetti, the Italian designer of the first moka pots, released a new design twist called the Mukka (pronounced *MOO-ka*) Express. Targeted toward moka pot users who typically make drinks with milk, like cappuccinos and lattes, the Mukka Express is essentially a standard moka pot that harnesses the pressure of the coffee coming from the lower chamber to aerate and froth milk in the enlarged upper chamber. While the "lattes" it produces won't match ones prepared traditionally, they are nonetheless pleasing and save considerable time. The Mukka Express is a worthy consideration if a significant amount of your moka pot brewing is for these "mixed drinks."

When shopping for moka pots, we recommend opting for a stainless-steel model. They cost more and are less plentiful than their aluminum counterparts, but then again, they won't disrupt the taste of the coffee. Another thing to consider when making your selection is another new twist: the electric moka pot. You'll give up a little control but gain ease of use and portability.

The Ibrik

These traditional Middle Eastern brewers, usually made of copper and brass, are essentially long-handled pitchers with narrow necks. They produce a strong, concentrated brew, often called Turkish coffee, that is served in very small cups (about 2 ounces).

Brewing with an ibrik (pronounced *e-brEEgh*) takes a little more time than most methods and requires careful attention, but it isn't too tough. Start with an ibrik that's sized for the amount you want to brew. When the pot's filled, the water should be a bit below the neck of the pot. This method uses coffee that's powdered—finer than any other method, including espresso. Set your grinder on its finest setting, or use a blade grinder to pulverize the coffee into dust.

Add the coffee and water to the ibrik, and set it on a medium-low heat. Now's a good time to add any sugar or cardamom you'd like, which is common with this method.

Cuppa Wisdom

Coffee should be as black as hell, as strong as death, and as sweet as love.

—Turkish proverb

After a few minutes the coffee will begin to froth; remove it from the heat just before it reaches the top. After the foam has receded, set the pot back on the burner with the heat turned down to low. Allow it to froth up and settle down twice more and then you're done. Serve into *demitasses*—espresso-size cups—and allow it to settle for a minute. Sludge in the cup is part of the deal, so you'll want to avoid the last sip or two.

The ibrik is another stovetop brewer, this one of Middle Eastern origin, that makes concentrated, espresso-esque brew.

Cold Brewing

The slow-cooker of coffee brewing, this method uses room-temperature water and very long brewing times to create a unique brew. Often referred to as Toddy brewing after a common commercial cold-brewing system, this method produces a rich, resonant concentrate.

Because you're using cool water rather than the near-boiling water typically employed in coffee brewing, not all of the same solubles are extracted when you cold brew. Most notably, the brew is lower in acid and has a much "rounder" flavor profile. Manufacturers of cold-brew systems often tout the low-acid angle proudly as a selling point for those who experience stomach upset from the acids in coffee. Reportedly, the reduction is as great as 67 percent less acid in the cup, and it's certainly worth a try if you experience stomach discomfort from brewed coffee.

But that's not the only reason to cold brew coffee. The resulting brew is fairly stable and can be kept in the refrigerator for at least a week. And because it's so concentrated, one batch of cold brew goes a long way. It holds up well in milk and makes a great *café au lait*. It's also handy for baking and cooking. If a "regular" cup of coffee is what you're after, try mixing it with an equal amount of water. Alternately, you can use it as a (loose) approximation for espresso and use it in the drinks and recipes covered in Part 3.

Utlizing long brew times and cool water, cold brewers produce concentrated coffee known for its smooth, low-acid nature.

Buzz Words

Much like a latte made with coffee rather than espresso, a **café au lait** (pronounced *o-LAY*) is a coffee-based drink made with milk. Typically, it's about half strong coffee and half milk.

Some more coffee drink lingo: a *cappuccino* (*cap-a-CHEE-no*), made with equal parts steamed and frothed (thicker) milk, is a classic espresso-based drink. Cappuccino's milder cousin, a *latte* (*LAH-tay*), is made with steamed milk and usually a small amount of frothed milk. (See Part 3 for more information on espresso drinks.)

Cold brewing is the epitome of easy. Coarsely grind up a pound of your favorite coffee; dump in approximately 72 ounces of fresh, filtered water; and set the concoction aside for 12 hours. When it's brewed, just filter and refrigerate.

Although you don't *have* to have one, a dedicated cold-brewing system, which costs about $35, makes this process simplistic by providing a brew bucket fitted with a reusable filter and bottom drain hole. Just dump it all in, wait overnight, and allow it to drip into the accompanying carafe.

Choosing the Brewer for You

Sorting through the multitude of brewing options can be a little daunting, but it needn't stump you if you ask yourself a few basic questions. Perhaps first is whether you mind the extra steps involved with manual brewing. If you do, you'll want to look at the automatic brewers (we recommend the vacuum pot). Next, ask yourself if you prefer very concentrated brews over traditional-strenghth coffee. If you do, take a look at the moka pot, cold brewers, and the ibrik.

For traditional brewed coffee, the drip brewers, vacuum pots, and French press are our primary considerations. None are a serious pain to clean, but the French press requires the most attention, including minor disassembly and more parts to scrub. If you're typically in a hurry or like to multitask, the press is the star because you only need to combine, wait, and plunge. For many, it's a question of cup clarity and body. If you want a sediment-free cup, the vacuum pot and the drip brewers meet your demands. Should a relatively full, complex brew be for you, press pots can't be beat. Can't decide? Consider multiple brewers, as many of these basic tools are fairly inexpensive.

Field Notes

Whatever brewing method you choose, resist the urge to brew up enough coffee for an entire morning's worth of drinking. Coffee's delicate flavors are at their prime right after brewing, so it's better to brew another batch if you think the coffee will be sitting for more than about 15 to 20 minutes.

Regardless of the method you select, try to choose a model that fits your typical brewing needs. Many are optimized for their maximum brewing capacity and underperform when brewing less. The press is a notable exception, as it enables you to make partial batches with relative impunity. Drip brewers rely on a thick bed of grounds for the water to pass through for best extraction, and if you make a small batch in a large-capacity brewer, your results will suffer. Moka pots, with their fixed space for grounds, nearly demand full batches; some models have an insert that can be used to reduce that space, but results are usually superior with properly sized brewers.

So although it can be a bit of pain to have to brew a couple batches when entertaining, it's probably a better comprise, from a quality standpoint, than brewing significantly below your brewer's capacity on a routine basis.

Selecting a brewer that's best for you can be challenging. To help you get a better picture for how the various methods stack up, check out the following table. The ratings are relative, with higher numbers indicating more favorable qualities.

Comparison of Brewing Methods

Brewer	Claim to Fame	Ease of Use	Cleanup	Cost
French press	full body	4	3	4
Vacuum pot	clarity	3	3	2–3
Manual-drip	clean cup	3.5	4	4
Flip-drip	self-contained	3	3.5	3
Auto-drip	convenience	4	4	2–4
Automatic single-cup	speed	5	5	2
Percolator	campfire comfort	4	3	4
Moka pot	stovetop espresso	3	4	3
Ibrik	Turkish coffee	3	4	4
Cold brewing	low-acid	5	3	4

The Least You Need to Know

◆ Each brewing method brings out somewhat different nuances in the coffee.

◆ French press–prepared coffee has more oils and solubles, resulting in a unique, full-bodied brew.

◆ Coffee made with vacuum pots and drip brewers is clear and flavorful but contains fewer oils and solubles, providing a "lighter" cup.

◆ Automatic brewers abound and are easy to use, but when shopping for one, keep in mind that they almost universally suffer from water-heating issues.

◆ While each has a unique flavor profile, moka pots, cold brewers, and ibriks all prepare highly concentrated coffee.

◆ Choose a brewer that fits your needs, as most perform best at their intended maximum capacity.

Chapter 7

Brewing Basics

In This Chapter

- Uncover secrets to brewing great coffee
- Learn the proper brewing technique
- Understand why water matters
- Discover ways to keep your beans fresh

Now that you have a solid background in coffee, let's talk about how to unleash the delicate goodness locked inside those beans. Coaxing the maximum flavor into your brew isn't difficult, yet many people struggle to reproduce the flavorful cups good coffeehouses offer. If you start with fresh, quality ingredients (coffee and water) and use proper brewing technique, you'll find that you can actually out-brew the cafés. While even the best technique won't compensate for stale coffee or water with a "taste," sloppy brewing can turn even award-winning beans to swill.

Let's take a look, then, at a few key considerations for producing coffee that enlivens the taste buds.

Good Water Makes Great Coffee

Really, brewed coffee is just flavored water. If you start with water that tastes funny, expect your coffee to taste funny, too. It's that simple, but it doesn't have to be that drastic to show water's influence in the cup.

Municipal water treated with chlorine can dampen the flavor of your coffee even if the water itself does not have a strong taste. Likewise, well water that contains a lot of dissolved minerals will not allow the coffee to shine to its fullest. Given that information, it might seem like the best answer is to buy distilled water. But without mineral content, which distilled water lacks, water cannot properly extract coffee and, therefore, produces lackluster brew.

So the best bet is to use filtered water. If you usually brew with tap water, give filtered water a try. In many cases, you'll be rewarded with a "fresher" or "clearer" taste, and it's one of the easiest ways to improve your brew.

Better Beans = Better Brew

Just as starting with inferior water clips the potential of your brew, so, too, does using less-than-high-quality beans. Unfortunately, it's not quite as simple as going to the store and buying coffee marked "superior quality."

Coffee is a complex product, and its quality is affected at numerous stages even before you purchase it. Therefore, put the odds in your favor by purchasing beans that are freshly roasted by a reputable roaster, ideally within the past few days. (Inquire for the roasting date if it isn't noted on the package.)

Coffee begins to stale after it's roasted, as carbon dioxide gas is released and exchanged by oxygen. Staling rate depends on storage (more on this in a bit), but if stored properly, coffee should remain flavorful for up to about 2 weeks. It will be at its peak from a few hours to a few days after roasting. Some people contend that coffee packed into one-way valve bags immediately after roasting remains fresh beyond 2 weeks, but we suggest not relying on this unless you must. Although coffee that's a little past its peak may still taste okay, you'll be missing out on all the precious nuances and varietal characteristics that its growers and roasters strived to highlight.

Field Notes

Coffee stales naturally after it's roasted, and even coffee stored under ideal conditions for more than about a week is hard-pressed to compare to freshly roasted coffee. Try to purchase only as much coffee as you'll use in the next week, regardless of how you store it.

Getting the Goods

In many parts of the country, there are more places to buy good-quality whole bean coffee than ever before. Even so, finding good coffee can be challenging for a number of reasons. For one thing, it's pretty hard to tell whether the coffee on a vendor's shelf was well prepared and well roasted, even if you can discern that it was roasted recently. The only real way to know is to taste it. The easiest way to navigate this concern is to purchase from a roaster-retailer, where you can sample a brewed cup before buying and where the beans are in fresh supply. Granted, you won't likely be able to try coffee from all the offered origins, but you will be able to get an idea for how that particular shop roasts and sample the quality it's offering.

If you're unable to purchase beans directly from a local roaster, try to choose a store that sells a high volume of the coffee you want. This is especially important for more expensive coffees like Hawaiian Kona and Jamaican Blue Mountain, which tend to turn over more slowly. Buying prepackaged coffee from grocery stores and small coffee shops can be a bit riskier. If no roasting date is noted, you're better off passing on the coffee.

> **Field Notes**
>
> Ordering online can mean fresh, quality coffee for residents of more remote areas and opens the door to trying coffees you might not otherwise be able to. Many roasters ship the day the coffee is roasted or perhaps the day after to allow the coffee to de-gas a bit prior to packaging. However, when ordering online, you can't first sample the beans and you pay additional shipping charges. Check out Appendix C for recommended mail-order roasters.

In an effort to extend coffee's shelf life, some roasters flush freshly packed coffee with nitrogen gas, which displaces the oxygen that would otherwise affect freshness. Doing so extends a grace period of sorts to roasters during the distribution process, allowing the coffee to travel farther and sit longer before being purchased. Notably, it has allowed roasters from other countries to more effectively compete with fresh product on the U.S. market. It doesn't impact or indicate quality in any other way, and once opened, the coffee degrades normally. While it can be helpful, the process has been employed perhaps as much for marketing as a tool for freshness. As always, look for a roasting date, and let taste be your guide.

Freshness Counts: Storing Your Beans

Most of us don't have a small warehouse of green coffee and the luxury of roasting as needed, so it's important to keep the roasted coffee we purchase fresh until it's needed. Light, moisture, heat, and oxygen are the primary enemies of coffee freshness, so it's best to keep your beans in an opaque airtight container. Glass jars with rubber seals also work well if they're kept out of direct sunlight.

If your coffee came in a resealable foil (and/or plastic) bag with a one-way valve, it will work well for storage; however, if your coffee was packed in a lined bag with a roll-down closure, it's best to transfer it to another container for storage.

Plastic picks up and retains odors and tastes, so it's best to avoid storing coffee in reusable plastic containers. Most resealable valve bags aren't very durable, so washing and reusing them until they fail probably won't wreak too much havoc; just be aware that it could.

> **Hot Water**
>
> Coffee packed into a tightly sealed container immediately after roasting can emit enough carbon dioxide gas to explode or rupture the packaging. To avoid this, use bags with one-way valves or otherwise vent the package (open it briefly) when storing just-roasted coffee. If you're opening the container or package to get beans for brewing, it's unlikely that you'll experience any trouble.

The Refrigerator

One common storage method *does* destroy delicate coffee flavors: the refrigerator. Many well-meaning coffee drinkers slip their beans in and out of the refrigerator, thinking it's a great way to keep them fresh. Coffee is indeed perishable, but it doesn't "spoil" in the same way your mayonnaise does.

So if the fridge isn't a good idea, why? There are two basic things that make the refrigerator an inhospitable home for your beans: rogue flavors and moisture. Unless you have a dedicated coffee refrigerator, your coffee will take on subtle flavors from the foods it is stored alongside of. But before you convert your old dorm room–size refrigerator into a coffee cooler, recall that moisture is a chief enemy of fresh coffee and that refrigerators are damp environments. Add to that the potential for condensation buildup as you take coffee in and out of the fridge for brewing, and you have a system better suited for ruining than for preserving coffee.

The Freezer

Freezing coffee may, however, hold some merit. We still consider it a last resort, but in some situations, it can mean the difference between stale and enjoyable coffee. There is a risk that the coffee may pick up subtle food flavors, but freezing is probably the best long-term storage method. It's particularly useful if you've come upon much more coffee than you plan to use in the next week or two.

To prepare coffee for freezing, transfer the beans into freezable airtight packages containing about enough coffee for a week. Store them away from the freezer door if possible (to avoid temperature changes). When you're ready for more beans, remove a package and allow it to adjust to room temperature and then transfer the coffee to your daily storage container. Do not return it to the freezer.

Field Notes _____

For those who live in areas where obtaining quality, fresh coffee is difficult, buying coffee in bulk or via mail order and subsequently freezing it is a workable solution.

Caution: Contents *Should* Be Hot

Often overlooked by beginning brewers, water temperature is critical to extracting the most flavor from coffee. The difference among coffees brewed at 175°, 195°, and 210°F is so dramatic it can be immediately recognizable by even the most casual of coffee drinkers. The difference is enough that you might not even guess coffee brewed at these various temperatures was made with the same beans.

Optimum water temperature for brewing coffee is 200°F, plus or minus about 5°F. If the water is too hot, you'll end up with coffee that tastes bitter or astringent. If it's too cool, you'll find the coffee will be flat and lifeless.

Field Notes _____

Preheat your equipment with hot water when brewing manually to prevent a drastic temperature drop when you pour in the brewing water.

A good way to control your brewing temperature is to wait to grind the coffee until right after the water comes to a boil. This way, the water will cool to the optimum 195° to 205°F and your coffee will be as fresh as possible when you brew.

We recommend brewing methods that involve manually heating the water. This is not to say all automatic brewers produce poor coffee, but it is indeed rare to find an automatic that can consistently match the quality of manually brewed coffee. In fact, at the time of this writing, the Specialty Coffee Association of America recognizes only one automatic-drip brewer—the most common type of auto brewer—as being able to maintain proper temperature throughout the brewing cycle.

It's important to achieve and maintain proper brewing temperature, and fortunately it's not too difficult. Bring water just to a boil, either on the stove or with an electric kettle, and then allow it to cool briefly before brewing. The rate at which the water cools will vary by environment and water volume, but 30 seconds to 1 minute is a good starting point. If you have a candy thermometer and the inclination, you can easily check this for your brewing conditions.

Coffee-to-Water Ratio

Although the recipe for brewed coffee is simple—or perhaps because of it—it's critical to get the ground coffee-to-water ratio right. Coffee tastes best when the resulting cup is about 98.5 to 99 percent water, with the balance being flavor elements extracted from the grounds. If the ratio is off much in either direction, you'll taste it and you probably won't enjoy it.

The first step to achieving this balance is to start with an appropriate dose of ground coffee for the amount of water you'll be using. Use a standard coffee scoop (about the same as 2 level tablespoons) per 6 ounces of water. Because the size and density of beans can vary, it's more accurate to weigh out the dose of coffee; shoot for about 9 grams per 6 ounces of water. Most of the time, however, the scoop method will get you close, and you can just fine-tune the proportions based on taste.

Field Notes

A "cup" in the coffee world rarely refers to a standard 8-ounce measuring cup. Rather, it variably refers to between 4 and 6 ounces. Often, American manufacturers reference a 6-ounce cup, while Europeans use a 4-ounce standard (sometimes called a *tasse*). For example, when buying a 3-cup French press, you're really getting a brewer with a capacity of 12 ounces—about right to fill 1 coffee cup.

Getting into the Grind

Just having the coffee-to-water ratio correct isn't enough, though; what's actually extracted counts. This is controlled by the interaction between the fineness of the grind and how long the grounds are in contact with the brewing water.

The grind you use for brewing should match the brewing method and brewing time. Coffee ground too coarsely (for its intended use) does not provide enough surface area, resulting in underextracted, weak-tasting brew. Conversely, if the coffee is ground too finely, you'll overextract the coffee due to the increased surface area and end up with bitter coffee and, possibly, a plugged brewer.

In the following table, we give you the recommended grind for various types of brewing methods.

Field Notes

It's convenient to have your coffee ground at the store, but doing so will negatively impact the quality of your brewed coffee. Grinding coffee increases surface area, and so it accelerates the rate at which it stales—immensely so. To avoid this, just grind as much as you need each time you brew.

Recommended Grind Settings

Brewing Method	Grind
French press	Coarse
Vacuum pot	Medium-fine
Drip	Medium
Percolator	Medium-coarse
Moka pots	Fine
Ibrik	As fine as possible
Cold brewing	Coarse

Grinding at home also allows for flexibility because you can adjust the grind as necessary to bring out the best in your coffee. Another benefit of buying whole-bean coffee and grinding at home as needed is the ability to test the same beans with various brewing methods. You'll find that the same coffee will express itself somewhat uniquely depending on the brewing method, and by experimenting, you'll often find a hidden "sweet spot" where a certain brewing method just seems to bring out the best in a particular coffee.

Hot Water _____

Flavored coffees leave behind oils that taint other coffees ground with the same equipment, so be sure to use a dedicated grinder when working with these coffees. Be wary of grinding your coffee at a store that sells flavored and unflavored coffees yet has only one grinder. When grinding, begin by grinding and discarding a small amount of your coffee to help minimize carryover tastes from the previous customer's coffee. (This applies to nonflavored coffees as well.)

Grinders come in two basic styles: whirling-blade grinders and burr grinders. The bladed variety is the cheapest, usually selling for around $20. If you're on a tight budget when shopping for your brew tools, the blade grinders are the ticket. These "grind" the coffee blender-style by smashing and chopping the beans into pieces. They're not a bad place to start, but they do have the drawback of producing inconsistent grinds. There are no grind settings, so you'll need to eyeball the results to achieve the desired consistency. Try counting as you grind (one Mississippi … two Mississippi …) to make the results a little more repeatable. Due to the heavy paper filters it employs, the Chemex pour-over brewer is a good match for a blade grinder because the powder inevitably created during grinding won't end up in your cup. Also, these grinders work well if you enjoy Middle Eastern–style coffee and are brewing with an ibrik.

Field Notes _____

Espresso brewing demands a very fine, easily adjustable grind. If espresso is part of your home brewing, you'll definitely want a quality burr grinder. Check out Part 3 for more information on choosing espresso equipment.

A burr grinder, which starts at about $50, employs two burrs that mince the beans as the beans are pressed between them. A key advantage of burr grinders is that they produce much more even grinds than do blade grinders. An even grind is important because it ensures proper (and consistent) extraction; with an uneven grind, some of the coffee may be overextracted (the smallest particles) while some is underextracted (the largest particles). Another perk of burr grinders is that the distance between the burrs can be controlled easily, making repeatable results a snap.

Making Your Bed

While not universally applicable to all brewing methods, many rely on a thick bed of grounds for proper extraction. Ideally, you should shoot for 1 to 2 inches of grounds, evenly distributed across the brewing chamber. Without proper grounds depth, the water will run through the coffee too quickly, resulting in weak, underdeveloped brew. If it takes too long for water to clear the grounds because they're too deep, you'll end up with the opposite problem—strong, overdeveloped brew.

Some brew methods, like moka pots for example, account for proper depth by using a specially sized insert that you fill with grounds; others, such as drip brewers, do not, and you must manage the depth of grounds. Brew baskets are sized accordingly to the brewer's output capacity, so you're likely to achieve the best results when making full or nearly full batches. Therefore, if you typically only make coffee for yourself or one other person, purchasing a 12-cup brewer is likely a dooming decision, as the grounds will be too spread out for proper extraction.

Wash, Rinse, Repeat

Coffee is an oily product, and unless you thoroughly clean your brewing equipment, these oils can spoil future brews. Anything that comes in contact with the coffee should be cleaned, using soap and warm water if possible, after each use. Be sure to disassemble the brewer, where applicable, and scrub each part. For example, if you're using a French press, be certain to take the plunger assembly apart and to thoroughly clean the screens, as grounds are especially likely to build up there.

Built-up oils will turn rancid and spoil your coffee, often imparting a sour taste. Old oils also can turn your coffee bitter; this is especially so when they're left on brewing surfaces—they are essentially re-extracted repeatedly. Keeping your equipment clean is all it takes to avoid these nasty tastes, so don't forget to wash!

Field Notes _____

In addition to washing your brewer and wiping out your grinder, don't forget to clean your storage containers and thermoses. It does little good to prepare a great cup of coffee and then pour it into a dirty carafe.

Hot Water _____

The use of soap in cleaning coffee equipment sometimes stirs a heated discussion, usually by a few who denounce it. While it's true that you'll be left with a bad taste if you don't rinse properly after washing with soap and water, we have never experienced any negative effects. On the contrary, washing with water alone does not sufficiently clean brewing surfaces and will result in eventual buildups of coffee residues—sure to spoil the brew.

Troubleshooting

Sometimes trouble brews more easily than good coffee, but you can often discern enough to correct the problems by employing your palate. Before you put your tongue to the task though, your first step should be to ensure that you're working with clean equipment and fresh, high-quality coffee and water. Assuming you are, you'll be on the hunt for one of two likely problems: underextraction or overextraction. To many, coffee that's been overdone tastes unpleasantly strong, bitter, or astringent. Underextracted coffee may taste weak, undeveloped, flat, or lifeless.

If you suspect you've overextracted your brew, examine the grind size and contact time used. Either make your grind a little coarser to reduce the coffee's exposed surface area or decrease the time the grounds and water are in contact. The principles of remedying underextraction are the same as with overextraction, just applied in reverse. Here, you've not gotten enough out of the beans, so try using a finer grind or extending the contact time. Incorrect brewing temperature can play a role in either case, so it's wise to be sure you're hitting that 195° to 205°F ideal range.

Troubleshooting Brewing Problems by Taste

If Your Coffee Tastes ...	It Might Indicate ...
Flat or weak	Freshness and/or storage issue
	Grind is too coarse
	Contact time is too short
	Poor water quality
	Water is too cool
"Off"	Freshness and/or storage issue
	Dirty equipment
	Poor water quality
	Improper water temperature
Bitter	Grind is too fine
	Contact time is too long
	Water is too hot
Chalky	Grind is too fine
	Poor filtration

Hold It! What to Do with Brewed Coffee

Drink it, naturally! However, plenty of situations exist in which you may need to hold brewed coffee for a while prior to serving.

Brewed coffee will taste its best when kept at approximately 175°F, give or take about 5°F, because the chemical compounds that make coffee flavorful are most stable at this temperature. The best way to achieve this is to decant the coffee into a thermos or carafe that's been preheated with just-boiled water; if you don't preheat, your brew will lose critical heat when it acclimates to the cool container. Avoid using heating plates, as the continued heat alters the taste and can impart burnt or bitter flavors. While perhaps less convenient, you'll enjoy better coffee if you brew another batch in lieu of drinking coffee that sat for more than about 15 to 20 minutes.

Field Notes

Serving coffee in preheated mugs ensures it'll be at its best when you sip. Just heat a little extra water and fill your mug so it can warm up while you brew. The difference is subtle, but you'll notice it, and it's why coffee shops keep cups on top of espresso machines.

Does this holding temperature sound a bit hot for your tongue? Well, it likely is, and so you should, obviously, allow it to cool slightly before drinking. You'll note that the taste of coffee changes a bit as the temperature does. This has to do with the way we perceive taste and the point at which certain aromatics are released. Because so much of what we taste relies actually on smell, it's important that the coffee is served hot enough (above the boiling point of the key aromatics). For many of us, the optimum serving temperature for coffee is between 155° and 175°F.

Hot Water

The best temperature (about 180°F) to hold coffee for the preservation of the compounds that control taste can cause severe burns. Allow it to cool before sipping, and take precautions to prevent spilling.

The Least You Need to Know

◆ The ideal brewing temperature for coffee is between 195° and 205°F.

◆ Light, moisture, heat, and oxygen are the enemies of coffee freshness, so coffee is best stored away from these.

◆ Coffee stales very quickly after it's ground, so it's best to grind immediately before brewing.

◆ The fineness of the grind should match the brewing method and the length of contact with the brewing water.

◆ Coffee is best served within 15 to 20 minutes of brewing and should be decanted to a thermal carafe if not enjoyed right away.

Part 3

The Espresso Family: Cappuccino, Latte, Americano, and More

Despite the fact that many espresso-based beverages—like lattes, cappuccinos, and mochas—are everyday favorites, a fair amount of confusion surrounds them. That's understandable when you consider the complex brewing and preparation processes—not to mention a lot of specialized terms and jargon.

In Part 3, we sort it all out, starting with a little background on espresso. We not only describe the drinks you're likely to encounter at cafés across the United States, but we also explain how to make them. In the process, we cover equipment requirements and the necessary techniques to produce awesome espresso shots and drinks. We're also very happy to share some special drink recipes from top baristi from around the world.

8

Easing Into Espresso

In This Chapter

- ◆ A look at various espresso myths and the real truth behind them
- ◆ A historical overview of espresso: machines, drinks, and popularity
- ◆ Learn how espresso complements today's coffee culture

Espresso is coffee, yes. But because each step in the preparation process for espresso is very important, brewing espresso is far more complex than coffee brewed by other methods.

If you've ever watched a barista preparing espresso in a coffeehouse, you understand what we mean. Watching the process can be dizzying, not to mention noisy, because it's a combination of taps, hisses, and whirs, and the barista closely monitors each step. Juggling settings on a grinder, machine, and steam wand (for the milk) requires concentration. And it's all done to extract a small but delicious shot of espresso.

What Is Espresso?

You probably already know that espresso is dark, strong, and served in a tiny cup. And whether it's a shot drank alone or mixed with steamed milk to make a latte or cappuccino, it's not just a plain cup of coffee. The taste is much sweeter, almost bittersweet.

Espresso is prepared from coffee that's typically roasted somewhere between medium and dark. Near-boiling water is pushed through roughly 7 grams of compressed coffee grounds. The finished shot should be approximately 1¼ ounces and *pulled* in about 25 seconds.

On top of the espresso—its hallmark touch—sits a frothy crown of golden red crema. This crema is the one determinant—even before taste—that the shot will be excellent or terrible. Even before they bring the drink to their lips, good baristi study this crema very intently after they've pulled a shot to look for certain visual characteristics that will influence taste. Crema on a shot pulled properly has tiny speckles and a stunning golden-red color. And a full, fragrant aroma tips off baristi to a good shot before even the first sip.

Buzz Words

Preparing espresso is often referred to as **pulling** a shot because early espresso machines required the barista to pull down on a lever. The phrase is commonly used today despite the fact that most espresso machines no longer require the effort.

If espresso were a personality, its mood could shift from bold to bright or take on bitter, sweet, or spunky notes. It all depends on the process, such as the kind of beans used, how many seconds it took to pour the shot, and whether or not the ground was fine enough. (In Chapter 10, we discuss more about the changing variables and how they impact the taste of espresso.) An attentive barista works with the espresso to ensure it expresses a sweet, sensual mood.

Espresso has cultivated many fans, people who appreciate not only the sophisticated attention it requires during preparation but also the big taste that's delivered in a small package. A shot of espresso is served in a *demitasse*, a small cup designed to hold up to 3 ounces.

Trying Espresso for the First Time

The unusual intensity espresso packs into such a small drink may surprise and overwhelm some palates. Americano (espresso with hot water) and con panna (espresso with whipped cream) are both excellent drinks to sample when first trying espresso. An Americano is roughly the strength of brewed coffee but all the flavor is powered by espresso. Con panna mixes the rich, sweet tastes of whipped cream with espresso. We also recommend a small cappuccino with a single shot for the espresso newbie, as the milk softens the power of the espresso but still allows the taste to shine through.

Another drink that helps take the edge off espresso for its new drinkers is a romano—espresso with lemon peel rubbed on the rim of the glass and served with a twist, which increases the perceived sweetness.

Espresso can be thought of like the vodka in a cocktail. It provides the base for a whole host of mixed drinks. Pairing it with different flavorings or styles of milk (steamed or frothed) brings out a new, distinct taste. Have fun with the experimentation, and don't feel inhibited!

Field Notes

For many, espresso is an acquired taste, so don't be disappointed if you don't fall in love the first time you try it. One way to ease into espresso is to try drinks made with espresso, like cappuccinos and lattes, which include milk as well.

Espresso Truths

Many myths and misunderstandings surround espresso. Let's debunk some of those myths now.

Espresso beans come from the same trees as coffee does. Although the coffee world has generally come to discover, through experimentation, which bean origins produce the espresso blends pleasing to most palates, or a coffee that holds its own as espresso, there are no right and wrong answers when it comes to what beans are used for espresso. Your local coffeehouse, if it has an on-site roaster, has probably spent a great deal of time creating a signature espresso blend, one that won't taste like another you could get across town.

Often, we hear that espresso contains more caffeine than coffee. That's not true. About the same amount of caffeine is extracted to make a single shot of espresso as an 8-ounce cup of coffee.

It's important to remember, too, that espresso is made to order, even if that means in your own kitchen. Just because an espresso machine sits on your counter doesn't mean you can keep a shot glass of espresso in wait for the time you plan to drink it. With coffee, we can make a pot and toss whatever we don't drink into a thermos for an hour later, and as long as the heat is retained, there will

Hot Water

Espresso is quite often mispronounced. To avoid sounding like an espresso newbie, be sure you pronounce it *eSpresso*, not *eXpresso*.

be relatively minor differences in the taste. Espresso isn't as forgiving. It should be drunk immediately after extraction or not at all. After espresso sits, the prized crema dissolves, as does the body to some degree, leaving one flat drink. It's the crema that holds all the delicate aromatics.

When preparing espresso at home, don't give into the temptation to pour it into a larger cup if you're worried about spilling when you sip or you enjoy the design of the larger cup better. Small cups are more appropriate due to size and crema retention.

Cuppa Wisdom

The customer must wait for the espresso. The espresso must not wait for the customer.

—Italian saying

And a final myth: espresso is difficult to prepare. By following instructions and having the proper equipment on hand (grinder and espresso machine), you can easily pour a sufficient shot of espresso. It's harder than making coffee in that it's not as automated and requires attentiveness to temperature settings, for instance, but with time and patience, anyone can do it.

The Evolution of the Espresso Machine

The coffee industry is just like other industries in that over time, technology improves and innovative products are introduced to the market, often replacing earlier versions. Even today, researchers are toying with the concept of a better machine, although what we have to work with at the commercial and residential levels is definitely adequate.

Field Notes

One of the earliest devices for making espresso, which you can still buy today, is the moka pot. Made of metal and designed for stovetop usage, the coffee a moka pot produces tends to be espressolike, with a different taste than coffee brewed in a vacuum pot, drip maker, or French press. It uses steam power to force water through a bed of coffee, but there's a limit to the pressure, which is key to good espresso. (See Chapter 6 for more on moka pots.)

Espresso Machines of the Past

It wasn't until the twentieth century that espresso came into its own, when steam pressure had advanced enough to be used on a commercial machine with success. In 1935, Francesco Illy substituted compressed air for the steam, which resulted in the first automatic machine, which was very similar to what we use today.

But even before Illy, attempts had been made to extract espresso at home by pulling hot water at high pressure. The first patents for home devices in Europe were somewhere between 1818 and 1824. In France in 1822, Jean Louis Rabout patented an extraction press, building on the momentum of other espresso inventions.

Then, in 1855, a more sophisticated version of the machine was showcased at the Paris Exposition. Here, Édouard Loysel de Santais demonstrated his machine, which had an elaborate system of tubes running to the coffee bed.

Field Notes

The Illy family has had several successes in coffee and espresso innovation and is considered the founding family of espresso. Their company, Illy, is still in operation, with its headquarters in Trieste, Italy, and sells coffee, accessories, a line of artist-designed cups and machines available in local retailers and via mail order.

According to historical records, the machine brewed 2,000 cups of coffee in an hour. The problem with de Santais's machine, despite its ingenuity, was that it was way too complex and sophisticated for the average user to operate. Its presence quickly fizzled, although it served as inspiration for other machine builders, who built on his concepts.

It wasn't until 1901 in Italy that the first commercial espresso-making machine was manufactured. Luigi Bezzera of Milan patented a single-cup espresso machine that was different from all others before because it poured a single shot into only one cup at a time, guaranteeing freshness in each cup. Now people could have espresso made to order.

In 1945, Gaggia, a manufacturer of commercial espresso machines, unveiled its lever-operated, spring-loaded machine, making the process of pulling espresso shots much, much easier. This marked the first time a machine could press hot water through a bed of coffee grounds, with pressures above those generated by steam pressure alone; this concept has become crucial to making a good shot of espresso. A piston on the machine was powered by a spring, which compressed by a lever. As the user pulled down on the lever, the piston pressed water through the coffee.

Hot Water

Attempts to preserve espresso for later only ruins the taste. If you'll notice, at a café, or even in someone's home, the espresso machine is fired up only just before someone wants to have a shot. That's the best way to make espresso.

Imprinted on the machine was the logo "Crema Caffe / Naturale"—"natural coffee cream." This refers to the ability to create crema, the prized crown on top of a great shot of espresso.

Cuppa Wisdom

If it keeps up, man will atrophy all his limbs but the push-button finger.

—Frank Lloyd Wright

About 10 years later, Cimbali (which still manufactures espresso machines) designed the world's first hydraulically powered piston espresso machine. A piston powered tap water with lots of force, requiring the barista to manually control different phases in the preparation process, which, as you might imagine, was quite a hands-on education.

An espresso machine called Faema E61 was unveiled in the 1960s. Water was heated upon request, instead of sitting in a tank, and a pump replaced the spring-driven piston. The E61 also employed a decalcification system, which kept the pump and heating mechanism from being destroyed by hard-water deposits.

Semi-automatic and automatic machines created during the 1980s and 1990s allowed the operator to dose and tamp the coffee but took over the role of maintaining water pressure. These machines also made repeatable results more attainable, so if a barista was happy with the outcome of the espresso he or she made, it was easier to do once again as long as he or she followed those same steps.

Home pump machines were also very popular during the 1980s and 1990s and really pronounced the idea of the home barista. The machines were relatively inexpensive and can still be found in housewares stores. Lightweight and simple to use, they introduced a lot of people to espresso, at about the same time coffeehouses were popping up all over the country, fueling a want for espresso.

Today in America we have lots of options for espresso machines and other accessories, in part due to a resurgence in making espresso at home. Although more people likely have a toaster than an espresso machine (because of the additional cost and because espresso is an acquired taste), we're seeing more buzz than ever before about the home barista.

At the Espresso Bar

Espresso's arrival in the United States started with the Pacific Northwest and New York City. Eventually, the craze for espresso spread to other cities, especially in college towns and arts communities. Café managers and baristi educated themselves—or learned from others—how to pull good shots and blend a solid, delicious choice of coffee beans into signature espresso.

Espresso drinks are the fanfare in a coffee-house. Before coffeehouses were predominant, it used to be that espresso was an after-dinner drink in a restaurant. Now it can be ordered, made, and carried off by the customer in a matter of minutes. Espresso drinks are the result of the barista's hard work, and when you see a signature drink on the menu, it's because the barista is not just following convention or going along with what other cafés are doing.

Field Notes _____

Today, espresso bars aren't only in hip, metro areas, or on a congested street of storefronts all lined up one after the other. You can find them inside grocery stores, commercial office buildings, department stores, and airports.

Speaking of drink menus, you've probably already noticed how the cafés you visit tweak the menu from time to time to bring in special flavors of the season, offering honey lattes, peppermint mochas, and—in fall and winter—flavorings of pumpkin and cinnamon. With a rotating menu of drinks, the customer gets added variety at little or no extra charge.

But don't forget that espresso is fun and not something to be intimidated by. If you enjoy drinking espresso at cafés, you might like tinkering in your kitchen to make similar drinks. Once you have the proper setup (espresso machine, grinder, and tamper) you're ready to start brewing and steaming.

Field Notes _____

To Americans, coffee initially was a delicious replacement to beer as a favorite break-fast drink.

Espresso as Flavor

Aside from treating espresso as a beverage, food manufacturers and chefs have begun to rely on espresso as flavor. Muffins, cookies, ice cream, and other foods and candies contain espresso, which borrows the flavors of a shot of espresso. We've even seen espresso-rubbed filet mignon on an upscale restaurant's dinner menu. And chocolate-covered espresso beans are often sold at candy stores alongside gummi worms, malt balls, and chewing gum. It's hard to not like the classic pairing of chocolate and coffee.

Surrounding all this is a keen appreciation for espresso culture, whether it's the operator of a machine or a doting customer. Now that espresso can be prepared at home, more and more people can safely say they've had good-quality espresso. It's no longer a mystifying, muddled concept. Instead, espresso has been integrated into our lives, whether as a countertop appliance or drink choice on a menu.

The Least You Need to Know

♦ Espresso is finely ground, dark-roasted coffee brewed by forcing steam under high pressure through the coffee. A single shot of espresso is $1\frac{1}{4}$ ounces.

♦ Espresso is more complex than coffee, due to its preparation.

♦ Espresso machines have evolved over the years, from complicated gadgets originally unavailable to consumers to push-button automatic all-in-one machines sold today.

♦ Natural steam pressure is not enough to properly extract espresso, which has led to the developments of many espresso machines and eventually, the kind of espresso machine we have today.

9

Navigating the Café Menu

In This Chapter

- ◆ Why coffeehouses are so popular
- ◆ What's in café drinks and, briefly, how they're prepared
- ◆ Discover how drinks and cafés vary across the country and around the world

Café, coffee shop, coffeehouse. Whatever you call it, it's still the spot where you go to grab a cup of coffee (or another beverage), meet friends, or get lost in a good novel or the morning newspaper. If you're a coffee or espresso drinker (and you likely are because you're reading this book), you probably have located a favorite café in your neighborhood.

When you're new to coffee, however, surveying the menu at a café can be rather intimidating. The cup sizes, for example, are unlike what you might find at a fast-food restaurant (small, medium, and large). Instead, you'll often see names like *venti* or *grande*, and ordering a drink means answering a series of questions concerning a coffee preference, milk type, and flavoring. That said, cafés do collectively share a loose menu of what have become classic American drinks prepared with espresso. In light of all this, a standard cup of coffee remains, with the flexibility to add sugar or milk to achieve a desired taste.

Our goal in this chapter is to explain various drinks served at cafés in the United States and fill you in on their ingredients and taste, as well as give you tips on how to customize them to your liking. Consider this chapter your guide to cracking the café-menu code.

Coffeehouse, Sweet Coffeehouse

In previous chapters, we've covered the history and social importance of coffeehouses across not only the United States, but also the world. Coffeehouses are where people can meet, get a drink, talk with others, and generally cultivate a feeling of community. Telecommuters might be searching for a home away from the home office; stay-at-home moms might desire a place to take their toddlers during the day. Wall outlets (for laptop computers), good lighting, board games, and picture books (for young kids)—these are telltale welcome signs for specific kinds of customers.

Field Notes

Coffeehouses often mimic their neighborhood surroundings to provide a comfortable and attractive environment for locals. That's why the same coffeehouse might not succeed in two different cities. If you're thinking of opening a coffee shop, carefully study the surroundings and think about what type of person might stop in on a regular basis.

Over time, cafés have expanded their menus to incorporate more than just what's in the pastry case. Customers have called for not just a muffin, but a sandwich or bowl of soup, not necessarily with a cup of coffee, but maybe an Italian soda or iced tea. Paninis—hot, pressed sandwiches—are a favorite within the Italian culture. Focaccia bread is often used to hold ingredients like mozzarella cheese, roasted red peppers, tuna, artichokes, and chicken, seasoned with such herbs as oregano, basil, and rosemary. Adding "meatier" items to a coffeehouse menu avoids an empty environment between lunch and dinner, when folks might crave more than a cup of morning coffee or pastry.

Some cafés have even started to carry gelato, a frozen Italian treat made with high-quality fruits, chocolates, or flavorings such as hazelnut, vanilla bean, or pistachio. Sold by the scoop, gelato is a sweet indulgence favored by many.

Another addition, designed to drum up more business in the evenings, is the number of beers and wines served by the glass.

But despite all the food and drink trends, the most important focus on a café's menu remains the same: espresso and espresso-based drinks. Barista staff, who are like bartenders, mixing and stirring, often add signature drinks to the menu, akin to what a chef might do at a restaurant. When a new recipe pleases the café staff, it's likely added to the menu.

On the Menu: Espresso Drinks

You probably don't go to a coffeehouse just for its comfortable couches and an opportunity to people-watch. Your experience is as much about the drinks you order, too. Whether you order it to go or for in-house, it's important that you understand what you're drinking. In Chapter 13, we provide instructions to make the drinks at home, but for now, think of this section as your primer or cheat sheet when placing your drink order.

In the drink descriptions that follow, we've tried to indicate drink size, as they can range from ¾ ounce for a short espresso shot to a 20-ounce latte. It's best to understand the drink's size before you order so you're not surprised later!

But don't be afraid to depart from the menu just a tad. You can customize your drink order to indicate a long or short espresso, which refers to the amount of water used to prepare the espresso (the amount of grounds remains the same). For instance, a short espresso, or *ristretto*, is between ½ and 1 fluid ounce. A double ristretto is 2 short shots of espresso. A *lungo* (*lun-gow*) refers to a shot of espresso made using more water, approximately 1½ to 2 ounces.

Another way to customize a drink is to add a flavoring syrup. There are many to select from, so pay homage to a favorite fruit or sweetener and enjoy the enhancement it brings to your drink.

Ready to step up to the counter and order? Here are descriptions of drinks commonly offered on café menus:

affogato   An affogato (*AW-fo-got-oh*) is a drink that isn't new in the culinary world but is

Field Notes _____

While it varies slightly from café to café, milk is usually steamed to a certain temperature, often between 140° and 160°F. You can usually ask the barista to make it a little cooler or hotter if you prefer.

Buzz Words _____

Ristretto (*wris-trett-oh*) is a shot of espresso that was prepared as "short," meaning it is only roughly ¾ ounce rather than the usual 1¼ ounces. A **lungo,** a long pull or double shot of espresso, is made with more than the standard amount of water (about an equal amount per coffee), and is typically 1½ to 2 ounces.

slowly making its way onto American café menus. Quite literally, it means "drowned" in Italian, which describes the pouring of espresso over vanilla ice cream. A newer adaptation is to substitute gelato for the ice cream. You might find some cafés using flavored gelatos or ice creams. A dollop of whipped cream is often added on top. This is a great dessert drink.

americano   An Americano (*a-mer-UH-con-oh*) is simply espresso diluted with water. You can order it with a single or double shot, depending on the strength you prefer. This drink is about the strength of brewed coffee and is most similar to filter coffee made in the United States. There is, however, a distinctive taste difference between an Americano made with dark-roasted coffee and one prepared with a medium-roasted coffee. This is a good intro to espresso for newbies because the espresso flavor shines through but its intensity is tamed with water.

brevé   Brevé (*brev-ay*) originated in Seattle. It is a latte made with frothed half-and-half instead of milk. Its texture, compared with a latte, is thicker and creamier.

cappuccino   A cappuccino (*cap-ou-CHEEN-oh*) is a very popular café drink. Hot, frothed milk is added to 1 or 2 shots of espresso. Classic Italian-style cappuccinos are served with $\frac{1}{3}$ espresso, $\frac{1}{3}$ milk, and $\frac{1}{3}$ foam in a 5- or 6-ounce cup. In the United States, the froth is often thicker and drier, causing it to sometimes float on top of the espresso and milk. True cappuccinos have a soupier foam that combines with the espresso to create almost a velvetlike texture, and remains wet for a longer period of time. Many people prefer a small dose of sugar with their cappuccinos.

chai charger   Chai (rhymes with *sky*) has its roots in India. Often when people first taste chai it reminds them of pumpkin, which is not far from the truth. When made from scratch, chai is essentially black tea mixed with spices such as cardamom, nutmeg, cinnamon, cloves, and ginger. However, in most coffeehouses, to save time, a chai concentrate is used and then added to milk and called a chai latte. To make a chai charger, the barista simply adds 1 or 2 shots of espresso to the chai latte.

espresso   Espresso is a highly concentrated beverage made when hot water is forced under pressure through finely ground and tightly packed coffee. It is made in less than 30 seconds and poured into a preheated 3-ounce demitasse cup. One shot is roughly $1\frac{1}{4}$ ounces. Doubles, sometimes called *doppio*, are not twice as strong or concentrated but merely 2 shots.

Heavy-bodied and bittersweet, when drunk on its own, espresso is too intense for some palates. Often it is enjoyed more when combined with milk

> **Cuppa Wisdom**
>
> I have measured out my life with coffee spoons.
>
> —T. S. Eliot

(steamed or frothed), ice, flavored syrups, or whipped cream, although espresso purists might disagree. We like to refer to espresso as the "vodka" in most drinks, meaning it's the base a drink is built upon.

espresso con Panna   Espresso con Panna is a shot of espresso topped with a dab of whipped cream, which softens the espresso's bite but doesn't abandon its taste. This drink is a nice introduction to someone who's not yet comfortable drinking espresso on its own but has maybe had and liked mochas or lattes.

espresso granita   Espresso granita (*graw-neat-a*) is not often served in the United States but still is a part of some cafés' culture. Brewed espresso is first frozen and then crushed. When served, it's topped with whipped cream and eaten with a spoon.

espresso romano   Espresso romano is a shot of espresso served with a twist of lemon on the side. This drink is prepared by taking a lemon peel (orange or tangerine may be substituted, too, to bring out different notes of citrus) and rubbing it on the inside rim of the cup. The sourness of the lemon increases your perception of the sweetness in the espresso, and so it's a good introduction to espresso.

Hot Water

Hot espresso drinks served in a café typically come with a saucer. If you ask for it to go, be sure to grab a java sleeve to wrap around the cup so you don't lose control of the cup and drop it.

frappé   (also called **latte granita**) If you've had a Frappuccino at Starbucks, you've essentially had a frappé. Served cold, it's freshly brewed espresso, milk, sugar, and ice blended. Sometimes cafés offer flavoring options such as vanilla, caramel, or chocolate.

honey latte   A honey latte is prepared like a latte with espresso and steamed milk, except honey is poured over the espresso before the milk is added, causing the espresso to taste sweeter than normal.

iced cappuccino   An iced cappucciono is essentially an iced version of a cappuccino, but it's not made by just taking a hot cappuccino and adding ice cubes to it. Instead, it's made by pouring just-brewed espresso over crushed ice and topping that with cold milk. Unlike a hot cappuccino, this drink is served in a glass, not a cup.

latte   Combining hot milk with espresso has long been a breakfast drink for southern Europeans. A latte (*LAH-tay*) is one such example. For the American version, shots of espresso are added to steamed milk.

> **Field Notes** _____
>
> To spruce up your latte, ask for a flavoring syrup such as vanilla, hazelnut, rasp-
> berry, or Irish crème. During the winter holidays, it's common for a café to roll out
> an eggnog latte, which simply adds eggnog to the milk for a sweeter, creamier
> taste. Peppermint mochas are a popular winter addition to café menus as well. If you
> haven't already experimented with flavorings, go ahead and start. You'll no doubt dis-
> cover a few favorites. (Most espresso-based drinks such as brevés, cappuccinos, and
> mochas can be flavored, too.)

macchiato In Italian, *macchiato* (*MA-kee-ah-toh*) means "marked." That's a good way
to describe an espresso macchiato. It's espresso with a thin layer of foam dabbed on
top.

mocha (including **white chocolate mocha**) A mocha (*MOW-ka*) is a serving of
espresso combined with intense cocoa and hot frothed milk. A white chocolate mocha
is prepared in the same fashion but substitutes white
chocolate instead of milk or dark chocolate. Cafés
use syrup, powder, or melted baking chocolate for
the flavor. Mochas are served both hot and cold, and
you usually have the option to add whipped cream
on top.

> **Field Notes** _____
>
> Peppermint mochas are a
> common café drink, mixing
> peppermint and cocoa flavors.

red eye (also called **shot in the dark** and **depth charge**) A red eye is espresso and
coffee combined, for an added jolt and flavor.

On the Menu: Nonespresso Drinks

Espresso drinks do not make up an entire menu at a coffee shop. Hot and cold beverages made with tea or coffee are important staples, too.

café au lait This is a favorite beverage in a café in France and a staple at many of
the country's bistros. Café au lait (*CA-fey oh-lay*) is half strong coffee with half hot
milk and is akin to a latte.

chai latte Earlier in this chapter you read about chai charger, which is a chai latte
and 1 or 2 shots of espresso. When made from scratch, chai is black tea mixed with
spices and milk, but in most cafes, in the interest of efficiency, a chai concentrate is
added to steamed milk to make a chai latte. No espresso is included in a chai latte.

drinking chocolate Within the last couple years, drinking chocolate has become a
popular drink at cafés. Only it's not like hot chocolate. It's a serving of less than 2

ounces of very, very rich chocolate, so rich that it would be nearly impossible to drink a mug even if it could be ordered that way. The drinking chocolate is prepared with a higher-grade chocolate (usually dark) and combined with steamed milk. Drinking chocolate has been popular in Torino, Italy, for quite some time, and the appeal has now spread to other countries, including the United States.

iced coffee   Iced coffee is not just hot brewed coffee with a few ice cubes dumped in. Instead, most commonly, the coffee has been cold-brewed and is poured over ice just before serving. Using the cold-brewed concentrate gives the coffee a rich, resonant taste that's lower in acid than hot brewed coffee. It's refreshing and is sometimes sweetened a bit.

Italian soda   In an Italian soda, sparkling water is combined with flavoring syrup—everything from peach to Irish crème to raspberry. It is served on ice in a tall glass.

shakes   Shakes, made with ice cream, need no explanation as they've been served at fast-food restaurants, diners, and ice-cream shops for decades. At a café, a shake might be flavored with coffee, espresso, or mocha (either brewed or as granules), borrowing notes from the drinks themselves.

smoothies   Smoothies have turned into a very popular drink recently, perhaps as the result of our society becoming more health-conscious. Smoothies are made with fresh or frozen fruits, fruit juice, and/or yogurt. Common fruits are mango, blueberry, strawberry, raspberry, and banana, but the possible combinations are many.

steamer   A steamer is milk that's been—you guessed it—steamed. You can select a flavoring syrup to add some punch to the milk. A head of froth is usually added on top as well.

white coffee latte   This is a drink that's new to many cafés, but you still may come across it. White coffee is coffee that's been underroasted and is often prepared as espresso. It has a peanutlike taste, which is why lattes almost always come with your choice of flavor syrups, so you have more activity in your mouth when you drink it. A white coffee latte has more caffeine than a regular latte because less caffeine has been burned off during roasting.

Regional Differences in Espresso

If, during your domestic travels, you've popped into coffeehouses in various parts of the country, you may have been surprised by what you sipped. Roast styles for espresso—and coffee even—are not the same in every city, and in fact, regional preferences have developed over time. Some exceptions are with larger chains such as Starbucks, where roast styles are mandated across the board, and in all retail cafés, which is usually based on roast style preferences in the city where the company is headquartered.

Cuppa Wisdom

You can tell when you have crossed the frontier into Germany because of the badness of the coffee.

—Edward VII

Generally speaking, however, people in the West Coast states—in particular the Pacific Northwest—prefer a darker roast for their espresso. Residents of the East Coast, especially Boston and Philadelphia, tend to like it lighter, although there tends to be a few departures. Coffee that's roasted to a full city is also popular in Florida and Georgia, and in Miami, with its large Cuban population, a dark-roast espresso spiked with sugar is a favored style. In New Orleans, the coffee (darkly roasted and with chicory) has become a trademark for the region, and it's commonly served with a beignet (fried doughnut) and milk.

Despite these geographical customs, if a roaster or café manager received his or her training in another region, influences from that region may appear in the coffeehouse. So it's always a good idea to get to know your local café scene and not assume that each one is following tradition.

When you start to compare the taste of espresso around the globe, that's when you'll notice true variance, especially in drinks in which espresso is only a small part and combined with milk that is steamed or frothed. In Italy, where espresso was practically born, locals enjoy their espresso with milk and as a morning drink.

We in the United States have amended our café drinks to the point where much more milk is added. It's certainly not a sin to do so, but it should be recognized that there's a notable difference between a cappuccino in Milan and a cappuccino in Manhattan. Italian-size cappuccinos are 5 ounces, but in America, cappuccinos are 8 ounces with 1 espresso shot added. Our "supersize" culture has brought 20-ounce drinks to café menus. Typically these drinks are very milky, often having only 2 espresso shots.

Milk and Sugar?

Sugar is the best way to sweeten any espresso drink you order. (Although for some people we recognize that pouring a packet of sugar into a cappuccino is not their idea of a desired taste.) Coffeehouses will have at their condiment stations either sugar packets or canisters to appease their sweeter-toothed customers.

All sugar is not the plain white stuff, though. Have fun trying out some of these different sugars to see how they change the way your drink tastes:

◆ Brown sugar

◆ Natural cane sugar (which has natural molasses notes because it's less refined)

◆ White table sugar

◆ Low-calorie/unsweetened or artificial sweeteners

◆ Sugar cubes

Another variable when designing your ideal coffee or espresso drink are the choices of milk: whole, skim (or nonfat), 1 percent, or 2 percent. The default milk used if you don't specify varies from café to café.

Cafés are becoming increasingly sensitive to special dietary needs such as for vegans (no consumption of animal products) or for the lactose-intolerant. It's often possible to substitute cow's milk with soy milk, although it may add between 25¢ and 50¢ to the cost of the drink. The quality of a drink made with soy milk continues to get better because advancements have been made that enable the soy to react better to the kind of heat that's required to make espresso, as well as frothed and steamed milk.

Field Notes

Cafés often offer a discount if you bring in your own mug and ask that the drink you order be poured into it. This is also a way to help the café reduce its reliance on paper products.

Coffee Drinks Around the World

When Kristine spent a week in Paris a couple years ago, she made it a point to try out various cafés and bistros to get a rich experience of how the locals drank their coffee. Sticker shock occurred after just her first café visit. In Paris, the price for a cup of coffee (called *café noir*) was around 4 euros, which translated to just under U.S. $5.

The service is much more upscale than in our country, though, which might make the price worth it for some. For example, a carafe of water is served with the coffee on a small tray, along with a cube of sugar and a dark-chocolate square. Famous cafés such as Les Deux Magots have their logo imprinted on the sugar cube and chocolate square packages.

Also, there's hardly a presence of to-go coffee served in paper cups. Parisians enjoy the opportunity to linger inside or in front of a café.

Cuppa Wisdom

After a few months' acquaintance with European "coffee," one's mind weakens, and his faith with it, as he begins to wonder if the rich beverage of home, with its clotted layer of yellow cream on top of it, is not a mere dream after all, and a thing which never existed.

—Mark Twain

This is true at cafés in other European cities, too. The fine detail and presentation associated with stopping for a cup of coffee at a café make the experience exquisite and not at all rushed. The entire experience is designed for a leisurely pace.

And in Italy, be forewarned that if you order a "latte," you will really get a glass of hot milk, because *latte* in Italian means "milk." Instead, ask for a "caffe latte," which is espresso and steamed milk. And if you ask for a cappuccino with or after your dinner, expect a bit of confusion from the waiter. Italians prefer to drink cappuccino in the mornings.

The Least You Need to Know

♦ The number and importance of coffeehouses has grown exponentially in the United States in recent years. It's easy to see why.

♦ Coffeehouses are a "third place" for many people, meaning the number of visits they make to a coffeehouse ranks third to the time they spend at home and at work.

♦ When ordering a drink at a coffeehouse, customize it to include a ristretto ($^3/_4$ ounce of espresso) or lungo (between $1\,^1/_2$ and 2 ounces espresso), instead of ordering the typical size of espresso ($1\,^1/_4$ ounces).

♦ Roast styles and drink preparation, especially the sizes offered, vary according to regional differences (customs, traditions, and preferences).

Espresso Equipment

In This Chapter

♦ Discover the differences amongst common types of home espresso machines

♦ Find an espresso machine to fit your needs

♦ Pick a grinder, the key to great espresso

♦ Learn about accessories that make brewing espresso a little easier

Making good espresso can be challenging, but it doesn't have to be. It does require specific equipment, though, in addition to proper technique. We touched briefly on espresso machines and other equipment in earlier chapters, but in this chapter, we look closer at espresso machines, grinders, accessories, and more. We cover the types of espresso machines available to the home barista and break down not only how they work, but also the pros and cons of each.

Unfortunately, related technology necessary to properly brew espresso doesn't come as cheaply as that for other coffee-brewing methods. The market is currently bursting with options at prices from less than $200 to more than $2,000, and as we examine the equipment options, we give you a realistic idea of what each costs. After you've read through this chapter, you'll be prepared to make informed decisions about setting up your espresso system as well as what it will cost.

Pumping the Black Gold: Pump-Driven Machines

Home espresso machines that use a pump to force hot water through the coffee grounds are capable of reaching proper brewing pressures and creating fine espresso. These machines are a diverse lot with design variations within each of the four main kinds of pump-driven espresso machines:

◆ Semi-automatic

◆ Automatic

◆ Super-automatic

◆ Pod-compatible

Right now this might all sound like space talk, but it's really just a handy way of categorizing how much of the espresso preparation the machine does and how much is left up to the operator. Prices range quite a bit within each group, though obviously, the more complex the machine (like many of the multifunctional super-automatics), the more it generally costs.

Speaking of costs, because all these home machines produce water pressure on par with the commercial espresso machines, they're best paired with grinders with near-commercial capabilities as well (unless, of course, your machine is a super-automatic or uses pods), which come with a price tag themselves. The high-pressure brewing environment magnifies any problems created by poor or inconsistent grinds. For example, if the grind size isn't uniform, the water simply rushes past the largest pieces as it follows the path of least resistance. This underextracts some of the coffee while overextracting the rest, leaving you with a cupful of unpleasant tastes. If you purchase a pump-driven espresso machine, you really need to pair it with a quality burr grinder that produces a consistent, easily adjustable grind. Because pump-driven espresso machines generally aren't available for less than about $200 (and many cost much more), it's easy for people to blow their budget on the machine and be too eager to save money when selecting a grinder.

Hot Water

Skimping on a grinder will only lead to frustration and poor results, so budget at least $125 to $175 for a grinder if you go with a pump machine.

The primary drawback of many pump-driven machines is their high cost. Though pump-driven machines start at around $200, expect to spend more for one that will withstand the rigors of routine use. It's still challenging to build a system with machine, grinder, and accessories for less than $500. In spite of the stiff initial invest-ment, it often pays off for those who spend a lot on drinks at coffee shops.

Simply Semi-Automatic

A good share of home espresso machines are semi-automatic, which means you have to prepare the shot and then activate the pump for the appropriate amount of time to complete the shot. Automatics, commonly used at coffeehouses, are much the same except that after you've prepared the shot and turned on the machine, it pushes a pre-determined amount of water through the grounds and then turns itself off.

Semi-autos are usually designed to be brewing workhorses, so their general layout is pretty straightforward. Typically, they have a rocker switch to turn on the pump and another to trigger the boiler to prepare steam for frothing milk. However, because brewing good espresso and making proper latte or cappuccino milk are not immediately easy tasks, it's not uncommon for these machines to come equipped with promising gadgets. The most commonly encountered are crema-enhancers and frothing attachments. Some of these are moderately suc-cessful, but their ultimate usefulness is often tempered by troubles with cleanup. This is especially the case with milk frothing attach-ments, so it's best to buy a machine that can be used with or without the accessories. Good milk-frothing technique takes a little practice, but if you plan to use a machine often enough to justify its high initial cost, you'll be whipping up liquid velvet for your cappuccinos in no time.

> **Field Notes**
>
> At the consumer level, auto-matic espresso machines actually tend to be super-automatics because they prepare the shot for you in addition to brewing it.

We recommend semi-automatic pump espresso machines for those looking to re-create the café experience at home and who are willing to invest a little time and money to the prospect. Turning out good espresso with one of these machines relies on your skill at preparing and pulling the shot, so expect to spend some time learning the art. Your first few shots are likely to leave a bit to be desired, but when you have it down, it's not difficult, and you'll find that you have a lot more control over the taste of your drinks than more automated machines afford. Look for easy-to-fill water reservoirs and key internal components, like boilers, to be made of heavy brass rather than aluminum.

Automatically Espresso

Automatic espresso machines are essentially semi-automatics that push a specific amount of water through the grounds when you activate the machine (enough for a single or double, depending on which button you press). You still must prepare the shot as for semi-automatics, so you'll still need a good burr grinder that produces even, adjustable grinds.

Automatics are fairly popular at the commercial level because they free up the barista while the shot pours because the pump turns off automatically.

> **Field Notes**
>
> You'd think automatic espresso machines would be all the rage, but they never seemed to catch on for home use, most likely because the high cost of the automatic metering components and touchpads makes it hard for them to compete. It seems consumers would prefer to realize the savings with semi-automatics and dose the water themselves or have the conveniences of super-automatics.

Super-Automatic Wonders

Super-automatic espresso machines approach, and in some cases surpass, the ease of preparing traditional, brewed coffee with an electric drip brewer. The reason some people find them so super is because they do most every part of the process for you. These all-in-ones grind, dose, tamp, and brew the shot at the touch of a button. All you must do—other than to keep the water reservoir and bean hopper full and occasionally empty the internal waste compartment—is push a button. Obviously, this significantly cuts down on the learning curve to making espresso as well as operator-caused troubles, such as poor extraction due to uneven tamping.

Unless you have a very large budget, super-automatics take care of the espresso preparation but leave it to you to create the final cocktail. As with many home machines, you're bound to come across a dazzling array of milk-frothing wonder accessories as you shop for your super-auto. Look for a steam wand that can function without attachments if possible, as most of them are more of a pain to use and clean than they are miracle micro-foam creators.

The entry-level prices of super-autos have come down significantly in the past 5 years, but those consumers seem to like most still tend to be quite expensive—typically more than $700. Sticker shock is common enough when eyeing a super-auto, but it's important to remember you're really purchasing two machines in one. And because it's difficult still to get into a good semi-automatic system for less than roughly $500, their prices aren't as high, comparatively, as they may first seem.

Hot Water

The level of automation with super-automatic machines doesn't, however, ensure you sweet-tasting espresso shots. It's still important to understand how espresso is made so you can easily fine-tune your pours and troubleshoot shots that are pulling improperly or tasting poorly. In most cases, though, this simply requires changing the grind setting appropriately (finer for shots pouring too quickly or coarser to help shots that are pulling too slowly).

A primary concern with super-automatic espresso machines is the reduced control you have over the quality of the shot. You can minimize this by looking for a machine that offers a lot of adjustability. Especially important is a wide range of grind settings. Also look for the ability to alter the ratio of water to coffee (at least to some degree) by setting how much water and coffee is used in brewing. It's a helpless and frustrating feeling to watch your several-hundred-dollar machine pour shots too quickly but be unable to correct it because you've run out of grind settings.

Field Notes

With the limited real estate available for countertop appliances in most kitchens, there's certainly something to be said for the smaller footprint a super-automatic has compared to a grinder-and-machine combo necessary for less-automated systems.

Another drawback to super-autos is one raised with nearly any electronic hybrid system: one component could fail prematurely. And because they handle the entire operation internally, if the grinder quits working properly, for instance, the whole system is disabled; you can't just buy another grinder and use the brewer in a semi-automatic fashion. No one likes to think about servicing their new espresso machine, but it pays to explore service options before you buy.

Pods: Prepackaged Convenience

Another approach to simplifying espresso preparation is to use pods, which as we mentioned earlier are prepackaged espresso doses loosely akin to teabags. Not only do these pods eliminate the need for a grinder, they also bypass the dosing and tamping step usually involved in pulling a shot of espresso. Pods allow you to bypass the learning curve involved with zeroing in on the right grind setting and perfecting your tamp so it's even and appropriately firm. Instead, just pop in a pod, push a button, and out pours the coffee. A pod machine offers much of the convenience of super-autos but typically at much lower costs because the machine is otherwise a modified semi-automatic. Moreover, without the expense of a quality burr grinder, you reduce your overall espresso budget.

Convenience often brings compromise, though. The primary issues raised about pod-based espresso systems are an inherent lack of control and troubles regarding the coffee's freshness. The high-pressure extraction of espresso acts like a magnifying glass of sorts, in that even small changes in the process can make a huge difference. It's just not as forgiving as brewing in a French press or drip brewer, for example. This is the case with grinding and brewing a shot and also for the coffee you use to do so. You can see the impact of coffee freshness very quickly with espresso. Taste and crema production are quickly zapped by stale coffee, and ground coffee stales very rapidly. Despite packaging that tries to forestall the evitable, pods almost universally bring a freshness handicap with them.

Another prime concern with pods is the degree of control that's lost because someone else has determined the fineness of grind and amount of coffee to use; you can't do much to troubleshoot pour problems, such as shots pulling too quickly. Indeed, oftentimes your only recourse is to be certain your machine is properly preheated and working normally. Pods also limit your selection of coffees, as you have to use ones specifically designed for your machine.

Field Notes

Manufacturers and roasters have made some efforts to soften the impact of some of the drawbacks associated with pod-based espresso systems. Led by Illy, a consortium of companies that make espresso pod products formed and adopted a common pod design known as E.S.E. (Easy Serving Espresso). Some pod-based machines still use proprietary pod configurations, but many now utilize E.S.E. pods. This has opened a lot of options for pod users and has kept prices competitive. Still, expect to pay roughly twice as much for pods as for whole bean coffee. Currently, pods most commonly are packaged in large quantities—typically more than 100—and cost between 40¢ and 60¢ cents per pod. Capitalizing on the increased choice the E.S.E. system has brought, some companies offer "gourmet" pods costing more than $2 each.

In addition to the increased flexibility of using a standard pod design, many pod machines now can be used with ground coffee as well. This best-of-both-worlds approach often involves using an adapter or a different portafilter, the handled filter holder where grounds or pods are placed. In some cases, though, performance is stronger using the method for which the machine was originally designed; so while having the capability to make espresso both ways is handy, you should still determine which you'll typically use and purchase a machine accordingly. These machines need to be paired with a high-quality burr grinder just as the semi-automatics do.

Piston

Sometimes called lever machines, piston espresso machines tackle the issue of generating enough pressure to properly brew espresso differently from how pump machines do it. Rather than using a rotary or vibratory to push water through the grounds, these use the compression of a piston to generate the necessary pressure. Generally operated by a lever, piston machines come in two basic varieties: those that employ a spring to control the pressure exerted and those that use operator strength.

Regardless of what powers the piston, these machines are considered manual espresso machines because the barista controls the process instead of an electric mechanism controlling it. Both types have a chamber above the portafilter in which the preheated brewing water is drawn as the piston raises. As the piston is forced back to its resting position, the water is pushed through the ground coffee in the portafilter. In the case of spring-loaded versions, a spring is compressed as the controlling lever is pulled downward and then as the lever is released, the spring steadily forces the brewing water out of the chamber and into the waiting grounds. Models without the spring mechanism use the same principle but reverse the lever movements—as the handle is pulled upward, the piston, too, is raised (and water readied) and then the process is completed as the lever is pulled back down.

Does preparing a shot with a piston machine sound a little like work? It can be, and that both attracts and repeals users. Operating these manual espresso machines doesn't require burly arms, but it does require extra attention to detail. The increased control over the process can be both a blessing and a curse. The learning process is generally much longer for manual espresso machines because it can be difficult to master a consistent pull and troubleshoot poor shots; the added variable can make discerning the root of the issue complicated and frustrating. On the other hand, the minimal machine intervention allows refined espresso skills to shine, and seasoned users often prefer the espresso they are able to coax out with a manual machine to shots they make with more automated machines.

In addition to requiring a bit more attention to brewing, these machines also demand more caution. Their boilers often become extremely hot on the exterior, and you must be careful not to burn yourself. Another potential for trouble occurs when using spring-loaded machines. Because the spring decompresses with the same force each time, if there's not adequate resistance, the handle is forced upward more quickly and could injure the operator.

Field Notes

We wouldn't consider piston machines dangerous, but they may not be the best fit for every household. Follow the manufacturer's instructions to steer clear of potential hazards.

Simplicity and control draws some people to piston espresso machines, but it's the elegant styling of many of these models, which harkens back to another era, that lures many. Indeed, if you talk to an owner of one of these machines, you're likely to hear a shower of romantic endearments for the machine and its aesthetics. To that end, models often are available in an array of polished platings, like gold, copper, or chrome.

If piston machines seem like the ticket for you, expect to spend roughly $600 to $1,000 (or more) to get set up, as you'll need a high-quality burr grinder in addition to the machine itself. A dazzling array of finishes and trims are available for the models currently on the market, but the selection of base models is somewhat narrow. Most of these lever machines are not of the spring-loaded variety, which tend to be more expensive and more difficult to find.

It's important to carefully consider your espresso habits and needs before you select a piston espresso machine. The boiler of a piston machine is also the water reservoir and produces hot water for brewing as well as steam for frothing, so it's important that the water capacity is adequate for your needs. And because this chamber is pressurized, you need to turn off the machine and allow it to cool down before refilling it.

Field Notes

While brewing with a manual espresso machine often requires using both hands, left-handed users may find operating the lever of some models a bit awkward. If you're a leftie, try out a few machines before purchasing.

This, obviously, means these aren't the best choice for entertaining or making a large number of drinks at a time. However, models are available in several boiler capacities, with common sizes being adequate for producing several shots of espresso or a few drinks requiring the use of the steam wand. The upside of the boiler design of piston machines, though, is steam on demand; you don't need to wait for steam production like you typically do with other machine designs.

Steam-Powered "Espresso"

Steam-powered espresso devices come in a variety of designs, but all use the pressure of steam trapped in a confined space to push water through the coffee grounds. There's a limit to how much force can be produced by steam pressure alone, and it's significantly below the amount generated by piston- or pump-driven machines described earlier or by those used at coffeehouses. For true espresso, water must be forced through the compressed grounds with 8 to 9 bars (or atmospheres) of pressure, which is roughly 118 to 132 pounds of pressure per square inch. Steam power alone musters just $\frac{1}{5}$ to $\frac{1}{3}$ of that pressure.

What's more, and perhaps a greater issue, is that to build steam pressure, the water must be raised above ideal brewing temperatures. In some cases, though, this is mitigated to a degree by heat loss as the brewing water travels to the coffee.

Does this mean you shouldn't purchase steam-driven espresso equipment? Not necessarily, but you should take this all into consideration when you make your selection. Most steam-powered espresso machines cost less than $100, and several options exist even for those with $50 budgets (not including a grinder). Additionally, the budget-minded will appreciate that these machines don't require as high-quality of grinder as do more powerful espresso machines. That said, they still aren't a good match for blade grinders; the best results come when these machines are paired with grinders capable of producing a consistent, fine grind. If you already have a burr grinder you use when brewing coffee with other methods (like drip or French press), it's likely it will work when brewing with steam-driven espresso equipment.

Espresso equipment falls roughly into two categories: enclosed systems that are heated on the stove (or other heat source) and espresso machines that resemble semi-automatic pump models, complete with a portafilter and steam wand. We've never had much luck with the latter and don't recommend them, as they tend to produce more hassle and mess than flavorful coffee. The brewers from the first group, most notably represented by the moka pot and its variants, are capable of producing a thin, cremaless espressolike coffee and may be worth consideration. They work best

Field Notes _____

Steam-powered espresso machines may especially be worth consideration if you prefer au laits or lattes that have a less-powerful coffee character or if you typically like a lot of other flavoring with them. An example of this might be mint mochas, in which the espresso provides a base for the drink but doesn't completely drive the flavor.

when used for making milk-based drinks, although you'll need a way to heat and froth the milk; this, too, can be accomplished relatively inexpensively (see Chapter 12 on milk preparation for more details).

Grinders

We discussed grinders a bit in Chapter 7 as well as earlier in this chapter, so by now you should realize that a good grinder is important to producing great espresso.

Espresso grinders employ burrs that mince the beans to size as the coffee is pressed between them. Whirling-blade coffee grinders just aren't appropriate for espresso extraction, primarily because the grounds they produce have a relatively broad range of particle sizes. It's key that the packed bed of espresso resists the pressurized water evenly, and if the grind is inconsistent in size, it won't; the water will blast a path around the largest particles, leaving some of the coffee overextracted, some underextracted, and the resulting brew unpleasant.

> **Hot Water**
>
> Far too many home baristi choose to save money when selecting a grinder only to later realize they've sabotaged their espresso efforts.

Grinding is a straightforward task, especially compared with extracting espresso, so it's easy to mistakenly assume all burr grinders are more or less alike. Don't be fooled. Look for a grinder that produces evenly sized grinds that are easily repeatable and highly adjustable. The importance of being able to make minute grind adjustments can hardly be overstated, as you'll need to fine-tune the grind as your coffee ages, the humidity changes, and for each coffee or blend (more on adjusting grinds in Chapter 11). What's more, you don't want a grinder that causes the coffee to be heated much during the process (as you'll lose flavor) or to pick up a static charge (unless you like the mess created by leaping grounds or coffee that sticks to everything it shouldn't).

Most burr grinders under $100 fall short for espresso use, despite usually being adequate for other brewing methods. Grinders that make the cut do vary considerably, both in price and features, so you need to carefully consider your needs and budget.

One of the first differences you'll encounter is the type of burr employed, which falls into two primary categories: flat (sometimes called parallel) and conical. Both styles can produce excellent results, although our slight preference goes to conical burrs for their longer cutting surfaces, which allow lower rotation speeds. However, we don't recommend selecting a grinder on burrs alone, and many quality grinders on the market use flat burrs.

The speed at which the motor-driven burr turns (note that one remains stationary) has a significant impact on the amount of heat and static generated during grinding. The most effective way to reduce these two unwanted effects is to grind at slow speeds. This can be done either by using internal gears to reduce the speed of fast-turning motors or by employing a direct-drive system a low-RPM (rotations per minute) motor. Both are significantly better than high-speed models, but the latter are the most effective and desirable. Unfortunately, quality costs once again, and direct-drive models, which tend to be essentially light-duty commercial grinders, cost more than $200.

Some higher-end models also incorporate a *doser*. Whether to purchase a grinder with a doser is more a matter of personal preference than performance and is certainly not necessary. If you do use a grinder with a doser, beware of a couple traps their handiness presents:

- Don't fill the doser with ground coffee or scrape excess coffee back into it.

- Always grind coffee for each shot immediately before brewing. Preground coffee stales quickly and doesn't resist water to the same degree freshly ground coffee does and will, therefore, throw off the consistency of your shots.

> **Buzz Words**
> A **doser** is a chamber with a horizontally positioned paddle wheel that's operated by the flick of a lever. Each pull of the lever causes the fins of the internal wheel to push out approximately the desired dose of grounds.

Espresso Accessories

In addition to espresso machines and grinders, you might consider adding a few accessories as you assemble your espresso-making system. Most of these things aren't necessary to produce good espresso, but they either make it easier or enhance the experience:

- Tampers

- Timers

- Demitasses

- Knockboxes

- Milk-making helpers

> **Field Notes**
> It's not a bad idea to check before you purchase a machine to see if either the tamper is adequate or if it can be replaced.

Although nearly all espresso machines are shipped with a tamper, they are invariably cheap plastic models that can break or are hard to work with. In some cases, like when the tamper's handle doubles as a coffee scoop, it's hard to imagine what the designer was thinking, as trying to exert proper force using a poorly designed tamper is more likely to end in a hand cramp than a properly packed puck of coffee.

Fortunately, aftermarket tampers are available in an array of styles and weights. You can spend much more, of course, but $30 to $40 typically buys a very nice tamper that makes pulling a great shot much easier. Some models allow for different bases to be screwed on to the handle in case you own more than one machine or you change machines (not all have the same size portafilter, so you need to be certain the one you have is properly sized). You can also find tampers (and bases) that are slightly rounded on the bottom and produce a concave surface on the compressed grounds, which some believe better distributes grounds and produces a slightly better pour than do totally flat-bottomed tampers.

Another accessory that can be very handy is a digital counter or stopwatch. Knowing how fast your shots are pouring helps you make adjustments as you perfect your shots. A properly timed shot can still taste poor, but it's perhaps one of the easiest and quickest gauges of how you're doing.

The cup you pull your espresso shot into is indeed important. Heavy (prewarmed) demitasses help keep the espresso hot and retain crema. Tall, narrow designs especially can help form and hold on to crema, and they're a good option when you're struggling to achieve a nice layer of crema.

After you've pulled a (properly prepared) shot of espresso, you'll be left with a steaming puck of compressed grounds in the portafilter. The easiest way to dispose of these spent cakes is by rapping the portafilter against a solid surface, which allows the grounds puck to drop out cleanly. Knockboxes are small portable pans with a bar across the middle that make the process easy and simplify cleanup. They won't take a big bite out of your espresso budget (typically $30 will buy one), but you can improvise by using the corner of a nonmetallic trash can.

Field Notes

Most espresso machine housings are metal, so it's nice to have a timer with a magnetic back so you can stick it on the machine in a spot that's easy to read while you're working—just be sure it's not hot!

Milk frothers, pitchers, and thermometers are all important items to have on hand if you plan to make milk-and-espresso drinks such as cappuccinos and lattes. (Check out Chapter 12 on milk preparation for details on properly equipping yourself to make these drinks.)

Selecting Your Espresso System

The sheer number of options on the market can make choosing an espresso machine and grinder (unless you purchase a super-automatic or pod-compatible machine) a confusing and frustrating experience. A good place to start the selection process is by reflecting on your drink preferences and budget. If you consider yourself a casual consumer of lattes or other milky espresso-based beverages—especially flavored ones—a moka pot or other machine that uses steam pressure for brewing may be a good fit for you. (In which case, you'll want to review our notes on moka pots in Chapter 6 on coffee brewing equipment.) This is also the best route for someone looking for a minimal investment. It won't match the espresso prepared with brewers that can muster higher pressures, but the espresso-esque brew from moka pots can certainly be good in its own right.

In our opinion, there's currently a lack of quality espresso brewers in the below-$300 range, and by the time you add the cost of a good grinder, it's quite challenging to pull together a quality system for less than approximately $500. The catch of the cheaper pump-driven espresso machines is that they require every bit as good of a grinder as expensive ones, so the overall system savings are often not worth the reduced quality that the cheaper models bring. There's not a direct, linear correlation between price and cup quality, but it can be generally said that you get what you pay for.

That said, several excellent options are available for those with $600 to $800 budgets (including grinder). The same range will get you set up with basic piston machine and grinder—just be prepared for a much longer learning curve. Expect to spend a little more for a quality super-automatic (or automatic) than for a semi-automatic and grinder.

Often another deciding factor is the degree of effort you're interested in investing, both during the initial learning phase and to brew a shot or make a drink. We believe the best espresso from any machine is had by those that understand the brewing process, but there's no doubt that brewing is less complex when using super-automatics or pods. It's hard to beat the push-button convenience of super-autos, and brewing with pods is barely more involved. A good super-auto offers a range of grind settings and dosing options paired with push-button ease but is likely to be on the more costly side. Systems based on pods tend to be much cheaper than super-autos and cost less than semi-automatics in that you don't have to buy a grinder. Semi-automatics that can be used with or without pods offer tempting flexibility, although they provide no savings because you'll still need a good grinder to use them without pods.

If cup quality reigns supreme for you, we suggest a good semi-automatic and high-quality grinder intended primarily for espresso or a high-end super-automatic. In this case, plan at least $800 to $1,000 into your budget, and don't be surprised if you fall in love with a system costing more, especially in the case of super-autos. A piston machine is also an option for those seeking espresso nirvana and is especially suited for diligent process-oriented enthusiasts willing to invest time to learn appropriate techniques.

Field Notes

We highly recommend sampling espresso brewed with pods before purchasing such a system, as pods rarely can compete with espresso brewed with freshly roasted and ground coffee.

Keeping these general guidelines in mind should help steer you to a system that fits your needs. And if the current cost of brewing good espresso at home is outside your budget, we think it's better to support your favorite local coffeehouse for the time being than to purchase cheaply made espresso equipment. While it's unfortunate that the initial investment is so high, it's even more maddening to try to coax passable results out of inadequate equipment.

The Least You Need to Know

- ♦ Espresso machines that use pumps or pistons to pressurize the brewing water are key to true espresso.

- ♦ Steam-driven machines make an espressolike beverage that is thinner, less dynamic, and inferior to espresso, but can be viable options if you want to produce milky espresso drinks akin to lattes.

- ♦ Pods are pretamped, preground doses of coffee that simplify espresso preparation but generally compromise coffee freshness and user control.

- ♦ A high-quality burr grinder is absolutely necessary for making good espresso.

Chapter 11

Extraction Basics

In This Chapter

- ◆ Uncover the keys to pulling great espresso
- ◆ Control your brewing temperature
- ◆ Tips on grinding and dosing for a great shot
- ◆ Ways to properly tamp or pack espresso

Pulling excellent espresso requires a keen understanding of the variables at play and the techniques to align them in your favor. In this chapter, we lay the groundwork so you can start pulling thick, gooey shots of delicious espresso soon after you warm up your machine. (Although all espresso machines operate with the same general principles, machines do vary, so be certain to read or watch any instructional materials that come with your equipment.)

For the purposes of best understanding the steps and influences involved in espresso extraction, we based this chapter on a semi-automatic pump-driven machine paired with a quality burr grinder that produces even and easily adjustable grinds. The same techniques are applicable when using a piston machine, automatics, and super-automatics—in the case of the latter two machine types, though, some of the actual labor obviously is handled by the machine. And because the best technique only serves to bring the most from the espresso ingredients (coffee and water), we also take a look at how flavor is influenced by the water and coffee you use.

Working With H₂O

Like coffee brewed using other methods, espresso is almost entirely water, so it's crucial that the water you employ is up to the job. Use only fresh, filtered water that tastes good to you. No, your espresso won't taste like shoe leather if you brew with water from the tap. But water from city treatment plants contains chemicals, namely chlorine, that can take the tasty edge off your shots. What's more, the amount of treatment city water demands varies and so, too, does the chemical makeup of the resulting water, if even slightly. By filtering your water (or purchasing prefiltered water), you reduce one variable that can play on the outcome of your shots.

Field Notes _____

Some folks initially balk at the notion of paying for a filter or buying water especially for brewing, but the quality in the cup benefits for it. And if you've invested hundreds of dollars in good espresso equipment, we think you owe it to yourself to spend the little it takes to use good water.

Rural water supplies, although free of chlorine, can present their own issues, including unwanted chemicals or high mineral concentrations. When you've mastered your espresso technique and can consistently pull sweet, rich shots topped in delicate red-brown crema, give your tap water supply a try and see which shots you prefer.

Using distilled water is sometimes suggested because it not only navigates the issue of water purity, but also prevents scale buildup caused by minerals collecting in brewing equipment. We don't recommend using distilled water, however, as the flavor constituents in coffee are best extracted by water that has some mineral content. In addition, some machines rely on water's ability to carry an electrical charge, which distilled water cannot do. Water that's low in calcium and magnesium leaves the least amount of residue, and these minerals can easily be reduced by simple softening filters, which includes some pitcher-style filtration systems and inline filters that are available for some espresso machines (typically higher-end models).

Another water caveat is to be certain to flush out stale water that's been sitting in your machine before each brewing session. Not only does this mean discarding any water left in the machine's reservoir (assuming you can empty it easily) but also purging the water resting in internal tubing. Simply operating the pump a bit will usually do an adequate job. If you feel the need to empty the boiler—when, for example, the machine has been unused for several days—the relatively small boiler size of most home machines makes this a quick job. Simply run a few ounces through the *grouphead*, the area where the portafilter locks into place, and then use a steaming pitcher or similar receptacle and fill it using the hot-water delivery function built in to most machines. As an added bonus, this procedure helps get the metal in the portafilter and *group* up to proper temperature (more on this in a bit).

> **Buzz Words** _____
>
> The **group** or **grouphead** is the part of the espresso machine that dispenses the brewing water and into which the portafilter locks. They are usually made of thick metal to retain heat. In the center of the group, directly above where the portafilter rests, is a screen called a *dispersion screen*. Sometimes called a *shower screen*, it ensures even distribution of the water as it exits the group into the waiting portafilter.

Coffee and Espresso Blends

The market is flush with blends specifically designed for espresso extraction, but it's important to remember that any coffee can be used for brewing espresso. The intense nature of espresso does, however, make some coffees more suitable than others (to the likes of most palates, at least).

Experiment, Experiment

When you're first mastering espresso technique or breaking in a new machine, we highly recommend using a coffee you've had properly prepared as espresso in the past as a reference; if it's a coffee you can taste as espresso at a local café, all the better. Once you've got the technique down, we strongly suggest you pull a shot or two of espresso with every coffee that comes into your house, whether it's labeled for espresso use or not. Ideally, cup the coffee (or brew it using another method) and pull shots with it.

Granted, you may be in for a shock from time to time, like the first time you sip a shot of a straight winy Kenyan, but no doubt you'll find some that really strike a chord with your palate—that holiday blend you'd been enjoying in the French press may just become your new favorite espresso! Perhaps most important, though, you'll start to understand how a coffee's flavors translate into espresso and what your preferences are.

Consider the End Drink

As you experiment and explore coffees brewed as espresso, be it single-origins or blends, you'll probably find that your preferences vary based on the intended end-use, and understandably so. You can't really expect the espresso you love drenched in a milky latte to be your favorite when drunk straight. It takes a whole lot of muscle to carry through the milk, so much that it's likely to overpower the palate when sampled on its own.

Likewise, some of the most delicious straight espressos just don't come through with enough power in beverages that include milk, especially if the milk is high in fat content, like in the case of a brevé. To this end, we've seen roasters with as many as a half dozen different espresso blends, each with its own personality and intended purpose.

As you evaluate coffees brewed as espresso, consider all the possible uses of it and choose your coffees based on how it will be consumed.

Blend Your Own

At some point, you're likely to want to explore creating your own blends, and we wholeheartedly encourage you to do so. While some would have you believe that blending for espresso is an esoteric craft, the principles we outline in the cupping and blending chapter of this book (see Chapter 5) will serve you well as you create your own espresso blends—as long as you're mindful of how coffee tastes are translated by the espresso brewing process.

Your greatest aid in blending for espresso will be recognizing the tastes each single-origin coffee brings to the blend. And there's no better way to learn that than to pull shots with the single-origin coffees individually, just as you would cup each component coffee before blending to best understand what it has to offer to a blend.

Controlling Temperature

The temperature of the brewing water used to extract espresso is hugely important to the resulting taste—just as it is for other brewing methods—but is generally out of the control of the home barista. In many cases, the extra money spent on higher-end espresso machines goes toward providing you with heavier components that can better maintain and control brewing temperature. Unfortunately, because the boiler temperatures of home espresso machines are largely outside your control, there's little practical use for long discussions about precisely the best brewing temperature. That said, you certainly have your role in helping the machine maintain a proper temperature and can exert some degree of control.

One the most important things you can do is to allow your machine to heat up fully before brewing. Your machine's instruction manual will provide details, but in addition to simply allowing your espresso machine some idle time before brewing, you can run a bit of water through the portafilter to help heat the grouphead and portafilter metals. Another aid to maintaining proper temperature is to leave the portafilter in the grouphead whenever possible, removing it only for the time necessary to load the grounds into it and set up the shot.

Regardless of how diligent you are about allowing your machine to stay hot, you're still not in control of the actual water temperature used in brewing. Thousands of dollars are sunk into commercial machines to ensure proper brewing temperature, and most of us simply can't afford that kind of technology for the home. We're not helpless though, and with a little extra time and effort, repeatable, proper brewing temperatures can be achieved.

Although it may slow you down just a bit, we recommend a technique often referred to as *temperature surfing*. The goal is to produce a predictable chain of events that leads to a temperature that produces great shots. The procedure is easy and simply involves running water through an empty portafilter until the machine's boiler temperature drops below its lower threshold, causing it to cycle and begin heating the water. After the heating cycle has finished, pull a shot. Now repeat the cycle, causing the boiler to kick on again, but this time wait a bit after the machine reaches temperature before pulling a shot—say 20 seconds.

Field Notes

If you find you're running water through your machine either to help heat the portafilter or during temperature surfing, use the hot water to pre-heat the cup you'll be using for the shot as well.

Continue to do this in 10- to 20-second increments until the shot tastes best to you. You've now discovered the machine's temperature sweet spot, and you can hit it again every time you pull a shot. For example, if you've determined shots taste best from your machine when pulled 40 seconds after the boiler shuts off, all you have to do is trip the cycle and wait 40 seconds after it finishes before pulling a shot. It wouldn't be practical on a commercial level in a café, but it usually works just fine at home.

Pulling Shots

Perhaps the most important thing to remember when setting up a shot is that you want to end up with a bed of grounds that will uniformly resist the pressure from the brewing water. If it doesn't, your shot will be inferior; it's that simple. Water, like electricity, follows the path of least resistance, so only give it one option: evenly saturating the entire bed of packed coffee.

Five primary things upset this even resistance and cause poor extractions:

◆ Grinds that aren't of a consistent particle size

◆ Unevenly distributed grounds before tamping

◆ Unlevel tamps

◆ A too-light tamp that allows the pressurized water to blast through the grounds

◆ A broken seal between the packed grounds and the basket, which results from tapping the side of the portafilter with too much force

All these instances result in a puck of coffee that gives water an option other than to slowly and evenly flow through the entire bed of coffee. And water, with its carpe diem–like attitude, will take advantage of every such opportunity and ruin your plans for a perfect espresso. The resulting shot will have unwanted bitterness and will likely be thin as well.

Field Notes

Due to the geometry of single-dose filter baskets, most people find making great espresso with them more challenging than when using double baskets. Therefore, we recommend you practice and hone your technique pulling double shots. When brewing a double, you can place a demitasse or shot glass under each of the portafilter's spouts to easily make two single shots.

The good news is that avoiding these issues is a given with good technique, and the actual act of preparing and pulling a shot is a fairly simple ritual that, once learned, becomes second nature. It's merely a matter of managing variables by employing good, consistent technique and making adjustments along the way as needed.

The complexity of pulling shots lies in the fact that the web of variables that combine to hold up a good shot also makes it sticky to troubleshoot a poor shot. However, after you've learned what influences a pour, it becomes easier to not only discern what's not working properly, but also to keep the operation running smoothly in the first place.

Let's take a look first at how the overall process should go, and then we'll delve more into some underlying complexities.

Here's a quick overview of the process of pulling a shot of espresso:

1. Remove the portafilter from the grouphead of the preheated machine, and wipe it dry with a clean towel. (Use care, as it'll be hot!)

2. Grind the coffee and fill the portafilter until heaping.

3. Using your finger or the back of a butter knife, evenly distribute the grounds so they're flush with the top of the portafilter, scraping off and discarding any excess grounds.

4. Rest the portafilter on its spouts on a countertop while holding the handle. Keep the top of the portafilter parallel to the counter. Holding the tamper like you would a doorknob, lightly compress the coffee by pushing straight down as you keep your wrist straight and the tamper level.

5. Tap the side of the portafilter lightly with the handle of tamper.

6. Tamp the coffee as you did in step 4 but use approximately 30 pounds of pressure (see the "Tamping Your Way to the Top" section later in this chapter). As you finish your tamp and while you're still applying a bit of pressure, twist the tamper to polish the surface of the grounds.

7. Brush away any loose grounds along the outside edges and protruding tabs of the portafilter.

8. Firmly lock the portafilter into the grouphead.

9. With a preheated cup or cups in place below the spouts, activate the machine's pump and start your timer.

10. Carefully watch the espresso pour and stop the pump and timer when the espresso begins to suck in as it drops to the cup and appears thinner and lighter in color. Ideally your timer should show 25 seconds, give or take 5 seconds, and you should have about 1¼ ounces espresso.

Hot Water _____

Good, reliable espresso pours are made possible by machines that maintain consistent temperatures. To that end, quality portafilters and groups are made of heavy, plated brass or other metals and remain very hot at all times. Be very careful as you work with espresso machines, and avoid touching these metal parts. If it's not plastic, it's probably hot.

Now that you have an idea of how espresso brewing works, let's examine the process more closely. It can be roughly broken into three parts: dosing, tamping, and extracting.

Dosing

You'll sometimes hear that the proper dose for a single espresso shot is 7 grams coffee (or 14 grams for a double), but you'll rarely see it dosed by weight because practical espresso dosing is a matter of volume. When you've properly dosed and tamped the correct amount of ground coffee, there will be roughly a scant ⅛ inch clearance from the top of basket to the coffee. If the basket you're using has a dosing line on the inside, you should be able to see it. This space is necessary to allow the coffee enough room to expand when it's saturated with water.

To dose a shot of espresso, grind enough coffee to make a small mound above the rim of the portafilter but dry out the filter basket (which should be resting in the portafilter) before you fill it. Wiping out the basket first not only removes rogue grounds, it also ensures a good seal between the basket walls and the coffee.

Next, use the back of a butter knife or your finger to evenly disperse the grounds across the basket. We prefer to use an index finger with slight downward pressure, but you can substitute a knife if you prefer not to touch the coffee. Push the grounds from one edge of the basket until they begin to overflow on the opposite side and then reverse the procedure, pushing the grounds to the opposite edge. Do the same again, pushing the grounds from one edge and back, but make these strokes across the basket approximately perpendicular to the first path. On the last stroke, push the remaining heap over the edge of the portafilter and into a waste receptacle. Don't reuse these grounds.

With time, you'll learn to grind only enough for the shot and the amount wasted will be minimal. Discarding a few grounds is better than ruining an entire shot with left-over grounds.

Field Notes

An easy way to check for proper dosing is to prepare a shot as normal and lock the portafilter into the grouphead. Wait a moment or two and then remove the portafilter and examine the top of the puck. If you see a dimple in the center of it (caused by pressing against the screw that holds the dispersion screen in the group), something is amiss with your dosing and/or tamping procedure. Also, check the dispersion screen for signs of contact with the grounds.

Overdosing

Overdosing is a technique that seems to be popular right now and has been for several years, especially at the café level. It's not uncommon to see coffeehouses pulling double shots of espresso using baskets made for triples, which affords the use of 50 percent more grounds.

One common overdosing technique, other than using a larger basket, is to firmly rap the portafilter on a countertop before distributing the grounds, as this settles a bit more coffee into the basket. Another technique is to actually overfill the filter basket by allowing a slight mound of grounds above the top rather than scraping the grounds off flush with the rim.

Field Notes

Triple baskets aren't typically available for home machines, although those that use the standard commercial portafilters may accept triple baskets.

Overdosing somewhat covers for less-than-perfect technique and helps build extra crema in the cup. It can cause troubles, though, too, especially if it means the expanding coffee grounds don't have room to swell and end up pressed against the dispersion screen. Therefore, we think it's best to save dosing experiments until you're consistently pulling beautiful shots with standard dosing techniques.

Tamping Your Way to the Top

Tamping or packing the ground coffee into a firm puck is important because it prepares the grounds to evenly resist the pressurized brewing water, which ensures good extraction. Fortunately, it's pretty straightforward.

Ideally, the tamp should be level and applied with about 30 pounds of pressure. What, your arm didn't come standard with muscle memory that can accurately and reliably produce 30 pounds of pressure? No worries, you can build up your muscle memory by practicing your tamp on a bathroom scale. Practice until you know the feel of the appropriate pressure and can do it over and over.

Field Notes

The more consistent your tamp, the better, as you want this variable in the process to be as close as a constant as possible. Don't change your tamp to remedy extraction troubles; change your grind instead.

To execute a proper tamp, rest the portafilter on a counter so the top of the basket is level. Then grab your tamper as you would a doorknob with the butt of the tamper just into the palm of your hand. It should feel fairly natural and your hand shouldn't be cramped. (You may want an aftermarket tamper if the one supplied with your machine is flimsy, small, or otherwise ill-conceived.)

Keeping your wrist straight and your elbow in the air, place the tamper levelly on top of the ground coffee and push down lightly. Don't get hung up on the exact pressure applied at this point, but do apply about the same light pressure each time. The purpose of this first packing is much the same as drilling a pilot hole before turning in a screw: to set the stage and to ensure a perfect outcome.

Next, give the portafilter a light rap on the side with the *handle* of the tamper; using the business end will damage it. This will knock loose any grounds hanging on the sides of the basket. There's no need to use much force here, and doing so can cause the seal between the coffee and the basket to be disturbed, opening an escape route for the water.

Now, give a final tamp using the full 30 pounds of pressure and as you release pressure and are exerting just a few pounds of force, twist the tamper to polish the surface of the coffee. This will further keep the puck from pitting under the pressure of the water. Now all that's left is to wipe the top of the portafilter—namely the protruding tabs—free of any remaining grounds.

Field Notes

If you're having trouble achieving a nice, level tamp, first be certain you're resting the portafilter on the counter so the rim is parallel to the countertop. Next, as you tamp but before you apply much pressure, allow your finger to explore the lip of the filter basket. You'll easily be able to detect if more of the tamper is sticking out of the basket on one side or another. Make the necessary adjustment, check it again, and then tamp like usual.

Extracting All the Good

With your shot properly dosed and tamped, all that's left is to lock it into the machine's grouphead and activate the pump. If all goes well, your shot will begin oozing out the spouts a few seconds after you turn on the pump and finish right around 25 seconds with roughly 1 ¼ ounces of espresso crowned in a rich, red-brown crema. Different coffees may taste best to you with slightly different pour times, but you should shoot for your pours running no faster than 20 seconds and no slower than 30 seconds. Altering your shot times is simple, given you have a quality burr grinder and you're tamping consistently. To increase the pour time, just increase the fineness of the grind. If your shots are running more slowly than you'd like, simply make the grind a little coarser.

> ### Field Notes
>
> If you're having trouble deciding when to end your shots by sight, get them as close as you can and then send your taste buds to work. Using separate cups, collect and compare the espresso produced during the first, second, and final 10 seconds of a 30-second pour (collect more often or pull a longer shot if it helps). This lets you better associate the appearance of the pour to the taste of the espresso, and you'll quickly learn what you want to avoid.

While your target is a 25-second shot, we recommend using the clock only as a guide and referencing it *after* the pull is complete. As the espresso is dribbling into the demitasse below, keep your eyes on it. Take note of its apparent thickness, its color, and how it hangs or falls into the cup. It's time to call the shot and turn off the pump when it begins to lighten in color and viscosity. The espresso will also tend to suck in as it thins out, with the two streams approaching each other a bit. The shot is spent at this point and is beginning to extract undesirable flavors. Your espresso will vary based on the coffee you're using, but it should generally be very thick and mouth-coating and be topped with a rich red-brown crema. If possible, start with a coffee that you've had prepared as espresso at a coffeehouse so you have a good benchmark to replicate.

To help you determine the volume of espresso, especially until you have the hang of things, you can pull espresso into shot glasses or similar receptacles. Restaurant-supply stores and specialty coffee shops often sell one with marked gradations to simplify matters. Another method is to pour the appropriate amount of water in the cup you'll use ahead of time so you know what you're aiming for, and because it's preferable to pour the shot into the cup in which it will be served, this tactic is particularly handy. But unless you plan to compete in barista championships, worry more about how your espresso tastes than if you have $\frac{1}{8}$ ounce too much or too little.

A standard shot is $1\frac{1}{4}$ ounces, but you might want a bit more or less espresso in your pour. You could try a ristretto, a restricted or short pull with a volume of roughly $\frac{3}{4}$ to 1 ounce. Naturally, it's a matter of taste, but many who enjoy espresso straight find the additional concentration of a ristretto very appealing. Ristrettos also carry

Field Notes _____

If you have a machine that automatically pushes a prede-termined amount of water through the grounds and is pour-ing shots too quickly despite all the adjustments you make, you can still get decent espresso. Watch the shot pour, and when you would like to end it, just remove the cup and replace it with another. Just discard the undesirable end of the shot.

through milk very well. The opposite of a ristretto, a long pull or lungo, is a shot that's roughly 1½ ounces or more.

Regardless of the total volume extracted, the time to do so should remain constant. When you can pull a good standard-volume shot, making a ristretto or lungo is just a matter of tweaking the grind. For a lungo you'll want more water to pass through the coffee in the same time as a normal shot, so make the grind a little coarser. For a ristretto, grind the coffee a little more finely. Remember to keep your tamp consistent for all pulls.

Espresso Cleanup

Making espresso can be a bit messy, but fortunately cleanup is usually just a matter of a few extra minutes before you put the machine away at the end of a session.

The spilt grounds and dribbles of espresso on the counter call for attention, but the machine itself also needs to be cleaned. Just as you wouldn't attempt to make a fine meal using a pan with caked-on and spoiling food, you shouldn't expect to prepare a good shot of espresso with a dirty machine. Coffee oils and residue build up on the machine, in (and under) the filter basket, and on the portafilter. If these deposits aren't removed, they bake on and can become rancid, which spoils crema and imparts a bad taste.

Hot Water _____

When bad, bitter-tasting shots appear seemingly out of no-where, dirty coffee residues are a prime suspect. Give your machine a thorough cleaning.

After each brewing session, remove the filter basket from the portafilter and clean them both. A small, flexible brush can help you clean the spouts, which are often overlooked during cleaning routines. You can purchase cleanser specifically for cleaning up coffee and espresso residues, and it helps to periodically soak your portafilter and baskets in the cleaning solution. (Note, though, that most will break down plastic, so keep the portafilter handle out of the solution.)

In addition to scrubbing clean the portafilter and filter baskets, you'll want to do some simple cleanup of the machine. Following the manufacturer's instructions, be especially sure to clean the grouphead and dispersion screen after each use.

Hot Water _____

You might hear about a cleaning procedure called *backflushing*, which uses built-up pressure to free residues within the espresso machine. It's appropriate for commercial machines but usually isn't for home models. Follow the manufacturer's guidelines, as backflushing a machine that's not intended for such treatment can cause damage and possibly void warranties.

The Least You Need to Know

◆ Espresso shots, regardless of size (single or double, ristretto or lungo) should pour in roughly 25 seconds.

◆ Increasing the fineness of grind increases the time it takes to extract the same amount of espresso. It allows less fluid to be extracted in the same amount of time.

◆ A coarser grind allows shots to pour faster.

◆ Don't change your tamp to alter your shot times. Keep it consistently at 30 pounds of pressure.

Milk Preparation

In This Chapter

- Learn how to steam and froth milk and understand how these techniques affect espresso flavor
- Examine milk steaming and frothing products
- Got milk? (or not)
- Latte art: Picasso in your cup

When used to prepare an espresso- or coffee-based drink, milk becomes the crème de la crème. A pillow of foam on top of a cappuccino or a latte of steamed milk with espresso is nothing short of pleasing. Milk adds sweet, nutty characteristics to the espresso or coffee and can, in fact, take espresso from slightly bitter to slightly sweet.

Steaming and frothing are the two major milk-preparation techniques baristi use to make the diverse array of espresso drinks on the menu. In this chapter, we give you tips on how to steam and froth with skill and grace. By the end of this chapter, you'll know both the science and the art behind milk preparation in the coffee world—after all, it's not just an act of calculation; it's also about being an artist.

Steaming and Frothing Defined

The terms *steaming* and *frothing* are often used interchangeably when describing the technique used to properly make coffee shop drinks such as lattes, cappuccinos, and café au laits. The processes of preparing steamed and frothed milk are basically the same, with some subtle variations. Remember, though, that "steamed" and "frothed" milk are distinct products.

Frothing means you're adding air—more than if the milk was simply heated or steamed—to create a dense, velvety milk. It's this texture that gives a well-made cappuccino its signature silkiness and mouthfeel. Steamed milk has some air incorporated into it so it thickens a tad, but it's more fluid than frothed milk.

For both steaming and frothing milk, you're going to need the following items:

◆ A 12- to 20-ounce capacity stainless-steel pitcher specifically designed for heating and conditioning milk. We recommend a stainless-steel pitcher, which costs around $10 or $15. (A nonplastic container will do in the meantime if that's all you have access to.)

◆ An instant-read thermometer with a clip you can attach to the side of the pitcher. Knowing the temperature while the milk is heating is very, very important. An instant-read thermometer costs around $10 and has a dial on top and a probe that goes down into the milk.

◆ A steam wand. Multiple-holed tips are most efficient, but whatever your steam wand came with will work; replacement and substitute tips may be purchased relatively inexpensively.

Most espresso machines today have a steam wand—a small, thin metal pipe of about ¼ inch in diameter—on the side or front of the machine. The steamer tip should contain three or four small holes, which helps push steam from the espresso machine into the milk.

Field Notes

Rather than thinking of prepared milks for your drinks as falling into two dichotomous categories, consider where their degree of texturing falls on a continuum, from not at all (no added air) to extremely thick and stiff.

Later in this chapter we talk about stand-alone options such as a milk whip and a frother that looks just like a French press. But we recommend using the steam wand on your espresso machine, especially because the machine is already warm when you make the accompanying shot or shots of espresso.

Preparing Latte Milk and Cappuccino Milk

Pumping volume into milk is an easy process once you get the hang of it. Really, this is all you have to do:

1. Pour cold milk into the pitcher.

2. Insert the tip of the steam wand just below the milk's surface.

3. As the milk expands, bury the steamhead by lowering the pitcher to keep the wand just underneath the surface.

4. When the milk reaches 80° to 90°F, sink the wand farther into the milk.

5. Offset the submerged steam tip to one side of the pitcher to encourage whirlpooling.

> **Field Notes**
>
> Whether you're making latte (just a little incorporated air) or cappuccino milk (substantial amounts of incorporated air), be sure to purge the steam wand before and after so any remaining steam can be released. (Purging is simply allowing a puff of steam by turning the knob or opening the steam valve briefly.)

6. At between 140° and 160°F, remove the wand from the milk. Note that the temperature will creep a bit at the end; the amount varies among espresso machines.

Sounds pretty easy, doesn't it? Let's get into a little more detail.

Stretching the Milk

Hot milk is an important part of a latte, steamer, or café au lait. The first stage of preparing your milk is called *stretching* because it's during this step that you add the most air, which results in significant increases in the milk's volume. When a lot of air is added to the milk, as for cappuccinos, the surface of the drink changes and becomes satiny and chiffonlike and resembles the consistency of melted ice cream. Keep these images in mind as you teach yourself how to prepare milk, as they are what you ultimately want to achieve in appearance.

> **Buzz Words**
>
> **Stretching** milk means you're incorporating air into the milk, increasing its volume.

To stretch milk, you need a pitcher and an instant-read thermometer. To start the process, pour cold milk into the pitcher until it is about ⅓ full. The pitcher should ideally be straight-walled, with tapered sides and a pouring spout. Keep in mind that once the milk is aerated, it will expand, and if you pour in too much milk, you won't have enough room to properly expand it.

Field Notes

This may sound strange, but to help you get the hang of frothing, try purposefully scalding milk (taking it to a temperature of 175°F). This will show you what to avoid and why overheating ruins milk and makes poor milk for espresso drinks. Compare this with milk heated at varying temperatures up to 160°F, and you'll be able to taste the difference instantly and be better equipped to evaluate your milk.

Before you use the steam wand on your espresso machine, run the steam for a second, putting an empty cup or steaming pitcher under the steam wand to collect any condensed water that might remain.

Now you're ready to prepare your latte milk. Gently place the tip of the steam wand just under the milk's surface. At first, finding the proper positioning of the milk may be tricky because you can't touch it with your fingers or hand, but instead have to observe how the tip of the steam wand responds.

Hot Water

Wipe off the steam wand after each use. If you don't, over time it will, in all seriousness, resemble a corn dog.

If you hear a loud whooshing noise and milk is splattering, your tip is too close to the surface and simply needs to be dropped a bit (raise the pitcher). On the other hand, if you don't hear a gentle sucking sound, the tip may need to be nearer to the surface (lower the pitcher). Don't worry, you'll get it after a few times.

Then open the steam valve so a full flow of steam comes through. As the milk expands, drop the pitcher slightly so the tip of the steam wand always remains just under the milk's surface. Don't stretch the milk past 80° or 90°F, as you'll only produce an undesirable mess of large bubbles. Instead, stop the aggressive aeration process by plunging the steam wand well into the milk, beginning the second phase of milk development: conditioning.

Conditioning the Milk

After you've stretched the milk by adding air, it's time to condition it a bit to whip the bubbles into a tight structure and achieve a uniform texture.

To froth the milk, keep the steam wand submerged in ¾ of the pitcher's volume. Whirl the milk aggressively for at least 30 seconds if possible. Avoid the temptation to move the pitcher up and down or even back and forth. Any exaggerated movements you bring into the process will only result in too-aerated foam. Lots of big and unevenly sized bubbles make this an easy mistake to spot.

Remove the wand from the pitcher when the thermometer reaches a few temperatures above 140°F. *Absolutely do not allow the milk to reach a temperature of above 160°F, or the taste and texture will suffer.*

You should now be looking at *microfoam,* foam composed of small, dense bubbles. Now, shut off the steam flow and remove the wand from the pitcher.

Hot Water _____

Don't feel tempted to brew espresso and froth milk simultaneously, because it will only get you stale-tasting coffee and brown foam. Also, consumer machines are generally not designed for this and can't maintain ideal temperatures for brewing and steaming at the same time.

Buzz Words _____

Microfoam is the name for optimum bubbles, ones that are not big but are instead tiny and packed densely together.

Cleanup is very important to avoid bacteria in the pitcher or on the steam wand. Take a wet rag and move it along the steam wand, removing any remaining milk, and release a burst of steam.

Do not allow the heated milk to sit for too long. While it's not always practical to have a just-brewed shot of espresso waiting, you should begin work on that immediately after the milk is done. If the milk ends up sitting in the pitcher for too long, swirl it manually a few times. Also, sometimes there are extra, unneeded bubbles in the milk after it's been heated. If this happens, simply tap the pitcher on the counter gently and they'll disseminate.

Your goal as a barista is not only to obtain a rich, thick foam, but to also be sure it combines well with the milk. Otherwise, you'll end up with a thin layer of milk separated from a dense, foamy top. When you're done preparing the milk, be sure to combine it with the espresso right away. You won't see baristi at cafés using a spoon or spatula to pour the milk over the espresso, but as a new barista, consider using those utensils to help you. With a spoon or spatula, hold the foam back while you pour the milk and push a little foam into the cup. With practice and well-prepared milk, you can learn to pour milk for lattes and cappuccinos without needing a spoon. As a general rule, the faster you pour the milk, the more foam will make it to the cup.

If done right, your conditioned milk should contain no large bubbles at the surface and be glassy and shiny. There might even be a slight reflection so it resembles a mirror or a whitish chrome.

Choice of Milk?

You might have a standard milk choice (skim, 2 percent, whole, etc.) for drinking or pouring on your morning cereal, but for making espresso drinks, we recommend using whole or 2 percent milk, as they both contain the fatty proteins that really help fluff up the foam and hold the drink's volume while you're sipping. But there's no reason why you can't still use 1 percent or skim milk if that's your preference.

In this section, we break down the disadvantages and advantages of each milk type, to prime you for what to expect when you begin to experiment at home. For beginning baristi, milk with a higher amount of butterfat will make for easier frothing, so that might be good to begin with.

Whole Milk

When you order a drink at a café and don't tell the barista what type of milk you want, he or she will probably use whole milk. Whole milk has more fat and vitamins—both aids to achieving the best froth possible. And because whole milk is about 3.5 percent fat, you're able to stretch the milk more aggressively than all other milk types.

Skim (or Nonfat) Milk

Skim milk is a healthier option because most of the fat has been removed. However, fat aids in the development of good structure in frothed milk, so it's more difficult to achieve proper texture with nonfat milk. Milk that doesn't contain any or very little fat separates quickly in the pitcher, and there's a high chance you'll get a dry foam on top and runny, thin hot milk underneath.

If you do decide to use skim or nonfat milk, serve the drink immediately after you've steamed the milk. As we mentioned earlier, you can stall the milk if the espresso shot isn't yet brewed, but unfortunately, you cannot do that as well if you're using nonfat milk. Whirling the milk in the pitcher won't keep it fluffy, and it will soon fall flat.

> **Cuppa Wisdom**
>
> You should respect each other and refrain from disputes; you should not, like water and oil, repel each other, but should, like milk and water, mingle together.
>
> —Hindu prince Gautama Siddhartha

2 Percent and 1 Percent (Low-Fat) Milk

At many cafés, you'll probably find a middle-of-the-road option—2 percent or 1 percent (also called low-fat) milk. This satisfies both the barista (who needs fat to make foam) and the customer (who wants to avoid those extra fats for health reasons). In terms of the stretching and conditioning process, 2 percent milk is much more forgiving than 1 percent milk.

Nondairy Milk Choices

More and more cafés are offering soy, rice, and almond milks as substitutes for cow's milk. It's usually at an additional cost, between 25¢ and 75¢ per drink, depending on the drink's size. The reasons for this preference vary, but most likely, these milks appeal to customers with certain dietary needs—vegans (no consumption of animal products), the lactose-intolerant (not able to digest dairy), or those who simply want to drink healthier.

Usually you can find all these milks at your local grocery store, so if you don't want to give up your espresso-drink fix and are looking for a dairy-free option at home, you have plenty of options. In this section, we provide tips on how to manipulate the foam and steam so the quality comes pretty close to what you might get if you were working with cow's milk.

Soy Milk

When you use soy milk in an espresso drink, you get a boost of high-quality protein B vitamins and iron. Some soy milk products are fortified with other vitamins and minerals and also serve as a source of calcium, vitamin D, and vitamin B_{12}.

Field Notes

If you decide to use soy milk at home, use it within 7 to 10 days after you open the carton or jug to ensure freshness.

It's rare to find a barista at a café who hasn't poured an espresso drink with soy milk. More and more customers are drawn toward healthy options, so it's become a regular staple at coffeehouses.

Here are some tips on how to achieve the same level of greatness with soy milk as you do with cow's milk:

- Slow down your process and pay attention to each step as the main variable (the milk) is different and will react differently to steam.

- Give less air to the milk in the beginning; otherwise, the soy milk will become too frothy.

- Remove the steam wand sooner than if you were working with cow's milk; instead of waiting until the temperature of the milk is around 150°F, remove the steam wand at 140°F. Soy milk can begin to burn not long after 140°F—not to mention it produces an undesirable burnt-bean smell.

Rice Milk and Almond Milk

Compared with soy milk, rice milk tends to be flat and doesn't hold foam very well. The same is true for almond milk, although its inherent flavors are delicious.

We encourage you to try different brands of rice and almond milk, because they change all the time—and improve in quality—due to an increased demand for milk substitutes, not just in espresso drinks but for cereals and baking.

Stand-Alone Milk-Frothing Devices

If you're unable to use a steam wand attached to an espresso machine, you can still froth and steam milk using a French press–style frother or a milk whip. Both are inexpensive and don't require an electrical outlet to operate. Try them and see what you think!

French Press–Style Frother

In Chapter 6, you learned about the French press and its use in brewing coffee. A similar-looking model is designed for frothing milk and, in fact, is very easy to use with just a few pumps of the plunger when it is in contact with hot milk. The cost is around $15 to $20, for either glass or plastic.

To use, simply fill the jug with hot milk and then press the plunger up and down a few times, creating a whirlpool effect. In about 30 seconds, you get thick, creamy milk to top off your cappuccino.

The frothed milk is similar in texture to whipped cream and silky smooth. It's not as airy as if it were produced with the help of an espresso machine's steam wand, but it's still sufficient. One disadvantage with this product, other than having to tap into your upper-arm strength (meaning several good, strong, and steady pumps), is that it creates another mess to clean up.

Handheld Frother

Another product that works separately from the espresso machine to froth milk is a handheld milk frother, or the milk whip. These battery-operated frothers are either plastic or stainless steel and cost between $10 and $20.

To use, you simply stick the frother in your heated milk, push a button, and soon you have frothed milk. It only takes a couple minutes to get the milk to the approximate consistency. Plus, these frothers are portable, so if you desire a cappuccino in your hotel room or around the campfire, no problem.

Latte Art

Have you ever ordered a drink with espresso and milk (such as a cappuccino or latte) at a café and gazed down into a design in the milk? If so, you've seen latte art. To do this, the barista pours or etches an illustration into the top of the milk using certain pulls of the pitcher and twists of the wrist. While not all cafés add latte art to their drinks, many do, especially if there's a focus on quality and gourmet beverages. Perhaps in time you'll have a signature design atop the milk on drinks you prepare at home!

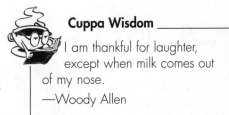

Cuppa Wisdom

I am thankful for laughter, except when milk comes out of my nose.
—Woody Allen

There are three latte art forms baristi use most often: single leaf (also called *rosetta*), heart, and apple. Know, though, that these are not the only designs possible to make. Very skilled baristi tinker around with different designs of their own creation, such as flowers, spiders, and other symbols—something to set their drinks apart. It's much like how a bartender might dress up a standard cocktail with personal touches.

Buzz Words _____

In latte art terms, a **rosetta** is a single-leaf design in the top of the milk.

Latte art has become so common, but at the same time there's still plenty of room for art and innovation. Millrock Latte Art Competition, presented by *Tea & Coffee Trade Journal*, is held four times a year and in different regions of the United States. This competition is an opportunity for baristi to showcase the hard work and originality they put into these drinks. Baristi take immense pride in their latte art, and fortunately, there is a lot of appreciation for it as well. Several websites showcase galleries of the beautiful designs that can be created.

Creating Your Own Latte Art

In this section, we walk you through the steps to make each of the three most-common designs: rosetta (single leaf), heart, and apple. For all three designs, your shot or shots of espresso should be just brewed and waiting in the cup. The easiest way to showcase the latte-art designs is to pour the milk into a wide-mouth cup so you have more room to create the design.

To make a rosetta design, begin by holding the cup at an angle, with the back raised and the edge closest to you a bit lower. Your first pours of milk should be in the center of the cup and straight down. When the cup is about ¼ full of milk, shake the pitcher from side to side to form the leaves of the rosetta design. Keep pouring in the center of the cup and shaking the pitcher. After about five shakes, move the pitcher back toward you, oscillating it in tight movements. Draw through these leafs with a final pour of milk.

Leaf design is among the most common of all latte-art designs but is also a good opportunity to showcase a barista's talent.

The heart and apple latte-art designs are actually fairly simple to make. (That said, you may not nail these designs on your first attempt, but maybe after a few practice sessions.) Before pouring, swirl the pitcher so the milk and froth stay compact and don't separate (which would create unwanted layers in your drink; the goal is to keep the foam intact). Keep the cup slightly inclined toward you, and pour milk into the center of the cup with a light circular motion. When the cup is half full, return the pitcher back toward you, slightly and with a semi-rotating movement, not as aggressively as you shook the pitcher when creating the rosetta. Don't move backward as much, either. When you see a ringed circle form, take a slow sweep through across the cup with your pitcher to form a multilayered heart.

The heart design is easier to pour, making a good first design for beginning latte artists.

To create the apple, simply follow the directions for the heart, but reverse the direction of your final stroke to make the stem.

Although not seen as often as the leaf and heart, the apple design is a simple adaptation of the heart design.

Etching

Etching is fairly rare, although you will find some cafés that train their baristi to do it well. To etch, a barista uses an etching tool—such as a tall spoon, thermometer needle, butter-knife blade, or a stirring straw—to make small indentations into the foam or steamed milk, either straight lines, diagonals, or half-moons, whatever is needed to create a desired illustration.

While sometimes considered lesser than free-pour latte art, etching is still a legitimate form of latte art.

The best kind of foam is one that is settled and dense, so as to retain the etched lines; otherwise, they'll dissolve into the milk and all beauty will be lost.

In some cases, chocolate syrup and powdered chocolate are used to "draw" the design onto the milk, creating a stark contrast between dark-brown and white. Otherwise, a simple indentation will work. Examples of designs using etching are crosses, diamonds, small dots, and anything that can trace an already-existing design, framing it essentially. Simple words like *Love* have been etched into the foam atop a cappuccino, too.

Etching is very time-consuming, especially in a high-volume café where the barista is making drinks one after another. It's easier to do at home, as you're not so rushed and can really focus on creating artful designs. Give yourself a lot of practice in etching, and remember, a poor etching design still tastes delicious. So even if your diamonds look more like curlicues, you can still take a sip and enjoy.

The Least You Need to Know

◆ Milk should not exceed a temperature of more than 160°F while steaming or frothing.

◆ If you're not using an espresso machine (preferably with a multiple-holed steamer tip on the steam wand), you can use a milk whip or a French press–style frother to do the job.

◆ Latte art is created in three common designs: rosetta, heart, and apple—but with some practice and your imagination, the sky's the limit!

◆ Etching requires practice and precision to add an additional design to a drink's surface.

Drink Making

In This Chapter

◆ Learn to prepare espresso drinks like a professional barista!

◆ Follow recipes developed by award-winning barista champions from around the world

◆ Discover how to incorporate the proper glassware and garnishes for each drink

In this chapter, we give you instructions on how to prepare common espresso drinks, bringing together the information you learned in Chapters 11 and 12 about the techniques involved in preparing espresso and milk. Our hope is that you'll not only feel confident in following these recipes, but that you'll become a home barista in your own right, tinkering with milk, espresso, and flavorings to create signature beverages.

Making Café Drinks at Home

All the drinks in this chapter can be adjusted for taste. You can substitute ristrettos for standard-size shots, or single espresso shots for doubles, or vice versa. In addition to altering the amount of espresso you use, consider experimenting with the coffee used to prepare espresso, because different coffees produce a different taste in the drink.

What Size?

It's a challenge for us to narrow down and define cup sizes, so we're going to give you approximations so you can match an appropriate cup with the drink you're preparing:

◆ A latte bowl is a wide cup with a handle, and is typically at least 16 ounces.

◆ A pint glass is the same glass used to pour tap beer into at bars.

◆ A demitasse is a tiny 3-ounce cup used to serve shots of espresso.

Unless otherwise stated and whenever possible, pull your espresso shots into the cup you'll serve the drink.

Flavorings and Garnishes

An entire industry is built around flavoring, so your options are nearly endless. You can buy bottles of these syrups in a plethora of flavors. For those who are so inclined, organic and sugar-free versions are available, too. If you're going to flavor your drinks, these flavored syrups are hard to beat. But you can also substitute with natural extracts like the kind used for baking, such as peppermint, vanilla, or almond extract.

An advantage of the flavored syrups—or disadvantage, depending on your perspective— is that they are already sweetened. Each manufacturer has developed a formula, so it's worth sampling more than one syrup before you decide on one. For example, if you wanted mintier but not sweeter, you would need to find a different manufacturer instead of just adding another tablespoon of the same mint syrup.

Spices (like nutmeg or cinnamon), chocolate shavings, and whipped cream are simple add-on toppings, and people tend to either love them or hate them. Part of this senti- ment may be fueled by a romanticism for traditional Italian espresso drinks that don't include these garnishes. We encourage you to stay true to your taste buds, however. If you like a topping of whipped cream, or the sweetness of a particular flavor, you're not ruining the taste of a cappuccino or a mocha. You're adapting it, and that's what makes drink making a lot of fun.

Drinks at a Glance

Before we get to the actual recipes, here's a quick cheat sheet that covers the basics of how to make each drink, including what to serve the drink in and what to garnish with (if anything) to make you look like a coffee-shop pro—at home!

affagato *Serving ware:* Sundae dish. *The setup:* Pour 2 freshly brewed shots of espresso (ristrettos work best for their short, concentrated nature) over a scoop of vanilla ice cream or gelato. *Garnish:* Whipped cream and/or chocolate shavings.

americano *Serving ware:* Coffee mug. *The setup:* Pull your espresso (no more than 2 ounces) and top off with hot water. (Many espresso machines have a hot-water jet for this purpose.)

brevé *Serving ware:* Latte bowl or pint glass. *The setup:* Pull a double espresso and pour over it steamed half-and-half like you would for a latte. Pour into a bowl or glass.

café au lait *Serving ware:* Pint glass. *The setup:* Steam together equal parts cold-brewed coffee and milk.

cappuccino *Serving ware:* Cappuccino cup. *The setup:* Pull shot of espresso into the cup. Pour in steamed milk from a pitcher, quickly so the heavier foam falls into the cup along with the milk. For cups smaller than 8 ounces in size, start with a single shot of espresso; for larger cups, use a double shot.

Hot Water

Take caution whenever serving hot drinks in glasses without handles.

chai charger *Serving ware:* Latte bowl. *The setup:* Prepare your favorite chai recipe (or use a prepared concentrate) and drop in a shot of espresso. *Garnish:* Cinnamon stick (optional).

eggnog latte *Serving ware:* Latte bowl or pint glass. *The setup:* Pull a double shot of espresso and steam together equal portions of milk and prepared eggnog. Slowly pour the steamed mixture over the espresso. *Garnish:* Sprinkle the top with nutmeg or cinnamon.

espresso con Panna *Serving ware:* Small (5-ounce) cappuccino cup. *The setup:* Pull a single or double espresso (your preference) and top with whipped cream.

espresso granita *Serving ware:* Sundae dish. *The setup:* Brew espresso and freeze in ice-cube trays. Crush or shave the cubes using a blender or ice shaver. *Garnish:* Whipped cream.

espresso romano *Serving ware:* Demitasse. *The setup:* Rub a lemon peel on the rim of the demitasse and then pull a shot of espresso into it. *Garnish:* Lemon peel twist.

frappé (also called **latte granita**) *Serving ware:* Pint glass. *The setup:* In a blender, combine a double shot of espresso, 1 tablespoon sugar, 5 or 6 ice cubes, a dash of salt, and approximately 6 ounces milk. (Use these proportions as a guide and tweak to your taste.) Optionally, add 1 tablespoon or less flavored syrup. *Garnish:* Whipped cream.

honey latte *Serving ware:* Latte bowl or pint glass. *The setup:* Prepare 2 shots espresso and pour over 2 tablespoons honey. Mix. Steam the milk as you would for a latte, and slowly pour over espresso and honey.

latte *Serving ware:* Latte bowl or pint glass. *The setup:* Pull espresso (2 shots for a drink that's more than 12 ounces). Slowly pour steamed milk over the espresso.

macchiato *Serving ware:* Demitasse or a small cappuccino cup (for a double macchiato). *The setup:* Froth milk and spoon a couple dollops over espresso.

Field Notes

Many traditional espresso drinks can be served on the rocks (with ice). In most cases, the preparation is quite similar. If possible, froth your milk cold using a French press–style frother or milk whip. Otherwise, forgo frothing.

mocha *Serving ware:* Latte bowl or pint glass. *The setup:* Pull double shot of espresso and mix with chocolate syrup or cocoa powder. Pour on top milk that's prepared as you would for a latte. *Garnish:* Whipped cream.

shot in the dark (also called **red eye** or **depth charge**) *Serving ware:* Coffee mug. *The setup:* Combine a shot of espresso and brewed coffee to fill the mug.

steamer *Serving ware:* Latte bowl or pint glass. *The setup:* Steam the milk and add flavored syrup.

Drinks of Champions

In Chapter 14, you'll read about two competitions that spotlight the barista profession and the art of preparing an espresso drink: the World Barista Championship and the United States Barista Championship. Each is held annually and brings together the best baristi. As a requirement for competing, the baristi must prepare a signature drink during the competition, showcasing their abilities to not only practice proper techniques but demonstrate their creativity.

We talked to several of these all-star baristi who were happy to share a couple of their own creations and give you step-by-step instructions on how to make the drinks as they did.

Insieme

by Sammy Piccolo, World Latte Art Champion (2004) and Canadian Barista Champion (2003, 2004, 2005)

1 egg yolk	Dash curry
¾ oz. raw sugar	4 oz. homogenized milk
1 oz. bittersweet chocolate	Enough espresso for 4 shots

Makes 4 drinks

Buzz Words

Insieme means "together" in Italian and is symbolic of how coffee and the World Barista Championships bring people together.

1. Whisk together egg yolk, sugar, chocolate, curry, and milk in a bowl.

2. Pour mixture in a steaming pitcher, and steam until the pitcher is too hot to hold.

3. Extract 4 shots espresso (1 for each glass). Pour steamed mixture over espresso shots.

Le Baron

by Jónína Soffía Tryggvadóttir, Iceland Barista Champion (2005)

1 tsp. hazelnut syrup	1 TB. whipped cream
1 (1-oz.) shot espresso	Handful of finely chopped hazelnuts (optional)
5 TB. plus 1 tsp. whole milk	
½ oz. dark-chocolate bar with praline filling	

Makes 1 drink

1. Pour syrup in the bottom of a brandy glass and top with espresso.

2. Warm milk and mix chocolate with it. Pour milk-chocolate mixture over syrup and espresso.

3. Top drink with lightly whipped cream, and garnish top with nuts (if using).

Kaffa Amubi

by José Miguel Coto, Costa Rica Barista Champion (2005)

Makes 1 drink

1 cup water

1 *Maracuya*, cut in half, rinds and seeds intact (may substitute passion fruit or orange)

2 TB. sugar

1 (1-oz.) shot espresso

3 ice cubes

Pinch nutmeg

1. In a pot or casserole dish, combine 1 cup water, 1 Maracuya half, and 2 tablespoons sugar. When mixture begins to boil, remove the pot from heat and let it rest for 5 minutes.

2. Remove Maracuya rind and seeds and then combine sugar in a mixer at medium speed until a syruplike texture is obtained. Let the syrup rest for 10 minutes in the refrigerator before continuing.

3. Place 1½ ounces cold Maracuya syrup at the bottom of a martini glass.

4. In a shaker, mix espresso, ½ ounce cold Maracuya syrup, ice cubes, and nutmeg. Shake.

5. Slowly spoon mixture over cold Maracuya syrup in the martini glass.

Buzz Words

Maracuya is also called passionfruit. It is a round fruit about the size of a lime and has a tart taste.

Hemispheres

*by Sammy Piccolo, World Latte Art Champion (2004) and
Canadian Barista Champion (2003, 2004, 2005)*

2 egg yolks

2 TB. sugar

3 oz. hot water

4 (1-oz.) shots espresso

½ oz. caramelized pear purée

1 pt. heavy whipping cream

5 tsp. confectioners' sugar

2 oz. vanilla syrup

5 vanilla pods

Makes 4 drinks

1. Combine egg yolks, sugar, hot water, and espresso shots in a double boiler. Using a hand blender or a whisk, blend ingredients until they're consistent, and heat mixture until hot.

2. Remove mixture from heat and pour over caramelized pear purée.

3. In another bowl, whip whipped cream, confectioners' sugar, vanilla syrup, and vanilla pods until you've achieved a thick consistency but can still pour it easily into espresso mixture.

4. Pour 1 ounce whipped cream mixture on top of drink, creating a circle as you do so.

Field Notes

Hemispheres incorporate ingredients from the three hemispheres that are represented at the World Barista Championship.

Sweetness

by Bronwen Serna, United States Barista Champion (2004)

Makes 1 drink

¼ tsp. clover honey (Snoqualmie Valley works best)

1 (1-oz.) shot espresso

1 oz. half-and-half

Valrhona unsweetened dark-chocolate powder

1. Preheat a 4-ounce espresso cup (with a spoon in the cup) with hot water.

2. Add honey to espresso cup and pour espresso over honey to incorporate the flavors. Mix. Top with steamed half-and-half, and sprinkle with dark chocolate powder.

3. Mix again before enjoying to fully integrate half-and-half and chocolate with the flavors of honey and espresso.

Field Notes

Sweetness is a twist on the traditional macchiato served at Hines Public Market in Seattle. When shopping for ingredients, find a honey that will go best with the flavor of the espresso.

Black and White

by Joseph El Khoury, Lebanon Barista Champion (2004, 2005)

½ oz. coconut syrup

1 (1-oz.) shot espresso

8 ice cubes

1 oz. vanilla extract

1 oz. coconut milk

Makes 1 drink

1. Pour coconut syrup into a martini glass.

2. Add espresso shot and 2 ice cubes to a shaker, and shake.
   Strain espresso from ice and pour it over syrup.

3. Shake together vanilla extract, coconut milk, and remaining 6
   ice cubes. Gently pour vanilla mixture over the espresso.

Field Notes

Black and White is a popular beverage served at Casper & Gambini's, a coffee-house in Beirut. It's a shot of espresso topped with coconut milk and organic home-made vanilla cream.

Affagato Gianduja

by Bronwen Serna, United States Barista Champion (2004)

Makes 1 drink

1 scoop cream- or vanilla-flavored gelato

⅓ cup Nutella spread (adjust for taste)

1 shot espresso

Valrhona unsweetened dark-chocolate powder

Field Notes

Affagato is a traditional Italian drink made with vanilla gelato or ice cream and espresso. It can double as a dessert.

1. Chill the glasses/cups in which the drink will be served. (Smaller-sized martini glasses or 3-ounce demitasses work well.)

2. Mix 3 parts gelato to 1 part Nutella spread. The mixture will melt, but it should not be liquid. You only need to mix so Nutella is streaked in gelato.

3. Put a spoonful of the mixture into the chilled glass/cup.

4. Make espresso, and pour shot over mixture.

5. Top with dark-chocolate powder and serve. Swirl ingredients around to incorporate.

Flower of Siam

by Khun Supot Leesuwattanakul, Thailand Barista Champion (2005)

1 (1-oz.) shot espresso

Crushed ice

³/₄ oz. pasteurized milk

¹/₂ oz. sweetened condensed milk

¹/₂ oz. prepared Jasmine tea

Whipped cream (enough for garnish)

Green tea powder

1 orchid flower

Makes 1 drink

1. Pour espresso over crushed ice for a few minutes and allow it to cool. Do not use the serving dish for this, just something to hold it for a few minutes.

2. Pour pasteurized milk, sweetened condensed milk, Jasmine tea, and crushed ice into shaker. Shake well, and pour into a serving glass.

3. Gradually pour espresso into mixture. Garnish with whipped cream, and sprinkle green tea powder over whipped cream. Decorate with orchid.

Tonka Mocha

by Mark Koncz, Hungary Barista Champion (2005)

Makes 4 drinks

6 to 7 tonka beans

8 oz. just-boiled water

1 cup sugar

2 oz. Captain Morgan black label Jamaican rum

4 (1-oz.) shots espresso (French-roasted Mexican Maragogype)

1⅓ oz. liquid Valrhona hot chocolate

Ice cubes

2 (1-oz.) shots espresso

Dash sugar

Crushed ice

Cocoa powder (enough for sprinkling)

Field Notes

Tonka Mocha is an alcoholic beverage served cold. It's easier to make when you prepare the tonka syrup before serving. To make a stronger frappé foam, use a double shot of espresso per serving instead of a single shot.

---

1. Cut tonka beans into small pieces, and steep in just-boiled water for about 8 minutes, stirring often.

2. Carefully remove beans from water, and stir in sugar until dissolved and mixture forms a syrup.

3. In a shaker, combine 1 ounce tonka syrup with rum, 4 espresso shots, chocolate, and several ice cubes. Shake and strain into 4 martini glasses.

4. In a blender, combine 2 espresso shots and dash sugar with crushed ice. Mix at high speed until well blended.

5. Top drinks with this frappé foam and sprinkle with cocoa powder.

Black and White Coffee

by José Miguel Coto, Costa Rica Barista Champion (2005)

³/₄ fl. oz. honey

¹/₂ egg yolk

1 fl. oz. buttermilk

Pinch cinnamon

1 (1-oz.) shot espresso

4 fl. oz. milk

Bitter-chocolate shavings

Makes 1 drink

1. Pour honey in a warmed martini glass.

2. Beat egg yolk, buttermilk, and cinnamon in mixing bowl.

3. Steam mixture to 165° to 170°F. (If you don't have an espresso machine, warm up the mixture in a pot or casserole slowly for a few minutes, always stirring and being careful to not let it boil.)

4. Slowly spoon hot mixture over honey and then add espresso.

5. Steam milk to 175°F and top drink with foam. Garnish with bitter-chocolate shavings.

Field Notes

Black and White Coffee is a smoky, hot cup of coffee perfect for cold days and nights.

The Least You Need to Know

◆ Garnishes are optional finishing touches on drinks and should reflect your personal style and tastes.

◆ Iced versions of traditional drinks can easily be made by substituting cold, frothed milk for heated milk.

◆ Several kinds of glassware are available for serving espresso drinks. Each is chosen to show off the drink's best attributes, but is not crucial to the taste of the drink.

Chapter 14

The Barista

In This Chapter

◆ Understand who a barista is and what he or she does

◆ Discover competitions that spotlight the profession

◆ Learn about training opportunities and schools designed specifically for baristi

In some ways, a barista can be likened to a bartender or a chef, an artist in his or her own right. Each pull on the espresso machine or frothing of milk is done with precision and care, and is the result of intense practice. Making a delicious espresso drink for customers requires the barista to pay attention to temperature, product quality, and food chemistry. Being a barista at a café is a demanding job.

Even though you don't have a line of folks standing in your kitchen waiting for lattes, you can still learn from the techniques professional baristi use. At home, you'll be using similar equipment and have to learn how to balance the various accessories so everything is timed as it should be.

In this chapter, you learn more about the profession and how it is woven into American café culture, along with tips on how to be an artisan barista at home. You may even decide that you want to be a professional, paid barista, or take specialized training courses.

Meet Your Friendly Barista

Europe is ahead of the United States in terms of its appreciation of baristi. There, the profession is not always viewed as simply a stopping gap between careers or a paying job during college studies. Here, unfortunately, the job is lumped into the retail-service sector and does not always pay enough for a barista to support a family, which naturally deters some from pursuing the profession.

Unlike bars (at least in most cities), coffeehouses are open from morning to sundown, although a select few, especially if they're near a business district, may close down by dinnertime. The barista might be an employee who works a changing shift, sometimes pulling shots of espresso for morning commuters and maybe still making mochas for the night owls. This can be a changing set of drink orders and requests, so it's important that the barista really know the menu and customers' needs.

We're sure you've been in line at a coffeehouse at least once, pondering the menu board, when the barista gestured to you and asked what you'll be drinking today. This is a good way for the café workers (often a team of two: a cashier and a barista) to keep the line moving and not have customers walk away because they're waiting too long for their beverage. It also makes the barista's job less frantic when the drink orders are paced out, and so angry customers aren't dishing out their complaints while he or she is making splendid, delicious drinks.

The downside of being a barista is the historically low pay. Very rarely does a barista earn more than $10 an hour before tips. A barista might earn more than this in certain cases, such as in an expensive restaurant, a high-end resort, or at a large corporation where he or she might have an opportunity to train other employees, but such opportunities are often few and far between. An accomplished barista sometimes earns more, too, and has the opportunity to enter national and international competitions.

Field Notes

If the barista does a good job preparing your drink, the best way to offer your appreciation is to leave money in the tip jar, usually located near the cashier. Just like servers at a restaurant, baristi count on tips as part of their wages.

Another way a barista can increase his or her wage is by taking on a managerial role. Each café's work environment varies, but typically there's one lead barista who will, for example, oversee product inventory, train employees in working the espresso machine/preparing drinks, and help incorporate menu changes.

Traits of a Good Barista

Just like a bartender or an employee in a food-focused environment, a barista must be friendly and efficient at the same time. If a customer has a special request, it should be filled promptly but not at the expense of another customer's time. In a sense, it's a juggling act to please so many customers all at once.

Sporting a smile helps the customer feel relaxed. Some of our favorite encounters with baristi over the years were with ones who served our drinks with a smile. And it may sound cheesy, but displaying a friendly attitude is always appreciated when handing over one's cash.

Baristi should also be very knowledgeable and able to teach customers quickly about drinks on the menu, as well as decode customers' needs and be able to recommend a macchiato over an espresso con Panna, for instance. A good barista must also have a creative streak and be willing to develop new drinks and try new drink-prep techniques. Sometimes these new drinks coincide with the seasons (such as a peppermint mocha or a pumpkin latte), and other times they're designed to be vastly different from what neighboring cafés are offering.

What a Barista Can Teach Us

We realize that, particularly if you live alone or are the only coffee drinker in your household, you probably aren't preparing drinks for anyone other than yourself. However, there may be occasions when you're entertaining and want to serve mochas after dinner or want to relax with a drink far more rich than a cup of black coffee.

Precision is very important when preparing espresso drinks. Before beginning to prepare the drink, you should have a good idea of what kinds of beans you'll use and if any whipped cream or flavored syrups are needed. Having chilled milk on hand is necessary as well. Just like when you set out to bake a cake, you should take inventory of the ingredients in your pantry so you aren't running off to the grocery store in the middle of the process.

Attentiveness is a hallmark trait for a good barista. He or she needs to communicate with the cashier regarding drink orders, as well as carefully monitor the espresso machine, grind settings, milk steaming, and the crema. As you can imagine, even after just a few shifts in a coffeehouse, a working barista increases his or her competence and breeds an ability to move fast through each process, because there's a continual line of customers to serve. When you're making drinks at home, after a while, you'll be able to do each step quickly and efficiently. Over time, you'll see that not only are your drinks better, but they are made in less time.

> **Field Notes**
>
> Just like chefs bring their own signature creations to a new restaurant, a barista might tack on signature drinks to a menu of coffee drinks that showcase his or her ability to merge flavors and textures inherent in coffee and espresso drinks.

And just as a barista has to be open to change or unanticipated kinks in the process, so should you. If one of the steps goes wrong, you can either start over or return to the process with follow-up modifications. We're sure you've seen an instance when a barista's lineup of drink orders was disrupted due to an incorrect fulfillment (say the customer ordered a mocha with skim milk and instead got a white chocolate mocha with 2 percent milk) or a customer's dissatisfaction. Knowing how to keep the line moving—and in your case, the process flowing—is key.

Also, it's rare that a barista is able to work in complete silence. Knowing how to tune out surroundings (but of course not the customer's requests or communications with the cashier) that aren't important to the drink's creation, such as the music played in the café or noisy customers, is very important. For someone who thrives best in a quiet environment, the first few days on the job as a barista might be frustrating.

Yes, There Really *Is* a Barista Champion

You may be surprised to learn that the world's best baristi actually have a place other than their coffeehouse employer to show off their talents: the World Barista Championship. Many nations also have national championships for this purpose. So do

American baristi, at the United States Barista Championship and also at regional competitions. These competitions serve two purposes: they provide a showcase for skilled and accomplished baristi, and set benchmarks for other baristi to reach toward.

World Barista Championship

The World Barista Championship takes place each spring and is jointly run and organized by the Specialty Coffee Association of America (SCAA) and the Specialty Coffee Association of Europe. The championship started in 2000 in Monte Carlo as a rather generic idea to bring together the best baristi from around the globe and after intense study and a judging process crown an official champion. Although the goal was to attract worldwide representation, only 12 baristi entered the competition. Robert Thoresen of Norway was the winner of that first competition.

The following year the SCAA took a turn hosting the World Barista Championship at its annual conference, which was held in Miami that year. (The World Barista Championship is now held in the United States every 3 years, and in other countries during the off years.) Martin Hildebrandt of Denmark took first place out of 17 contestants.

Field Notes

To read more about the World Barista Championship, visit their website at www.worldbaristachampionship.com. Results from the current and previous years are available here.

At the 2002 World Barista Championship in Oslo, Norway, Fritz Storm of Denmark beat out 23 other baristi to win. Then, the next year, the championship really peaked in popularity due to its broadcast on national television from the host city of Boston. More than 20 million Americans viewed clips of the event on morning television, which had 28 baristi competing for the crown. Paul Bassett of Australia was the winner and the only non-Scandinavian to win thus far.

In its fifth year (2004) the World Barista Championship headed to Trieste, Italy, a city with a rich history of coffee and high-quality espresso, a backdrop quite appropriate for picking out some of the world's best baristi. Thirty-four baristi competed, which showed that the number of interested competitors was growing. It's worth noting that in many cases the cost to attend the championship may have deterred potential competitors, particularly those from impoverished nations. Tim Wendelboe of Norway captured the judges' highest scores and won the 2004 competition.

In 2005, 35 countries competed in the World Barista Championship, which was held in America's coffee capitol, Seattle. The winner was Troels Overdal Poulsen of

Denmark, giving further clout to Scandinavia's reputation of having many skilled baristi, and residents who drink a lot of coffee and espresso.

United States Barista Championship

Each spring the United States Barista Championship is held at the SCAA annual conference. Its primary purpose is to select a country representative for the World Barista Championship.

Field Notes

The United States Barista Championship was originally called the North American Barista Championship. The name was changed because Canada began hosting its own championship for Canadian residents.

Since 2002, the U.S. Barista Championship's first year, only one non–West Coast resident has won. That was Matt Riddle of Intelligentsia Coffee in Chicago, during the 2006 U.S. Barista Championship in Charlotte, North Carolina. But there's definitely been representation from other geographic regions in the championships, which might lead to a winner from those areas in future years and supports the idea of skilled baristi being in places outside of the Pacific Northwest.

In 2005, Phuong Tran, a barista at Lava Java in Seattle, took first place at the U.S. Barista Championship when the championship was held in her hometown. The previous year she took second place when the championship was held in Atlanta, losing to fellow Seattle resident Bronwen Serna of Hines Public Market. Heather Perry, a Southern California barista, won in 2003 at Boston, and the previous year Dismas Smith, then of Zoka Coffee & Tea in Seattle, took first place when it was still the North American Barista Championship.

Each winner of the U.S. Barista Championship earns a trip to the World Barista Championship. Costs for hotel, airfare, and ground transportation for a week are covered by the SCAA and a $1,000 cash prize is awarded. During some years, sponsors gift the winner with prizes, too.

Field Notes

To keep up to date on the United States Barista Championship contestants and champions, visit www.scaa.org/about_usbc.asp. Judge score-sheets are also available if you're curious to learn what defines a barista champ.

Winning a U.S. Barista Championship (or World Barista Championship) is more than just a new title for a barista. It's also the pathway to a career of promotions. For instance, opportunities to market a product line (such as syrups or milks), open up a consulting or training business, and appear in television commercials have been offered to previous winners.

Some winners have become trainers and consultants after a win. Just as other professions have winners presiding over the industry, as a benchmark for success and artistic reach, the championships exist for baristi worldwide.

In preparation for the U.S. Barista Championship, 10 U.S. regional barista competitions are held throughout the year. These competitions are hosted by coffee shops and open to any barista who resides in that geographic region. The winning barista from each competition automatically earns a spot in the U.S. Barista Championship, jumping to the semifinals and skipping the first round.

Scoring for Champions

For both the U.S. Barista Championship and the World Barista Championship, each barista contestant is required to prepare, in 15 minutes or less, 12 espresso drinks: 4 each of the following: a single espresso, a single cappuccino, and a signature beverage of the barista's own creation. (Each of the 4 sensory judges receives 1 of each drink, which is why 12 must be made.) A signature beverage often plays off of the geographic region in which the barista lives. For instance, a Thai barista might incorporate coconut milk into the drink's taste, while a Mexican barista might opt to include native spices in the drinks. Various types of glassware that go beyond the typical café mug or glass—like serving in a coconut shell—are sometimes used, too, to present flair and originality. Also, a signature beverage must not contain any alcohol, which includes alcohol-based extracts like vanilla.

The championship is organized into 3 segments of 15 minutes each: preparation, competition/performance, and cleanup. And just like with a figure-skating competition, music (of the barista's choice) is played while the barista is onstage.

Scoring is handled by seven judges, including a head judge who strictly offers oversight of the process and does not contribute any numerical scores. (More on that later.) Four of the judges are sensory judges, and another two are assigned as technical judges.

A technical judge's job is to examine the barista's workstation during the competition for

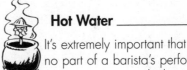

Hot Water

It's extremely important that no part of a barista's performance go unseen, which is the main reason for having more than one judge examine a skill set, especially in a situation where a blink of an eye or momentary distraction could take one judge's focus off of a competitor. Sometimes obstructed views are only for a moment, but missing that moment could be crucial.

cleanliness and hygienic procedures, following food and drink sanitation standards, and using proper techniques. Although this judge does not actually taste the drinks, he or she does look at how the barista is handling equipment, including cleaning the portafilter before dosing, extraction techniques, and milk frothing techniques. A sensory judge evaluates the barista's creativity in preparing the drinks, taking into account visual appearance of the drinks and how they taste. A sensory judge looks at such things as the quality of the espresso blend, the temperature of drinks and cups, and whether the correct accessories are served with the drink (spoons, for example).

Two different score sheets represent the separate judging areas (technical and sensory). Either a score of between 0 and 6, or a yes or no answer, is assigned to a category. Whoever earns the highest score on his or her assigned score sheets is named the champion.

Barista Schooling and Training

Twenty years ago most if not all barista training in the United States was a product of mentoring or learning was done by reading printed materials or self-published training sheets. Often a new barista learned the ropes from a longtime barista at the establishment where they both worked. Today, however, a greater number of opportunities exist for baristi who want to study up on their craft. Just like culinary school is on top of current trends and offers instruction to students, so do coffee-related schools.

For instance, at their employer's discretion, baristi can attend a short-term, intensive training. These trainings rarely last for more than a week, aren't too disruptive to the home café's scheduling needs, and don't take the barista out of work for a long time. Also, if the training is away from the café, there won't be any interruptions or distractions for the student barista. Sharing of ideas and thoughts is important, too, and a lot of this occurs when baristi from different cities get together to study their craft.

Cuppa Wisdom

By learning you will teach; by teaching you will learn.

—Latin proverb

Today we're seeing more of a hybrid of the two training options (on-site mentoring and off-site schooling). If a café has more than one location and employs many baristi, clinics or workshops may be hosted at the café periodically to keep baristi up-to-date on beverage trends or techniques. No transportation costs are required, just time away from the pressure of customers for a couple hours and then it's back to work.

Several cafés are beginning to open up these classes to consumers. They're separate from the employee training programs and are often held at night or on the weekends to accommodate those people who work during the day.

In just a few hours, customers can learn their way around an espresso machine and in time know how to make a latte or cappuccino at home. One might think the class deflects a customer's interest in the café, but actually the opposite is true. The customer begins to view the café staff as experts, and not only that but also friendly enough to help in any buying decisions they might make for setting up a system at home.

Hot Water

There's no nationwide certification for baristi, nor is there one recognized around the world. We caution readers to look into the programs because the idea of certification in the United States is so new. A couple certification programs exist at this time, but nothing seems to have really caught on as a standard in the industry. Scrutinize the programs carefully and balance what you think you're going to get out of it with what it will cost.

At the time of this writing, several roaster retailers around the nation have small start-up programs. These don't appear to be intended for mass schooling but do offer short-term training.

Seattle Barista Academy

At Seattle Barista Academy in Seattle, Washington, there are four tracks for learning: home, beginner, intermediate, and advanced. Taught by skilled baristi and café managers, students learn tips of the trade in steaming milk, grinding espresso, and tamping the grounds during either a half-day class or a 3-day-long training. The classes are held twice a week in various locations, including Portland, Oregon; Los Angeles; and Seattle.

American Barista and Coffee School

American Barista and Coffee School (ABC) opened in 2004 in Portland, Oregon. Its target student is not just a barista, but also owners and managers of coffeehouses who attend the school for business-management courses. Hands-on workshops for baristi are in a lab and last for 3 days.

For café owners, two seminars are offered at ABC. One is a 5-day seminar for new, start-up cafés. Another is a 2-day workshop for people who have owned a coffeehouse for quite some time but may want to learn about new techniques and ways of doing business.

Instructors at ABC are senior coffee-industry consultants. In 2005, ABC began teaching abbreviated versions of their courses to consumers. ABC also publishes business manuals and videos to help café owners in managing their company.

Coffee School Down Under

Coffee School in Australia is committed to teaching working baristi and coffee aficionados two things: coffee art and how to be a good barista. Classes last just a half day, which allows a traveling American to take advantage of a few classes and still have time to explore the outback.

The London School of Coffee

The London School of Coffee opened in 2004 but by the end of 2005, it had already completed a set of 10 classes, from barista basics to designing one's own espresso blend to tips on how to open a coffeehouse. In 2005, 14 classes were offered in the first half of the year, covering a lot of the same topics, but also adding a course in iced drinks.

> **Field Notes**
>
> In Appendixes C and D, we give you a list of online resources that can help you learn about a lot of what you will encounter as a barista, whether it's in your kitchen or as a profession. Study that list and take advantage of the opportunities if you want to learn more.

There are three learning tracks for an overview class for baristi: basic, middle, and advanced. So those with little or no experience, as well as baristi who are very comfortable behind an espresso machine, have an opportunity to learn. The cost for a class is on average 135 British pounds and lasts for 1 day. Half-day and 2-day courses are also offered.

Copenhagen Coffee Academy

Another schooling option, also in Europe, is the Copenhagen Coffee Academy in Copenhagen, Denmark. Five high-level executives in the coffee industry—ranging from a biologist who has studied the chemistry of espresso to Troels Overdal Poulsen, who won the World Barista Championship in 2005—serve as instructors. Some of the classes are very specific, such as how to become a world barista champion, while others are more general, as in latte art.

> **Field Notes**
>
> Building on the same energy and spirit as the championships, in 2003, U.S. baristi organized themselves into the Barista Guild of America. The guild is an offshoot of the SCAA and is intended for working baristi (necessary for membership) to share ideas and elevate their art. Furthering the art and the profession of the barista is the main goal, and the guild also serves as a tool for creating connections, in particular the online forums. Although still young, the guild has quickly become popular among working baristi, who for years worked in isolation without any formal professional networking group.

Other Instructional Avenues

But there's also another training method that's survived the ages: printed books and materials about all things coffee and espresso. Books like the one you're reading now are great to reference from time to time, whether it's the first time you're pouring a shot or when you want to study roast styles.

And with the advent of the Internet, even more information is available instantly at your fingertips. If you're a budding barista, hop online and see what you can find. Forums are particularly helpful to learn what other baristi are doing wrong and right, but be wary of bad information that's published on the Internet. By now you've probably learned that anybody can publish online, and so it's important that your facts are from reputable sources in the industry.

And of course baristi sharing notes among each other continues to be a good way to spread useful knowledge. Check out the bimonthly *Barista Magazine*, where you'll find articles about the profession as well as product news.

Where Baristi Work

Not so long ago, when a popular restaurant chain with a thick menu of lunch, dinner, and dessert items was moving into our town, we noticed an employment ad for a barista. This piqued our interest because up until then we hadn't seen that type of job at a large restaurant. The ad detailed the skills necessary, and it was obvious that the restaurant chain was searching for a savvy, competent, and experienced person to handle the restaurant's espresso drinks menu. But the truth is, in the 2 years since we saw this ad, times have changed. More and more, we are seeing that nontraditional businesses are employing baristi.

The face of coffeehouses is perhaps different. Espresso bars (and sometimes carts) are set up in laundromats, train stations, surfboard-rental shops, movie cinemas, banks, and grocery stores. Baristi also work at airports, department stores, and at university and corporation cafeterias. While out running errands or socializing with friends, oftentimes a steaming hot beverage isn't too far off.

> **Field Notes**
>
> Espresso carts have been a fixture in Seattle's caffeinated culture since the 1970s, but they're becoming more and more popular in other cities as well. Now you can find someone operating an espresso cart at business functions, street fairs, and farmer's markets. Espresso has become akin to offering cotton candy, hot dogs, or sodas at events.

And let's not forget about drive-thrus. As Americans continue to use their automobiles to get to work and other activities, being able to drive up to a window to order a latte to put in the car's cup holder is certainly appreciated. Starbucks has added many retail drive-thrus to its company, but many independent cafés are either entirely drive-thru or have added a drive-up window to the business.

The SCAA estimates 100,000 people in the United States are employed as baristi. It's likely that in the not-so-distant future we'll see even more espresso carts, in lieu of cafés, because it's a career alternative to owning a café but without the expense. It's also a way to put into practice and make money from a passion for coffee.

The Least You Need to Know

- Being a barista is not as easy as it might look. The profession has a need for artisans at the espresso machine.

- The Specialty Coffee Association of America estimates that 100,000 people in the United States work as baristi.

- Since 2000, the World Barista Championship has crowned baristi who win during an intense annual competition. Only one non-Scandinavian has won, and never an American.

- There is no national or global certification for baristi, although plenty of training programs are available.

Part 4

Tea: From Crop to Cup

Tea is an exciting beverage, thanks to its nearly endless variety (even if it all does come from a single plant). Part 4 is dedicated to shedding light on the world of tea and making it more accessible. First we catch you up on tea's long history and explain how tea is produced. We also explore all kinds of commonly encountered teas as well as many tisanes (or herbal "teas").

When you've finished Part 4, you'll be able to explain not only why oolongs are a unique subclass of teas, but also how and why oolongs vary. After exploring how to best unlock the flavors in tea, we close by taking a look at how tea is celebrated around the world.

Chapter **15**

The History of Tea

In This Chapter

- ◆ Learn the difference between specialty teas and commodity-grade teas
- ◆ Read about the discovery of tea and how it spread across continents and cultures
- ◆ Trace the evolution of tea culture in America
- ◆ Discover why tea was considered a form of medicine and a means of currency

The specialty tea culture is driven by aroma and appearance. How a tea tantalizes and entices the eyes and nose are important factors in determining how it will taste. Is the tea grassy? Bitter? Buttery? These are just a few examples of sensations encountered when tasting teas. Unlike coffee beans, where all beans essentially look alike (but do have different cup characters), tea varieties rarely resemble each other in appearance. Although all teas are grown from the same plant species, the defining characteristics lie mostly in how the tea is processed.

Fortunately, for tea drinkers, there's been a recent expansion in the availability of *whole-leaf teas* as opposed to teabags. Many cafés and restaurants now serve whole-leaf teas for their tangible and visual nature and above all, quality. When the leaves are whole and unbroken, the flavor's full intensity appears in the cup. On the flip side are teas graded as *cut-tear-curl* (*CTC*). These crushed bits of tea leaves are the result of mechanical processing and not necessarily love and care. CTC leaves are commonly used to make tea bags.

In Part 4, we introduce you to a variety of specialty teas, from black to green to white to *tisanes*. You learn where these teas are grown and under what conditions, how they taste, tips for brewing and blending (creating a signature blend of many teas) them, and finally, building off of this knowledge, how you can host a cultural tea custom or ritual. Outside the United States, tea is often considered a sacred beverage and is so rooted in culture that its presence continues to be celebrated today.

It would take a very long time to sample your way around the teas of the world—it's estimated there are over 2,000 tea types. And that's what makes the journey of learning about tea fun—it's endless. It's also affordable, with the cost per cup relatively inexpensive for the consumer.

Buzz Words

Whole-leaf teas are such that the leaves are large and intact. To earn this grade, the tea leaves cannot be broken. **CTC** (which stands for **cut-tear-curl**) black teas are produced by machines that lightly crush the leaves to begin oxidation while chopping it into small pieces. The teas are commonly used for bagged teas and tend to be of lower quality than traditionally produced orthodox teas.

Tisanes, sometimes called herbal teas, are considered nonteas because, instead of tea leaves, they consist of the flowers, leaves, and roots of other plants. Tisanes are typically caffeine-free. Learn more about tisanes in Chapter 18.

What Is Tea?

Tea leaves—whether green, black, oolong, white, or pu-erh—sprout at the top couple inches of the *Camellia sinensis* plant and are then picked by workers. These leaves are leathery in texture and with strong veins. Workers at tea gardens cultivate the plant either from seedlings or cuttings from a parent plant that has been a good producer. It takes about 3 years for a tea plant to be ready for harvest, and the height of harvestable plant should be a minimum of around 3 feet. A *Camellia sinensis* plant can grow much taller, but much of the time it is pruned. These plants contain caffeine, so you won't ever find a caffeine-free tea leaf that grew on this plant, although some tea-plant varietals are naturally low in caffeine.

Even if you've not seen *Camellia sinensis*, you've probably already noticed the vast variety of teas—how the dry tea leaves look and also what color the water in your cup turns when the leaves are added. A cup of tea can be sage, crimson, amber, or shades of gold, and these are only a few examples.

Tea is grown primarily in China, India, Japan, Sri Lanka, and Taiwan, comprising a tea belt that runs mostly through Asia. Tea is also commercially grown in Russia, Kenya, and Argentina, although teas from these nations are not commonly found at the retail level in the United States. One commercial tea garden exists in South Carolina, and Hawaii is trying to raise specialty teas, but it may be a while before we see those teas on grocery-store shelves.

> **Buzz Words**
>
> All tea leaves come from the *Camellia sinensis* plant. The leaves are picked from the top of the plant.

> **Field Notes**
>
> For about 25 years at the beginning of the nineteenth century, tea was grown in South Carolina as an experiment. While it prospered, it also proved too expensive to produce commercially. Currently, and with the help of a strong culture of tea-lovers in the United States, there's a small movement to revive those fields in South Carolina and try to turn them into a profit.

Areas where tea is grown are commonly called gardens, no matter what the size. And while topography changes from country to country, even within the tea-growing nations, some landscape conditions are necessary for the *Camellia sinensis* plants to prosper:

- The climate should be tropical or subtropical.

- The recommended elevation is between 3,000 and 6,000 feet, where the air is cooler and slows down leaf growth.

- Rainfall should be between 80 and 100 inches per year, and even though monsoons are a threat in many of the tea-producing countries, as long as they're not extreme, the tea will be fine. Regular, seasonal monsoons cause the plants to go through a growth spurt, which only aids them.

You may have seen the word *flush* used when referring to tea varietals. This is another word for the sprouting of new leaves and buds on the *Camellia sinensis* plant. Within one season, a plant will typically have up to three flushes, although it can certainly

Buzz Words _____

Flush is when new leaves and buds sprout on the tea plant.

have more or less depending on the gardens' caretaking and intent and growing conditions. First-flush teas are often prized for their delicate nature. Just like the Beaujolais wines of France are celebrated with each release, so are those first flushes of Darjeeling in early spring.

Darjeeling, a region in India, is well known for the different flavors that emerge with each flush. Each flush tastes different, creating a lot of variety even in one type of tea.

Types of Tea

Teas come in a few main varieties:

- Green
- Black
- White
- Oolong
- Pu-erh

A tea earns one of these names not because of how it was grown—because all tea comes from the same plant—but in how it was processed.

Green teas are considered by many to be the most healthful. People in China and Japan consider it not only necessary but also practical to drink green tea daily, as it's thought to aid digestion. Many Americans consume green tea as an accompaniment to a diet or weight-loss plan. Green tea has about one third the caffeine of black tea, so it's a good choice for people who are cautious about caffeine.

Field Notes _____

Green teas represent most of the teas grown in China, although green tea is also grown in Japan, where matcha (a powdered type of green tea) is used in the traditional tea ceremony.

Black teas are fully oxidized and often have a strong taste, which makes some people big fans of these teas. When brewed, black teas provide a reddish-brown infusion.

White teas are produced primarily in China and are considered a rare tea. The tips of buds, not the leaves, are picked and processed. White tea has a sweet and mellow taste and a bright orange-yellow hue in the cup when brewed.

Oolong tea looks different from other teas in that the leaves are twisted as the final stage in processing, bringing added flavor when brewed. Oolongs are mostly produced in India and China. In Chinese, *oolong* translates to "black dragon."

Pu-erh (pronounced *poo-air*) teas are named for the providence of Yunnan in China. While they are indeed robust in flavor, the teas also are an acquired taste. Pu-erh teas are commonly sold in cakes or bricks. To brew, you just break off a chunk.

> **Cuppa Wisdom**
>
> You can never get a cup of tea large enough or a book long enough to suit me.
> —C. S. Lewis

Tisanes: Herbal Infusion

Outside the five major tea types are tisanes, which are also referred to as the nonteas. No doubt you're familiar with chamomile, rooibo, peppermint, lavender, and fruit-flavored (blueberry and strawberry, for example) teas. These are all tisanes.

In Chapter 18, we discuss the world of tisanes and the ingredients they might contain, such as dried fruits, spices, herbs, and leaves. Tisanes are usually bold in color and have a lot of dimension.

The Discovery and Spread of Tea

Tea has such a deep, rich history that it traces back several centuries—so many centuries, in fact, it's impossible to say what year and in what city tea was first drunk, because it's debatable. While the details are different from parable to parable, we do know that tea was first discovered in China around 2700 B.C.E., according to written records.

Emperor Shen Nong (dubbed a "Divine Healer") is credited as being the first to find tea. According to legend, water was boiling in his garden when a *Camellia sinensis* leaf fell into the pot. Sometimes the best culinary discoveries happen by accident!

Knowledge of tea spread throughout China, across different dynasties at the same time. Historical accounts vary, mainly because there was not one word used for "tea," making it difficult to translate meaning in records that were kept. But around twelfth century B.C.E., King Wen, founder of the Zhou

> **Field Notes**
>
> Steeping the tea leaves was a culinary concept that had not yet been discovered, so the leaves—raw, pure, and not blended with any other ingredients—were simply tossed into a pot of boiling water.

dynasty, was given teas as a form of tributary offerings from tribal heads. Tea was brought into a regal status at that point, and because it was still rare—successfully growing the tea was a concept still being worked out—it was considered even more of a jewel.

Tea in China

During China's Sung dynasty (420–479 C.E.), tea was highly regarded as a form of medicine, as a way to rid the body of light ailments or maintain good, strong health. Aiding digestion and liberating lethargy were the two most common prescriptions.

> **Cuppa Wisdom**
>
> One should clean out a room in one's home and place only a tea table and a chair in the room with some boiled water and fragrant tea. Afterwards, sit and allow one's spirit to become tranquil, light and natural.
>
> —Li Ri Hua, Ming dynasty scholar

The tea was bitter and unpleasant, perhaps due to primitive processing methods (raw leaves were dried and pounded, formed into cakes, and pieces later broken off for brewing). The taste improved during the Chin dynasty (557–589 C.E.) when people began experimenting with salt and spices to flavor the teas, changing the face of tea from medicine to gourmet product.

Word of teas spread to Japan sometime during the Sui dynasty when Buddhist monks who were in China temporarily brought some back home. This is when tea as currency emerged. (Tea tax was first recorded a few years later, during the T'ang dynasty, 620–907 C.E.) Tea leaves were steamed, pulverized, and shaped into bricks for easier trading and shipping, and also used as a form of currency when tea's value increased, which we will talk about later in this chapter.

Today, tea is a social phenomenon, a reason for people to meet, a beverage of comfort to a friend, and an accompaniment to a meal just as milk, coffee, soda, or juice are. But this culture dates to the Song dynasty (960–1279 C.E.), when tea was first equated with art and people began meeting over tea. Whereas before tea was drank mostly in private, residential settings, now there were tea rooms and teahouses—still popular in China today—in which to do the same. Exquisite ceramics emerged as servingware, too, a foreshadowing for the Yixing pottery teaware from China's Jiangsu province first used in the 1500s.

During the Ming dynasty (1368–1644 C.E.), the variety of teas blossomed. With variety came passion for the product and a sense of procurement in developing new kinds of tea via different processing methods. Trading came into play during the Ming dynasty, and that's how tea arrived in Europe. Also during this time, the types of teapots, kettles, and serving accessories expanded so that it was more than just pottery. Ceramics in the fabled blue-and-white designs we still see today were introduced. Up until this time, bricks and powder forms of tea were quite common and made the best sense for long trade route; now people could brew with loose tea leaves, too.

Tea remained China's hottest export, and when the means to ship globally improved, so did tea's economic impact on China. Starting in the early 1600s, tea had a dual role for the Chinese as a profitable business venture and also as a popular drink.

Later, during the nineteenth century, tea plants were exported from China to countries like Japan, Java, India, Sri Lanka, Russia, Iran, Turkey, Indochina, Taiwan, Sumatra, and the Fiji Islands. Some of these nations were successful in growing tea, but China remains a successful supplier of teas, as does India, Sri Lanka, and Japan, with India being the largest tea-producing country.

Field Notes

Lu Yu is a poet often associated with China's tea culture. In 1780 he wrote *Book of Tea*, which dissected the presence of tea in people's lives up until that point, how it was both an offering and medicinal beverage. Written almost like a manifesto, the book provided instruction in growing, preparing, and sipping tea.

Cuppa Wisdom

Tea, though ridiculed by those who are naturally coarse in their nervous sensibilities, will always be the favorite beverage of the intellectual.
—Thomas de Quincey

Tea in Japan

The Japanese have their own legend of how tea came to their country. An Indian monk who often fell asleep during his regular meditations vowed to never let this happen again. His solution? To cut off his eyelids. When he tossed those eyelids on the grass beside him, a tea plant blossomed, which allowed him to make cups of tea—and never be tired again.

As we cover in Chapter 20, the tea ceremony in Japan is an art form and embodies spiritual philosophy. Each utensil used must be handled in a set fashion, and the décor and ambiance has strict rules. But the focus is on stillness and appreciation, both for the tea and the host.

Tea in India

Today India is a country rich in tea gardens and tea drinkers, but it wasn't always this way. During the seventeenth century, teas were imported from China and access was reserved for the wealthy. All this changed when, in the 1820s, indigenous tea plants were discovered in India near its border with Burma. Now India could cultivate its own tea, an idea the British government favored. In fact, in the 1830s, the commissioner of Assam put in a request that the forested areas in Assam (in northwestern India) be replaced with tea plantings, using seeds from the plants found near Burma. Tea gardens were created soon after in Assam, as well as Darjeeling, growing high-quality black teas. Today, tea in India—black tea, which is the most common—is often served with milk, sugar, and spices (cardamom, ginger, and cinnamon, as well as others).

> **Cuppa Wisdom**
>
> We had a kettle; we let it leak: our not repairing it made it worse. We haven't had any tea for a week … The bottom is out of the Universe.

Tea in England

Until the late 1600s, tea was brought into England through Holland, a practice that ended when the British East India Company (a group of wealthy British merchants) convinced the monarchy to ban Dutch imports of tea, essentially creating a tea monopoly. Tea quickly became a popular drink, further fashioned by Charles II and his bride and their well-known tea-drinking habits. Reports are that tea replaced alcohol as the most popular beverage. Whereas women were expected to not drink coffee at coffeehouses during the 1700s—because coffee was considered a masculine beverage—it was perfectly fine to drink tea. Then, in 1717, Thomas Twining (the man behind Twinings, a tea company still in business in the United Kingdom) opened London's first teahouse: The Golden Lyon. Tea continued to attract people and, fortunately, the price was affordable.

> **Field Notes**
>
> England's appreciation for tea is quite sincere. High and low afternoon teas—with paradoxical meanings: high is casual; low is more formal—are offered in fine hotels, restaurants, and even at home.

Methodist reformer John Wesley argued that buying tea was a poor purchase and people should spend their money on food instead. Wesley chucked all this, though, when he became ill and someone offered him tea, which pleased him at the time. Dr. Samuel Johnson, who wrote the first English dictionary, referred to himself as a heavy tea drinker, thus passing this sentiment along to many through his writings. By 1800, it's reported that people in England were consuming 5 billion cups of tea a year.

Other countries, of course, caught onto the tea boom. Holland, Russia, Morocco, and Africa, and of course the tea-producing nations themselves all saw increased tea consumption. During the late 1600s, Russia and China signed an agreement to bring the tea trade across Mongolia and China, thus providing Russians with access to tea.

Tea in America

Tea has become very popular in America, with the culture of specialty loose-leaf teas growing. Articles in food and lifestyle magazines discuss not just the healthy aspects of drinking tea, but how to brew tea at home and procure fine-quality teas. In short, tea is part of the lifestyle.

Tea was the American colonies' third-highest import during the mid-eighteenth century, even though a limited variety of teas were available. To dress up their tea, people added sugar and peach-flavored leaves. Their love for tea really took a blow when King George declared a high tax on teas, which caused the

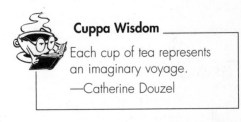

Cuppa Wisdom

Each cup of tea represents an imaginary voyage.
—Catherine Douzel

Boston Tea Party. On December 16, 1773, colonists dressed up like Mohawk Indians and tossed 340 chests of the tea into Boston Harbor, making a statement that tea was to be gone and coffee would replace it. Similar demonstrations were held in Philadelphia, New York, Maine, and North Carolina during 1773 and 1774 in response to the Boston Tea Party.

Then, in 1830, U.S. duties on tea imports were reduced and tea somewhat returned to its previous status as a beloved beverage. This time, though, tea shared the role with coffee, which had become increasingly popular during the time tea was scant. During the 1840s, new clipper ships (large ships designed to handle cargo) brought tea imports from China fairly swiftly, at least faster than they had been previously.

The United States Tea Act of 1897 was created and passed to set standards for not only sanitation of teas entering the United States but also their purity, to ensure low-quality teas weren't being masked as high-quality teas. The U.S. government appointed the Board of Tea Experts and Tea Examiners, whose main job was to examine and inspect all tea entering the country. That group is still active today.

In 1910, Thomas Lipton—who owned tea gardens in Ceylon (now Sri Lanka)—took a bold move and started to blend and package teas in New York. He started a revolutionary idea, where a tea branded in the United States was made available to Americans much, much easier than before, mostly through the 300 grocery stores he owned. Soon the teas became a common household product and continued to be that way into the rest of the century. Most grocery stores today carry Lipton teas.

Tea-Related Inventions

Over time, many products and new ways of thinking have been introduced to the tea world. One such invention was the tea bag. In 1908, John Sullivan, a tea seller in America, stumbled onto a new way to distribute his teas: in hand-sewn little bags with a string on the end. The teas were premeasured and made steeping much easier.

Tea remains largely a skilled-labor industry, but even so the reliance on technology to pick and process leaves has increased. Harvesting machines were invented during the twentieth century, allowing tea to be processed at a much faster rate, and coincided with John Sullivan's teabag invention, too. Along with cheaper labor, harvesting machines also brought lesser-quality teas. Instead of grabbing only the best buds, the machine might yank onto a branch or many leaves, not being necessarily discriminate as a person hand-picking would be.

And while tea was served hot for many, many centuries, finally someone had a brilliant idea to make it iced. At a trade exposition in the early 1900s, a British man decided to add ice to his hot tea, mostly to combat his customers who were suffering with the day's heat wave, starting what you might call America's love affair with iced tea.

Tea for Medicinal Purposes

As we mentioned earlier, after tea's discovery in China it was initially considered a prized, rare beverage and then a form of medicine. If someone was dealing with an ailment from a common cold to a life-threatening illness, tea was prescribed, not so much as the only treatment, but as a supplementary aid.

During the early 1600s, the Dutch East India Company, in an attempt to make extra money, began to market tea as an exotic medicinal beverage. The only problem with their plan was that the prices they put on tea were so high that only the very rich could afford it. So the idea never fully caught on. But when it became more widely available—crossing economic groups—people bought into it. In 1657, London's Garway's Coffee House was the first place to sell brewed tea as a health beverage.

Today a handful of tea purveyors market their teas according to health needs—such as sore throat, stomachache, or mental energy—as opposed to flavor or area of origin. Tisanes are probably the largest example; peppermint and ginger are suggested for curing upset stomachs and lavender is sold to promote drowsiness. Hundreds of articles are written about the health impacts of tisanes when suffering a cough, common cold, or other ailments.

Tea as Currency

Many instances in history exist where instead of coins or paper bills as a form of currency, people used tea. During some of the dynasties in China tea had such high economic value, it served as a method of payment. Countries that used tea bricks as forms of currency include China, Tibet, Siberia, and Mongolia. In fact, Siberians paid in tea bricks up until World War II.

In the 1800s, the British Empire was suffering financially but still wanted its tea. To import teas from China, it offered payment in silver, but when this was not enough, it paid with opium poppies, as the Chinese were fans of opium. The British East India Company sold off its opium crop in Calcutta for silver and stored the silver in Canton, where it was then traded for tea. But the arrangement soon took a downward turn. In 1839, the Chinese emperor demanded that 20,000 chests of opium be burned. This was the start of the Opium Wars; opium was deemed legal by the British and remained that way until 1908.

The Least You Need to Know

- Tea was discovered in China sometime around 2700 B.C.E. when an emperor was boiling water in his backyard under a *Camellia sinensis* plant. A single leaf fell into his pot, flavoring the water, and tea was born.

◆ All tea leaves and buds come from the sprouts on top of the *Camellia sinensis* plant. Today, some 2,000 varieties of tea have been identified and cultivated.

◆ The idea that tea has medicinal qualities was a widely accepted philosophy during the 1600s and is believed to be true even today.

◆ Tea had such great economic value during many of the Chinese dynasties that it became a form of currency.

Chapter 16

Growing and Processing Tea

In This Chapter

◆ Where and how tea is grown

◆ How the vast array of teas are made from a single plant

◆ A look at tea-grading terminology

◆ Ways tea is decaffeinated

It's hard not to fall in love with tea's amazing variety and complexity. Specialty tea shops often have a few dozen teas on hand, and their visual diversity is enough to challenge the notion that all teas come from the same plant. But all teas—whites, greens, oolongs, blacks, and pu-erhs—are indeed from the same bush, *Camellia sinensis*. From the small pellets of gunpowder green to the short, flattened leaves of a Dragon Well green, much of the variety you see in teas is the result of careful processing.

Tea also shows a lot of individuality in the cup, with flavor profiles ranging from the delicate and savory nature of a Silver Needle white tea to the malty boldness of an Assam black. And whether light and fruity best suits your palate, or it's a big, mellow cup you're after, you can find a tea that fits the bill.

In this chapter, we take a look at how all this diversity is coaxed out of the buds and leaves of a single plant.

Growing Good Leaf and Bud

As with coffee, the great care and attention farmers dedicate to producing high-quality crops is what separates specialty grades from ordinary or commercial crop quality.

New tea gardens and plantings are usually stocked with nursery-raised seedlings from cuttings and leaf clonings rather than seeds. This allows farmers to select hardy plants and those known to be good producers. After 2 years or so, when the tea plants have grown to roughly 5 or 6 feet high, they are pruned to about 1 foot tall. Regular pickings begin shortly after the bush is allowed to grow out a bit again. The plants are then kept to about waist tall.

The World's Tea Gardens

Camellia sinensis, the evergreen bush from which tea is made, is grown throughout the world but thrives in hot and humid environments. Although you're most likely to encounter teas from China, India, Japan, and Sri Lanka, tea is grown in many countries (more on this in Chapter 17).

Tea quality is affected by many of the same environmental factors that influence coffee quality, such as the soil, growing and weather conditions, and the specific varietal. The best teas are grown at relatively high altitudes in tropical and subtropical climes. The combination of humidity and altitude slows the plants' growth and produces better-tasting tea.

Made in the Shade: Gyokuro and Matcha

Gyokuro and Matcha, top grades of Japanese green tea, get part of their distinct tastes from the special preharvesting treatment they receive. Farmers cover or otherwise shade the tea bushes for approximately 3 weeks before picking, which forces chemical changes in the leaves and buds as they adapt to the reduced light. The process softens the tea's character a bit, imparts a little natural sweetness, and accounts for some of the higher cost of these teas.

Plucking and Harvesting

Most specialty tea is harvested by hand because superior teas start with careful plucking (save in Japan, where tea shears are typically used). Sorting during processing ensures that lower-quality material is removed, but it's important, too, that the tea be plucked and handled so it remains in good shape until it's processed.

Depending on the location and growing conditions, a number of pickings, or flushes, occur each season. Each flush has unique cup characteristics, which makes exploring the world of tea all the more interesting, as you can taste and follow the subtle changes in a given estate's teas with each successive flush, for example.

Tea Processing—What Color Is Your Tea?

Teas vary in flavor characteristics depending on the growing conditions, but the most dramatic variance in tea results from the specific method used to process the buds and leaves into dried tea. Understanding the primary processing methods and resulting tea types will help you get a good idea of what to expect when you encounter unfamiliar teas.

White Tea: The Innocence of Youth

While still somewhat new to many Americans, white tea is made using centuries-old techniques and is distinguished from other teas in several ways. White tea is minimally processed and composed of the tender young buds and leaves of the tea bush plucked in early spring. White tea can be made from any number of varietals, but modern white teas are made from a select few that are noted for their fleshy buds alive with little white hairlike fibers. While some white teas are made entirely of buds, like Silver Needle, others, such as White Peony, include the two uppermost leaves as well. Either way, these special teas offer a pale infusion with delicate nuances that are often sweet as well as savory. Most white tea is produced in China, although it is also made in India and Sri Lanka.

Producing high-quality white tea requires a lot of attention to detail from the tea maker. Timing is everything with white tea, and it all starts with the harvest. The buds must be plucked when

Cuppa Wisdom

The best quality tea must have creases like the leather boot of Tartar horsemen, curl like the dewlap of a mighty bullock, unfold like a mist rising out of a ravine, gleam like a lake touched by a zephyr, and be wet and soft like a fine earth newly swept by rain.

Field Notes

If you're new to white tea, White Peony (also known as Bai Mu Dan) is a great introduction. It has white tea's hallmark subtle nature, but its toasty nuttiness is more obvious to uninitiated palates. An added perk is that White Peony tends to be a relatively inexpensive white tea.

they're nearly ready to open, and rain and inclement weather can make this a tricky balancing act. After it's plucked, the tea must be immediately withered and then baked dry or steamed. Temperature and humidity greatly affect the process, and off colors and flavors can result if it's not managed well.

Green Tea

Sometimes referred to as unfermented tea, green tea is specially processed to preserve the green nature of the freshly harvested leaves by preventing the enzymes in them from oxidizing. To do this, the leaves must be heated to stop the enzyme activity. This can be accomplished in several ways, including roasting, pan firing, steaming, baking, sun-drying, or by combining two or more primary methods. The method employed depends on the cup profile the tea maker desires as well as local processing traditions. Most Japanese green teas are steamed, while the majority of Chinese greens is roasted or pan-fired.

Regardless of the method used to heat the leaves and stop the enzymatic activity, the leaves become supple and pliable, at which point they are rolled. The rolling process can be accomplished mechanically or by hand and helps determine the final shape of the tea leaves. How the tea is shaped depends on the region where it's grown and the grade of tea being produced. After the rolling phase is completed, which can actually involve several rolling steps, the tea is dried to roughly 4 percent moisture to ensure shelf stability. The resulting teas have a distinct vegetal character (think fresh peas or grass) and give a pale, relatively light-bodied infusion.

Ooh, Oolong!

Considered by many connoisseurs as the most complex type of tea, oolongs are allowed to oxidize to some degree before they're cured. This puts the character of these teas somewhere between that of greens (which are not oxidized) and blacks (which are fully oxidized).

Knowing the approximate degree of oxidation will give you a general idea of what to expect from the tea. Lightly oxidized oolongs tend to brew a relatively pale infusion and have somewhat delicate cup profiles akin to green teas but with fresh floral and fruity notes instead of the pronounced vegetal character. Heavily oxidized oolongs brew rich amber infusions much like black tea but with less heft and perhaps more finesse. They tend to be fruity, floral teas like their less-oxidized cousins but with more power in the cup. Regardless of the level of oxidation, oolongs tend to have "layers" of flavor such that each successive infusion uncovers a bit more of the tea's unique nature.

Produced primarily in China and Taiwan, the process for making oolong begins shortly after harvesting when the leaves are allowed to wither. The tea is then shaken to lightly bruise the edges of the leaves. This exposes the natural enzymes within the tea leaves to the air, allowing them to oxidize and staining the leaf a darker color. When the desired level of oxidation has been achieved, the leaves are fired to halt the process. The leaves are then rolled and dried to stabilize them.

> **Field Notes**
>
> Pouchong tea is a subcategory of oolongs that are lightly oxidized and have a sweet, delicate floral character. They are commonly used as a base when making scented teas.

Black Tea

The most commonly drunk tea in the United States, black tea is made from tea leaves that have been allowed to fully oxidize. The result is a tea that gives a reddish-brown infusion with sizeable body and power in the cup. The individual cup character of black teas depends, of course, on the region where it was grown, that season's climatic conditions, and the specific varietal from which the leaves are plucked.

To make black tea, the leaves are first allowed to wither after harvesting and are then rolled to start the oxidation process. Then the leaves are spread out and allowed to fully oxidize. At this point, the leaves turn a coppery red. The process is completed by firing and drying to halt the oxidation and to stabilize the leaves.

Black teas are often referred to as orthodox or CTC (cut-tear-curl), depending on their specific manufacturing process. Orthodox teas are produced in the traditional fashion, whereas CTC teas have been minced and curled into little balls by specialized machinery. Relatively good CTC teas can be found, but they're typically of lower quality than high-quality orthodox teas. Bagged black teas are commonly made from CTC teas.

Pu-erh

Named for a trade center in China's Yunnan providence, pu-erh tea (pronounced *pooair*) is in a class of its own. Having a robust, organic, or earthy character, these teas tend to be an acquired taste. Sometimes called an aged black tea, pu-erh teas are produced quite differently from blacks—and all other teas, for that matter. Pu-erhs are made from leaves and buds of broadleaf tea varietals that are withered and dried in the sun. From these sun-dried leaves, several forms of pu-erh are made.

The oldest type of pu-erh is variably referred to as uncooked or green pu-erh. Most commonly pu-erhs are found in compressed form, which may take the shape of bricks, round cakes, mushrooms, or even small bird nest–like bowls. To make compressed uncooked pu-erh, the sun-dried leaves are steamed until they're pliable and are then pressed to shape and dried. When dry, the compressed pu-erh is aged—often for years—which allows the tea to slowly ferment and change character. With time, the tea mellows and its flavor improves much as does the character of a fine wine that needs time for its youthful nature to mature. The same is true of loose-leaf green pu-erh, which is simply not steamed and compressed.

> **Hot Water** _____
>
> Age is complimentary to pu-erh tea, and so its price and flavor appreciate with time. Some aged pu-erhs, both loose and compressed, command hundreds of dollars, but even more recent vintages can cost quite a bit. Shady traders have sometimes counterfeited aged pu-erh cakes, so be sure you do your homework on the dealer and the particular tea before you plunk down a bundle on "vintage" pu-erh tea.

In the early 1970s, tea makers began to experiment with methods of accelerating the aging process, and by the middle of the decade, black or cooked pu-erh tea was born. The resulting method approximates the effects of the slow natural process but can be completed in a few months. The process begins just as it does with green pu-erh, but before the tea is finished (compressing and/or final drying), it is fermented in piles. The fermentation phase is essentially very carefully controlled composting. Depending on the size of the piles and the environmental factors such as temperature, tea makers add specific amounts of water. The tea is then carefully monitored and manipulated to ensure proper conditions and even fermentation. To help control the rate of fermentation, the pile may be covered or uncovered and is stirred regularly.

When the fermentation phase is complete, the tea is either dried as loose tea or first steamed and compressed. Like its more traditionally processed cousin, black pu-erh comes in a variety of shapes and sizes.

Making the Grade

After the tea is processed, it's sorted and graded by appearance and size, from whole leaves to dust. Grading terminology varies somewhat by region and also depends on the type of tea, but generally speaking, higher grades consist of whole-leaf teas made from young leaves and buds or entirely of tender buds; lower grades consist of broken leaves and dust, or fannings. While the primary grading criteria are not directly related to cup quality, the highest grade of any given tea is typically the best that tea has to offer. However, it's possible to find lower grades of quality tea superior in the cup to the finest grade of other teas.

So it's fair to wonder what the point of grading is. Separating the pieces of any given tea into like sizes ensures even brewing. It's the same concept as having a consistent grind when brewing coffee, and without it, brewing a good cup would be difficult.

Cup quality has more to do with the individual teas than their grades, so specialty tea buyers may have to sample a number of lots before finding one that fits the desired flavor profile. At the consumer level, considering grading isn't as crucial as choosing a specialty tea purveyor that wades through the masses of tea and only stocks the high-quality finds. It's better to drink a "common" grade of tea that excites your palate than a "reserve" grade of tea that's rather unremarkable.

Field Notes

Black tea has its own common grading system, and it's useful to be familiar with it. In fact, you've already stumbled onto it if you've ever wondered what made Orange Pekoe (pronounced *PECK-oh*) so orange. Rather than indicating the citrus flavor, the term refers to a specific grade of orthodox black tea.

Generally speaking, the younger the material and the larger the pieces that comprise the tea, the higher its grade. The primary grades, from lowest to highest, include pekoe, orange pekoe, and flowery orange pekoe. The terms *golden* and *tippy* refer to teas that contain some buds in addition to leaves, with tippy indicating more bud presence.

Decaffeination

A tea's caffeine content depends on the cultivar used, the growing conditions, and part of plant used (buds, leaves, or stems), as well as how it is processed. The U.S. Food and Drug Administration requires a 97 percent reduction in caffeine content before a tea can be labeled "decaffeinated," and although not perfect, modern decaffeination processes are very effective.

As it is with decaffeinating coffee, when decaffeinating tea, the challenge is to remove the caffeine without removing desired elements and, therefore, disrupting the tea's flavor profile.

Field Notes

Generally speaking, caffeine accounts for approximately 1.5 to 4.5 percent of tea's weight.

There are three primary approaches to decaffeinating tea:

◆ Methylene chloride

◆ Ethylene acetate

◆ Carbon dioxide

Each brings its own pros and cons.

Methylene Chloride

Methylene chloride is a very effective solvent for caffeine and is commonly used in decaffeinating tea. It can be applied either directly or indirectly. In the former scenario, the solvent is used to extract the caffeine from tea that's been premoistened with water. After the tea has been separated from the caffeinated methylene chloride, it's washed to remove the remaining solvent. Minute traces of methylene chloride are allowed to remain after the tea is washed, but it's not currently thought to be a health hazard.

> **Hot Water**
>
> Even though the level of methylene chloride is fairly small, some tea drinkers avoid teas decaffeinated by this method because methylene chloride is considered a probable human carcinogen by the Environmental Protection Agency.

Teas decaffeinated indirectly with methylene chloride—meaning the tea material and the solvent never actually interact—are first soaked in water. The caffeine-charged water is then treated with the solvent, which bonds with the caffeine. To remove the caffeine and methylene chloride from the water, the mixture is heated until they evaporate. The tea is then allowed to soak in the water again to regain some of the flavor components that were initially extracted along with the caffeine.

Both methods of decaffeinating with methylene chloride have a central drawback: the aggressive solvent extracts more than just caffeine from the tea. As a result, teas decaffeinated this way tend to have a less full flavor profile.

Ethylene Acetate

Decaffeinating tea with ethylene acetate is similar to using methlyene chloride. The solvent extracts the caffeine from the premoistened tea and is then removed and rinsed from the leaves.

Some tea drinkers feel better about the use of ethylene acetate because its materials occur naturally in some fruits and plants, including tea. In fact, teas processed with this method are often referred to as "naturally decaffeinated."

The ethylene acetate does, however, impact the tea's flavor. It tends to clip the cup profile a bit and can add an artificial fruitiness as well.

Carbon Dioxide

When highly pressurized, carbon dioxide assumes a super-critical state and has properties of both a solid and a fluid. At this point, it becomes an efficient solvent for caffeine. The compressed carbon dioxide is pumped into a chamber with the tea. It extracts the caffeine, and the carbon dioxide is separated from the tea and carbon filtered to remove the caffeine. Then the CO_2 is recycled, and the process repeats until the tea is sufficiently decaffeinated.

While the most expensive decaffeination method, compressed carbon dioxide is also the most selective solvent, which means more of the rest of the tea is preserved. Not only does this have less impact on the flavor, but it also ensures more of the tea's health-promoting compounds make it to your cup. Like those decaffeinated with ethylene acetate, teas processed using this method are often referred to as "naturally decaffeinated."

Do-It-Yourself Decaffing

Believe it or not, you can reduce the caffeine in your own tea at home. Simply infuse the tea for about 30 seconds and then discard the water, which contains a majority of the tea's caffeine. Naturally, caffeine isn't the only thing extracted, so the flavor may change a bit. The results vary somewhat by tea, but this method works well with most whole-leaf teas. This is especially handy in a pinch, but it's important to remember that the resulting drink will not be fully decaffeinated (reportedly 20 to 25 percent may remain).

The Least You Need to Know

◆ Tea—whether it's white, green, oolong, black, or pu-erh—is made from the buds and leaves of the tea bush, *Camellia sinensis*.

◆ White teas are made from young tea buds and leaves that are minimally processed.

- To preserve its green character, green teas are heated immediately after harvesting to stop enzymatic activity in the leaves.

- Oolong teas are allowed to oxidize to some degree, which determines if their cup character is more akin to that of greens (for lightly oxidized oolongs) or blacks (for heavily oxidized oolongs).

- Pu-erh tea is made from the sun-dried leaves of broadleaf tea varietals that are then aged, either through prolonged storage or by an expedited pile-fermentation method.

- Teas may be decaffeinated using methylene chloride, ethylene acetate, or carbon dioxide.

Chapter **17**

Teas of the World

In This Chapter

- ◆ The wonderful world of white teas
- ◆ A look at Japanese and Chinese greens
- ◆ Find out more about intriguing and unique oolongs
- ◆ Learn about classic black-tea producing regions and their teas

The world of tea is made rich and exciting by all the unique teas available today. And although only a portion of the diverse array makes it to the United States, still, American consumers can purchase literally dozens and dozens of teas. Add to that all the proprietary blends and combinations offered by tea retailers, and it's easy to become a little overwhelmed. If you've ever innocently dropped in to a tea shop just looking for a little black tea, for instance, and were barraged with 20 to 30 options, you know exactly what we mean.

No worries, though. It's all really quite manageable when you break it down a bit, and that's just what we do in this chapter. Teas vary somewhat reliably according to their types, and it's the most likely way you'll encounter teas, so we first break them down in that manner. Then, we explore some of the primary tea-producing regions and kinds of tea you're likely to find at your local tea shop. Our goal isn't to introduce every possible tea, but this chapter should equip you with the knowledge necessary to deepen your journey into the delicious world of tea.

White Tea

White tea—like the delicate silvery hairs on the backs of the young leaves and buds that comprise it—is cherished for its subtly and mildness. Today, you can occasionally find white teas from regions outside China, but the market is still largely dominated by Chinese whites.

Field Notes

If you run into a white from a region that doesn't tradition-ally produce these teas, look to the region's more typical teas for insight on how the white might taste. For example, a white Darjeeling tea is likely to show some of its signature fruity, mus-cat notes to the cup character.

The following are three whites—all produced in China—that are most commonly seen on the market:

White Peony   Sometimes referred to as Bai Mu Dan, White Peony is a classic. Mild like all whites but with less subtlety, it serves as a wonderful intro-duction to this gentle class of teas. It is made from the buds and surrounding two leaves. At once sweet and savory, White Peony expresses herbaceous and nutty notes in the cup.

Silver Needle   Alternately called Yin Zhen, Silver Needle is perhaps the best-known and most highly regarded white tea. It gets its name from the slender, needlelike appearance of the buds from a special tea bush varietal. Comprised entirely of buds picked in early spring, this prized tea is often more expensive and limited than other whites. In the cup, expect a natural sweetness to accompany subtle savory, slightly herbaceous notes.

Snow Bud   Xue Ya, or Snow Bud, is well regarded for its somewhat greener charac-ter than other whites. It does have the subtle sweet-savory character typical of this type of tea, but it also has vegetal notes akin to greens. Therefore, it makes a wonder-ful white for those who usually prefer greens.

Green Tea

Minimally processed, green teas have been traditional favorites in many Asian tea-drinking cultures. Not surprisingly, the nations consuming the most green tea—Japan and China—are also the most prominent producers. Occasionally, you'll run into a green tea from regions that traditionally produce black teas, like India or Sri Lanka. If you're familiar with the region's blacks, in most cases, these unique treats have fairly predictable flavor profiles. For example, a Sri Lankan (Ceylon) green is likely to display a crispness akin to its blacks, but with vegetal flavor notes.

Japan

Japanese tea is synonymous for green, as that's all Japan produces. Although agriculture land is at a premium, the Japanese are noted for their innovative tea farming practices. But the Japanese are such voracious tea drinkers and their culture so tea-focused, that the vast majority of its tea never makes it out of the country.

Generally speaking, Japanese greens are gently steamed rather than being fired or roasted like most Chinese greens. Their character is fresh and vegetal—from soft and gentle like buttered peas to more bracing and astringent—and is often described as "grassy." That may not immediately sound appetizing to everyone, but these teas have a large fan base devoted to their nourishing cup character.

> **Cuppa Wisdom**
>
> Thank God for tea! What would the world do without tea! I am glad I was not born before tea.
>
> —Sydney Smith

Following are some of the most common Japanese greens:

Gyokuro   Sometimes referred to as "precious jade dew," Gyokuro is Japan's most premium tea. It gets its darker, more saturated leaf color and unique cup character thanks to special handling before plucking. About 3 weeks before harvesting, the plants are covered or heavily shaded, which forces the plant to produce more chlorophyll (darkening the leaves) and lower quantities of tanninlike compounds (softening the flavor). This prized tea is often reserved just for special occasions, as its cost makes it hard for most to justify it as an everyday tea. Reserve grades of this smooth, refreshing green can easily run more than $15 an ounce, although less special grades can be found more inexpensively.

Matcha   This powdered green tea is a top grade of Japanese green and is whisked into a frothy beverage during the tea ceremony. Like Gyokuro, matcha is produced from plants that are shaded for about 3 weeks prior to harvesting. Once plucked, the soft, young leaves are processed like other greens before the stems and veins are separated from the rest of the leaf. Then, the tender remaining leaf particles are ground to a fine powder. Intense and simultaneously slightly sweet and astringent, this is a truly unique green tea.

Sencha   Known as an everyday tea in Japan, Sencha is actually available in a range of grades, from quite common and inexpensive to much the opposite. Unlike Gyokuro and matcha, Sencha is grown entirely in full sun. First-flush Senchas are prized for their mildness and fresh, vegetal character; subsequent flushes are brisker and more assertive in the cup.

Bancha   Because it's made from the older, tougher leaves after the harvest of the young leaves for Sencha, Bancha is considered a lower grade of tea. As you might expect, the coarser material used for Bancha gives a less refined, though somewhat milder, flavor than Sencha. All the same, this relatively cheap tea is worth trying and is naturally low in caffeine.

Houjicha   A relatively new tea (developed in the last hundred years), Houjicha is roasted Bancha. Also low in caffeine, Houjicha, not surprisingly, has a rich nuttiness and toasted character. Many are fond of its soothing flavor and relatively low cost.

> **Cuppa Wisdom**
>
> If man has no tea in him, he is incapable of understanding truth and beauty.
>
> —Japanese proverb

Genmaicha   Another favorite sporting toasty flavor notes, Genmaicha is Bancha mixed with puffed rice (some also add popped corn). Originally, the rice was added to stretch the more costly tea, but today Genmaicha has found a devoted following. Due to its popularity, it is now sometimes made using better grades of tea.

Kukicha   An example of another innovative way to produce more tea on the same acreage, Kukicha, or twig tea, has become a staple green tea. That's right, this tea has tender stems mixed with leaves, providing a unique, savory flavor that's become an everyday favorite. Kukicha is naturally low in caffeine and provides a nourishing infusion marked with subtle herbaceous and chestnut notes.

China

Although generally overshadowed by Japanese greens, China produces a substantial amount of fine green tea. A key difference is that greens produced in China are traditionally pan-fired to inactivate the leaf enzymes (as opposed to steaming, which is most commonly used in Japan). Tending to be somewhat less freshly vegetal and nuttier in character than their Japanese counterparts, Chinese greens certainly expand the variety available to green-tea enthusiasts. Be sure to check out China's offers in addition to Japan's as you explore the world of green teas.

Field Notes _____

Most tea importers are not native speakers of the languages spoken by the tea makers they purchase from, so some things—like proper spelling—have become blurred over time. Therefore, don't sweat it if you encounter a tea spelled with a slight variation to what you've become familiar. In all likelihood the teas are the same, and what really counts is how it tastes, right?

Some Chinese greens you're likely to encounter include the following:

Dragon Well   Also referred to as Long Jing, Dragon Well is one of China's best-known green teas. This traditionally processed tea, whose namesake is a local landmark, is pan-fired and then pressed flat. In the cup, Dragon Well offers delicate notes of steamed peas and chestnuts, complimented by a natural sweetness.

Gunpowder   Rolled tightly into tiny balls, gunpowder tea somewhat resembles its namesake. Add to that its dark color and tendency to be somewhat smoky in the cup, and you have a very distinctive tea. This hearty green tea is commonly used as the base for Moroccan-mint blends.

Pi Lo Chun   Sometimes also called "green spring snail," Pi Lo Chun gets its name from its tightly spiraled and rolled leaves. It has long been prized as one of China's best greens and, therefore, offered to emperors in tribute. In the cup, it's a smooth, gentle green that expresses its delicate vegetal character without being bracing or overpowering.

Green Pekoe   Gentle and soothing, green pekoe is a popular everyday tea with fans of Chinese greens. It also tends to be relatively inexpensive, so sampling this fresh, slightly sweet tea won't set you back.

Oolongs

With hundreds of different oolongs made, this class of tea epitomizes tea's variety. And while you'll occasionally come across oolongs from other regions, the vast majority is produced either in mainland China or Taiwan. Oolongs tend to have characters somewhere between those of greens and blacks, with more-oxidized teas being more similar to blacks. Regardless of their relative degree of oxidation, oolongs tend to release unique nuances of its flavor profile with each successive infusion.

These are some of the most common oolongs:

Pouchong   The most lightly oxidized of oolongs, pouchongs are in a class of their own. Floral, sweet, and delicate, these teas are an important stop on a tour of oolongs. Pouchongs make an especially good introduction to oolongs for green tea lovers.

Jasmine   Although sometimes green teas are used as a flavoring base for jasmine (either pearls or loose tea), many times it's actually a pouchong. These teas are traditionally scented by exposing them repeatedly to fresh jasmine blossoms, which are discarded after they have infused the tea with their soothing fragrances. Smooth and refreshing, jasmine-scented teas are widely loved.

Iron Goddess of Mercy   Also known as Ti Kwan Yin, this tea is one of the world's most highly regarded and pricey teas. Legend has it that this tea came into being after the Goddess of Mercy found favor with a local farmer and led him to a special tea bush. Falling about midway on the spectrum of possible oxidation, Ti Kwan Yins are fruity, floral teas with silky body and, oftentimes, a natural figlike sweetness. They can be pricey, but good Ti Kwan Yins go a long way, as their flavor just continues to unfold with infusion after infusion.

Field Notes

The world of tea is one of tradition, so you'll most likely encounter teas from Taiwan and Sri Lanka under their colonial names: Formosa and Ceylon, respectively.

Wuyi   Grown in the rugged and misty Wuyi Mountains, Wuyis have round profiles that are smooth and rich. A darker oolong, having been oxidized longer, Wuyi oolongs have fairly heavy body and often display notes of dried fruits. Boasting a broad fanship, these teas make a great introduction to oolongs for black tea drinkers looking to try this exciting class of teas.

Bao Zhong   Like a blast of wild floral notes, this lightly oxidized tea has earned a lot of fans. Bao Zhong is a classic Taiwanese oolong with savory green notes and a natural sweetness in the cup.

Jade   Another common Taiwanese tea, Jade oolongs are lightly oxidized. They have the typical oolong sweetness and bring a floral quality to the cup that conjures images of blooming lilac bushes in spring.

Tung Ting   Considered by some to be one of Taiwan's finest teas, Tung Ting is a lightly oxidized oolong. This ingratiating tea is gently toasty and mild with a light, floral character.

Oriental Beauty   Also known as Bai Hao, Oriental Beauty is at once delicate and rich. Moderately oxidized, this tea has a relatively full body and features notes of honey and fruit reminiscent of peaches.

Blacks

Whether it's taken black or with milk and sugar, black teas are the most commonly drunk teas in many Western societies. Black teas make up a large and fairly diverse class of teas, with most tea-producing regions creating at least some of these popular teas. The most commonly encountered blacks are made in China, India, and Sri Lanka. All black teas have been fully oxidized and tend to be fairly big-bodied.

China

China is the birthplace of tea and, appropriately, where the methods for making black teas were developed. The process of fully oxidizing the tea was first done to extend tea's shelf life so it could better make the long trade journeys. And that China's black tea hooked whole societies certainly serves as a testament to its high quality. Chinese blacks show up in a lot of blends, where they lend weight and depth, as well as on their own.

Here are a few Chinese blacks you're likely to find:

Keemun Perhaps the best-known Chinese black teas, Keemuns are regarded as some of the world's finest. Used in many signature breakfast blends, these teas are rich and complex with an elegant, winelike body and considerable heft. Some common flavor notes you might find in high-quality Keemuns include bits of caramel, cacao, dates, smoke, flowers, fruit, and a mellow, sweet earthiness.

Yunnan Another classic Chinese black tea, Yunnan teas are made in China's southwestern-most province of the same name. It's believed that tea is native to the area, which is home to ancient tea plants several hundred years old. Full-flavored and rich, Yunnan's teas have long maintained the attention of a large base of devotees.

Lapsang Souchong This distinctive tea gets its smoky pungency from special processing. Both during withering and final drying, the tea is heated over a pine fire. Although not everyone's cup of tea, its robust, hearty nature has won many faithful fans.

> **Field Notes**
>
> Sometimes you'll encounter teas, especially blacks, marketed as "self-drinking." This funny-sounding term is usually levied as a compliment and denotes a tea that tastes great without the addition of milk and sugar.

India

For years the British, who rightly suspected India as suitable for growing tea, tried in vain to grow Chinese tea cultivars in India. In 1823, however, a related tea plant growing wild in Assam was discovered, and soon India was on its way to becoming a high-volume tea producer. Today, India is one of the largest tea producers by volume and supplies a significant portion of the blacks—especially as CTC teas—consumed worldwide.

Let's take a look at the Indian black teas you're most likely to come across:

Assam   With its high altitudes and greenhouselike mix of high temperatures and humidity, it is not surprising that Assam teas make up about half of India's total annual production. In the cup, Assam teas are malty, robust teas with substantial body. This makes Assam a prime candidate—either as a base for a blend or on its own—for "breakfast" teas, both for its hearty flavor and its sheer power in the cup.

Darjeeling   This region's fame for its bright, fruity black teas—whether it's in the form of raisinlike flavors or those closer to apples—is due to a couple of factors. In the foothills of the Himalayas, Darjeeling has rich soil, sky-scraping altitudes and lots of cool, humid air. But Darjeeling has another trick up its sleeve: rather than growing the Assam tea-bush varietal, the more cold-hardy Chinese bush and related hybrids are raised. Good Darjeelings have a desirable astringency along with sweet notes of flowers and muscat grapes. The much-celebrated first-flush Darjeelings, the first pluckings of spring, are prized for their unique character, which has qualities of both greens and blacks. Second flushes tend to be bolder and rounder, with a more filled-out flavor profile.

Nilgiri   Nestled in the Nilgiris Mountains in the Southern India, this steamy growing region produces tea year-round and about one quarter of India's total. Big-bodied and packing plenty of strength, these smooth blacks make good bases for building blends.

Hot Water

As is often the case with popularity, India has struggled to keep counterfeiting from diluting the strong reputation its major growing regions—Assam, Darjeeling, and Nilgiri—have earned. This has been especially challenging in the northern regions of Darjeeling and Assam, which border tea-growing regions with much less notoriety and lower tea prices. For the most part, though, consumers needn't be too concerned about the authenticity of their Darjeelings if they're buying from reputable tea retailers.

Chai   Famous for its preference for combining tea with spices and milk, the Indian word for tea, *chai*, has become universal for tea doctored similarly. Expect teas sold as chai to be heavily seasoned with a variety of spices, such as cardamom, cinnamon, ginger, black pepper, anise, and clove. Many specialty tea blenders have embraced creating signature chais much as specialty coffee roasters have the classic Mocha Java blend, and it seems nearly all sell one or more unique interpretations.

Sri Lanka

Sri Lanka, India's island neighbor to the southeast, also produces a lot of high-quality black tea. Sri Lanka's interesting story began in the late 1800s, when a disease destroyed most its coffee trees. This forced farmers to look for alternative crops, and tea farming took off.

With year-round tea production and some of the world's highest tea estates, Sri Lanka was at one time—as recently as the early 1990s—the world's largest tea producer. Most of the Sri Lankan tea you'll find is labeled as Ceylon, the nation's colonial name. Akin to Indian teas, Ceylons brew a bright, copper-colored infusion that has ample body and is noted for its brisk nature. It has been a very popular tea iced, thanks in no small part to Sir Thomas Lipton.

Africa

While many of the nations along Africa's eastern coast produce tea, most of it is CTC-processed and used for bagged blends. Occasionally, though, you'll stumble across a well-prepared orthodox African tea (Kenyan is seen most commonly), which is a worthy treat. These teas tend to be fairly bright and lively teas with fruity flavor notes. They're usually medium-bodied and have a natural fruitlike sweetness.

Pu-erh

Made from broadleaf tea varietals in China, pu-erh is uniquely processed, and is, to many, somewhat an acquired taste. Available in both loose and compressed forms, it's most often seen compressed into various shapes. The most common shape is referred to as *toucha* and resembles tiny bird's nests.

Larger cakes, which may weigh several ounces, often demand considerable investment, so it's

Field Notes

Pu-erh's unique, rich flavors can be overpowering at first for some palates. One way to ease into pu-erhs is to try a pu-erh–based blend in which complementary tisanes, such as chrysanthemum flowers or ginger, are matched to the earthy tea.

often best to buy these directly from a tea shop. Doing so gives you an opportunity to sample a cup before buying a cake.

Blending In: Common Flavored and Blended Teas

Over time, blending trends have come and gone, but a few blends have been such crowd-pleasers as to become standards. Blenders often create their own slight interpretations of these classics, but the underlying blend stays fairly consistent across blenders.

Here are a few of the most frequently encountered blends:

Earl Grey   Flavored with oil of bergamot, Earl Grey is a traditional British blend. The teas used vary by blender, but you can usually expect a brisk yet silky cup profile and sweet floral and citrus notes.

Irish Breakfast   Bold and malty, this blend is driven by big-bodied Assams and can easily stand up to milk and food.

English Breakfast   Like its Irish cousin, English Breakfast teas are blended with food and milk in mind. Because fatty foods and drinks coat the tongue, delicate flavors in accompanying beverages are easily lost. English Breakfast blends traditionally rely on Indian, largely Assams, and Sri Lankan black teas to provide the necessary *oomph*. However, they tend to be somewhat less robust and heavy-bodied.

There you have it—your cheat sheet and starting point for exploring the vast world of teas! We covered a lot of teas, and you're bound to encounter others. Not to worry, though, as you can usually get a pretty good idea for how a tea might taste by knowing where it was produced. Also, you can use the teas you just learned about as a reference and ask your tea purveyor to compare a tea to one you're already familiar with.

Happy exploring!

The Least You Need to Know

- ◆ A key difference between traditional Japanese and Chinese teas is that the former are steamed and the latter are fired.

- ◆ Chinese greens tend to be nuttier and with a less-pronounced vegetal character.

- ◆ China produces the majority of oolongs.

- ◆ Assam, Darjeeling, and Nilgiri teas are named for their respective growing region in India.

- ◆ Pu-erh teas are a Chinese specialty and owe their intriguing, earthy flavors to unique processing techniques.

Chapter 18

Tisanes: The Herbal or Nontea Teas

In This Chapter

- ◆ What are tisanes?
- ◆ Discover rooibos and yerba maté
- ◆ Learn how to properly brew tisanes

Tisanes (*tee-sawns*), also called herbals or infusions, are actually nonteas. They're composed of fresh or dried fruits, flowers, seeds, roots, and berries. While completely different from the teas you read about in Chapter 17, which are made from leaves of the *Camellia sinensis* plant, tisanes still have a special spot in tea culture as self-prescribed medicinal beverages and also as aromatic wonders. Tisanes also have a caffeine-free advantage in most cases, appealing to people who cannot or do not want to consume caffeine.

You're probably familiar with some tisanes, such as chamomile and peppermint, but two have emerged in the past few years and gained acceptance: rooibos (*roy-bus*), from a red bush in South Africa; and yerba maté (*yur-bah mah-tay*), a drink native to South America.

We're seeing more and more varieties of tisanes, in part because they continue to be marketed as health-conscious—a big draw in today's specialty beverage world. They are also popular teas with children, as they are often sweet and fruity, more pleasing for their younger palates than, for instance, a pu-erh or green tea.

In the following pages, we explain the various tisanes, how to get the best flavor possible when brewing, and the folklore history of some of the most commonly used ingredients.

An Introduction to Tisanes

When talking about the history of tisanes, it's really more about the folklore in herbalism and apothecary. The interest in these two topics the monk population took during the Middle Ages helped to further the resources available to people, whether they were creating delicious infused drinks or trying to cure an illness. Monks studied intensely in Europe, balancing the transcription of ancient journals about herbs with the actual herbs they were encountering.

Field Notes

Many tisanes are full-bodied, and there's much intensity and flavor packed into the cup. Historically, tisanes were used for medicinal purposes and aphrodisiacs.

The Egyptians, Chinese, and Indians were practicing herbal medicine 4,000 years ago. Knowledge later spread to the British, Romans, and Americans. Information was passed on through the practitioners' careful note-taking, and over time, these notes were printed into books. One of those first books was the *Pen Tsao Ching* (or *The Classic of Herbs*) by Emperor Shen Nong, also credited with discovering the *Camellia sinensis* plant around 2700 B.C.E. Locals considered him an expert in herbal medicine, and his book detailed 300 known herbal remedies (which other herbal experts added to over time) and also outlined principles of Chinese medicine.

Simpling is a practice developed centuries ago—and still in place today—where only one herb at a time is experimented with to make a tisane, so you can learn what is good all on its own and what needs to be paired. The benefit of sampling is so you intimately get to know an herb's body, flavor, and—one by one—how it pairs with other ingredients.

You've no doubt seen several single-source tisanes on the market; peppermint and chamomile are two great examples. Because they taste wonderful on their own, there's not always a need to meld them with other herbs. However, not every herb is able to shine solo; some desperately need to be joined with another herb to create a positive flavor profile because their inherent taste is flat or weak.

Field Notes

Simpling is experimenting with one herb at a time to make a tisane. It's still common practice today.

When shopping for tisanes, look for the following:

- **Body.** Think of this as the platform for all other flavors in the tisane. You want to start with a full-bodied choice, to ensure dimension will be added to the cup.

- **Flavor.** While the definition of perfect flavor is going to vary depending on who you talk to, you should look for a complement of flavors, with high, middle, and top notes. In other words, no one flavor should be aggressive and overwhelm the other notes in the tisane. Flavor can be obtained in a tisane, not just with natural herbs but also with essential oils.

- **Color.** Color abounds with tisanes, whether it's the color of a brewed cup or a few ounces of dried or fresh ingredients that make up the tisane. Pretty much any color you desire can be obtained—although you probably already know that aesthetics does not drive taste in the tea world—from light yellow-green (chamomile) to a bright red (hibiscus).

Many of the tisanes currently available are commercially cultivated, but quality has certainly not been lost.

Common Tisanes

Two of the most common tisanes are rooibos and yerba maté, and it's only been within the last few years that many mainstream tea retailers have begun to carry them in the United States. Both have health benefits, are caffeine-free, and are quite distinct from all other tisanes.

Rooibos

Rooibos is sometimes referred to as Red Bush and marketed as a red tea. Rooibos comes from a red bush grown in South Africa's southwestern Cape region. (Historically Khoisan, Bushmen, and Hottentots used rooibos to make "tea";

commercial cultivation only began in the 1930s.) A bush can grow up to 5 feet tall, and its prickly leaves and stems are harvested in summer—which in South Africa is from January to March. During harvesting, the plants are cut so they're just 1 foot tall.

When brewed, rooibos is a stunning orange-red color. It tastes neither bitter nor sweet and is often blended with other herbs to create more body. Natives in South Africa add sugar and milk to rooibos, just as they do with black tea, but that's not commonly done here in the United States (so far). No matter how long you steep it, rooibos won't become bitter.

Recent studies have revealed that rooibos has much of the same antioxidant benefits of green tea but lacks caffeine because it's not from the *Camellia sinensis* plant. (Because it comes from the red bush, it is naturally caffeine-free, and also contains only about 5 percent tannin content.) Rooibos is also the only known natural source of aspalathin, a potent antioxidant. Tea purveyors have suggested that rooibos can help with allergies, insomnia, digestive problems, and headaches, but there aren't yet any scientific studies to back this up. In South Africa, rooibos is suggested to soothe infant colic.

Cuppa Wisdom

Great love affairs start with Champagne and end with tisane.

—Honoré de Balzac

Fermentation causes the rooibos leaves to be orange-red in color. With fermented rooibos, the green leaves and stems have been bruised and fermented and then immediately dried in the sun to prevent oxidation. Commercially processed rooibos is done in the same matter as it was hundreds of years ago by indigenous people, with a few tweaks changed due to the availability of sophisticated tools.

You can also find a different kind of rooibos called green rooibos, which is unfermented. Unfermented rooibos contains more polyphenol antioxidants, because some antioxidants are typically lost during fermentation. Green rooibos is tan-yellow when brewed. It's rare that you'll find green rooibos, but in case you do, at least now you know how it compares with regular rooibos.

Yerba Maté

Yerba maté is still fairly new to the United States, but it's become very well liked in a short period of time. The drink has its roots in South America—Paraguay, Brazil, Bolivia, Uruguay, and Argentina—and was introduced by the Guarani Indians of Paraguay and Argentina. Yerba maté is the name of the plant that produces it; its leaves are evergreen with four-petal flowers that are small and green-white. The plant also produces a red berry.

Yerba maté's hallmark is its grassy taste, and so it hasn't been the best drink to all people. Either you like it or you don't, and it tends to be an acquired taste. Combining brewed yerba maté with steamed milk adds a little bit of sweetness.

Yerba maté has also found followers among the health-conscious, as the drink provides a rejuvenating effect. Yerba maté does contain naturally occurring caffeine, however, so those following a strict no-caffeine diet should be aware. This drink does invigorate the mind and body, so it's considered a "natural" stimulant.

South Americans enjoy yerba maté for health benefits, too, and believe it boosts immunity, cleanses and detoxifies the blood, tones the nervous system, combats fatigue, stimulates the mind, controls the appetite, reduces stress, and eliminates insomnia. It's also been claimed to reduce effects associated with a debilitating disease.

> **Field Notes**
>
> In South America, yerba maté is commonly drunk in a small group, sharing the beverage by collectively drinking out of a gourd with a *bombilla* (*bahm-BEE-ya;* straw). When traveling throughout this region, it's not uncommon to see couples and groups sipping in a park in large cities, and in a more rural environment, ranchers doing the same.
>
> *Yerba maté* is often shortened to *maté.* You might find the abbreviated name on packaging.

A handful of tea companies in the United States market a line of maté concentrates flavored with lemon, chocolate, vanilla, and chai. These can also be added to steamed or cold milk, which may well be enticing to people who like a sweeter, creamier drink, or at least those who aren't interested in the dry, grassy version.

You may encounter both roasted and unroasted maté. Roasted maté is processed just like it sounds, by roasting as one would with coffee beans. The result is a bit of a dark-chocolate taste you would not find in unroasted maté. Some of the nutrients are thought to be lost when roasting maté.

More Sparkle in Your Cup

If we were to list all the possible herbs one can include in a tisane, it might read like a laundry list. Literally, the options are endless. Instead, we've listed the most common ones, which are affordable and easily obtainable, and will add sparkle to your cup.

Barley Roasted barley is popular with Koreans and the Japanese. It's caffeine-free, so it's considered a coffee substitute and sometimes drunk cold during the summer months. Barley has been cultivated since Neolithic times and was beloved by Egyptians and Greeks.

Chamomile Chamomile is used as a sedative or relaxant, something to drink before bed, as it calms the body and mind. Of all the tisanes, chamomile has one of the richest histories, stories that have crossed into different cultures that all had an appreciation for it. In ancient Egypt, it was dedicated to the gods and deemed a cure for acute fever. In Spain, it was called "little apple" and used to flavor light sherry. Incense was a popular use for chamomile in Rome, as were beverages. In fact, during the nineteenth century, a man who found chamomile growing in a coliseum there named it Roman Chamomile.

Chrysanthemum Many Chinese restaurants brew pots of chrysanthemum as a regular standard and a popular pairing with dim sum. Boiling water is poured over the dried white/yellow flowers, creating a sweet aroma and a delicate flavor. This tisane is known for its cooling properties and has been suggested for curing a fever, sore throat, and other heat-related illnesses.

Citrus There are many forms of citrus, but the most commonly used ones for tisanes are bergamot (an ingredient in Earl Grey) and dried peelings of lemon, lime, and orange. Bergamot is often used to cure nausea, common colds, and the flu, as well as ease pain associated with a tight chest, coughing, digestive problems, and sinus troubles.

Echinacea Tisanes with echinacea are often suggested for people suffering with a common cold or even the flu, and during the cold winter months—when a bout of flu is more likely to occur—it is sometimes drunk regularly, as a means of hopefully preventing serious illness. Native Americans relied on echinacea for tonic uses.

Fennel Fennel is commonly used in soups but also is popular as a tisane. The Mediterranean herb is licorice-flavored and was once listed as an official drug by the United States, designated for use in easing digestive problems. Not surprisingly, it's also a chosen herb for people with gastrointestinal and menstrual cramps, heartburn, and diarrhea.

Ginger   Real pieces of ginger root added to boiling water to make a tisane can help people with stomachaches, nausea, or motion sickness. Ginger has been grown in tropical areas of Asia since ancient times, and in the sixteenth century, it was introduced to Africa and countries in the Caribbean.

Ginseng   Ginseng is usually blended with other herbs to make a tisane. Chinese herbalism believes that ginseng can enlighten the mind, increase wisdom, and give longevity. Ginseng tends to have a strong, rooty taste that many find unpleasant, which is why it's blended with other herbs.

> **Field Notes**
>
> In the seventeenth century, it was common to have wildcrafted teas—teas collected from wild habitats all over the globe. The best example is ginseng, which during the nineteenth and early twentieth centuries, became virtually extinct. Today ginseng is grown commercially and still satisfies the buyer's need for a healthy boost. Wildcrafting of herbs still occurs in the Ozark Mountains as well as other rural spots.

Hibiscus   As you will read in Chapter 20, hibiscus is a popular beverage in the Middle East and is served both hot and chilled. In Japan, hibiscus is associated with longevity. Often hibiscus is blended with rosehips to make a beverage. Hibiscus contains citric acid and vitamin C and is also rich in calcium, niacin, riboflavin, and iron.

Honeybush   Honeybush grows in the Cape of South Africa, and while it's similar to rooibos, the taste is sweeter. The amount of honeybush commercially cultivated each year is growing, and in some countries, it's deemed a substitute for tea.

Kava   Kava has its roots in the South Pacific, where today it grows abundantly on Polynesian islands and is known to promote feelings of relaxation, create ease in talking, lessen depression and anxiety, and loosen tight muscles. Kava is a member of the black pepper family. In Fiji, Samoa, and Tonga, kava is drunk at ceremonies that honor visitors.

> **Cuppa Wisdom**
>
> Your head is affected most pleasantly. Thoughts come cleanly. You feel friendly … You cannot hate with kava in you.
> —Tom Harrison

Lavender   Lavender is known for creating a calming effect, whether it's through raw aroma or eating or drinking something that contains lavender as an ingredient. Lavender tisanes smell wonderful, and drinking them provides the added health benefit of quieting the body's nervous system. The flowering buds on top of the lavender plant are used to make tisanes, and the color of the drink is a light purple-blue. In Europe, it's common to use a lavender essential oil to cure anxiety and sunburn.

Lemon myrtle   Lemon myrtle comes from a tree native to Australia's Queensland region of coastal rainforest. The aroma is a combination of lemongrass, lime, and lemon.

Lemongrass   Food dishes from Thailand and Vietnam often include lemongrass. It wasn't until the 1970s that lemongrass started being used in herbal tea blends in the United States. Today it's commonly used for tisanes and acts as a central nervous system depressant as well as an antifungal aid.

Licorice   Licorice is sometimes used in a blend to hide the taste of bitter, unpleasant herbs. Native Americans in the eastern United States believed licorice combined with hot water could cure coughs. Egyptians, too, had faith in its healing properties (some have said that licorice sticks were found in King Tut's tomb), including soothing and coating a sore throat and preventing stomach ulcers.

Mint   Mint eases stomach pains but is also beloved for the bright, refreshing taste it brings. Crisp and astringent, it's a flavoring in everything from chewing gum to lamb and is very popular as a tisane. In the Moroccan culture, peppermint leaves are boiled in water with green tea and sweetened with sugar. Mint tisanes are great to drink after eating a heavy meal.

Rosehips   Often you'll a tisane that blends hibiscus with rosehips, which are high in vitamin C—more than that of oranges—and also serve as a laxative aid. Rosehips also contain vitamins A, B, E, and K, and because of its organic acids and pectins, rosehips has also been used as a laxative.

Rosemary   Rosemary is well regarded for its aroma and as a seasoning for lamb, but the herb can also stimulate circulation and get rid of migraines. Chinese doctors have blended rosemary with ginger to create a treatment for indigestion, insomnia, and malaria.

Cuppa Wisdom

As for Rosemary, I let it run all over my garden walls, not only because my bees love it, but because it is the herb sacred to remembrance, and, therefore, to friendship; whence a sprig of it hath a dumb language that maketh it the chosen emblem of our funeral wakes and in our burial grounds.

—Sir Thomas More

Sweet and Fruity Cups: Brewing Tisanes

In Chapter 19, we give you instructions for brewing tea. The methods are about the same for tisanes, but the variables are tweaked here and there to enhance the best flavor.

You should use about 2 grams tisanes per cup (about 1 teaspoon), but don't stick to this rule always. Depending on body, flavor, and intensity, a tisane may require more or less to satisfy the palate.

It's okay to use ceramic or glass teapots or cups, just as you would for teas. Metal is not advised, as it can sometimes leach undesirable metals into your infusion. Because tisanes have more volume than most other teas, you will want to use an infuser that fits snugly into the cup or teapot, as opposed to a wire mesh strainer or tea ball, which packs the tisanes very tight and does not allow enough space to circulate.

Generally speaking, steep tisanes 5 minutes. Of course, you should feel free to play around with different times, noticing how a few minutes longer or a few minutes left affects taste.

> ### Field Notes
>
> All tisanes can be brewed and served with ice to make an iced beverage. Some examples of iced tisanes are rose hips, lavender, and a blend that contains berries and hibiscus. To make an iced tisane, pour 2 rounded teaspoons dried herbs (3 if you're using fresh herbs) over ice cubes. Wait until the ice cubes have melted before drinking; the melted ice dilutes the strong herbs. You could also brew the tisane as you normally would—hot—and then chill it in the refrigerator. The beverage will, of course, need to sit for quite some time to cool down.

The Least You Need to Know

- Tisanes are not teas because they do not come from the *Camellia sinesis* plant.
- Two of the most popular tisanes are rooibos and yerba maté.
- It's best to infuse tisanes in something other than a tea ball or handheld infuser to allow the herbs to circulate as much as possible.
- Many tisanes claim to have health benefits, from relaxing to stimulating.

Chapter 19

Blending and Brewing Teas

In This Chapter

◆ Learn why blending matters: uniqueness and enhanced flavor

◆ Get tips on blending teas at home

◆ Discover the keys to bringing out the best from each type of tea

From garden to teacup, making great-tasting tea is at once an art and a science. But it's during blending and brewing that we consumers get to have an active hand in the process. In this chapter, we provide an overview of the blending process as well as some practical consideration to bear in mind as you begin designing your own blends. We then take a look at how to best bring tea's flavors to the cup—whether it's a delicate white tea or a bold pu-erh.

When brewing, you want to pay close attention to water temperature and infusion time, but even before this, you're faced with a lot of options about what kind of teapot or infuser to purchase. We explore some key points to consider when shopping so you can find one that fits your brewing needs.

Blended Teas = One-of-a-Kind Flavor

The world of teas is endless, comprising many different flavors, colors, and cultural origins. The number of single-origin teas is projected to be around 2,000, but when you add blended teas to that number, it becomes immeasurable.

When blending, tea manufacturers combine teas with one another or add ingredients like essential oils, dried fruits, herbs, and spices. Aside from creating a unique tea, there are several other reasons to blend:

- Flavor—both introducing and contrasting
- Adding body
- Aesthetics (texture and color)

Because the market of teas can shift—one year's crop of a certain tea might be quite different from the previous or have a distinct contrast to the next—tea manufacturers have relied on blending. If the tea is of a lesser quality, they can still have a consistent flavor profile by adding a few ingredients. This is also a solution for teas that are difficult to find consistently, or if a natural disaster wrecks a crop one year, making it unavailable.

Also, from a marketing standpoint, tea companies can really pull away from the pack if they have signature, branded teas no other company has. For instance, apricot–Earl Grey–raspberry–spice (we're just making this up) is less likely to be sold at a competing tea company than Darjeeling first-flush tea. In some cases, a company might give a fun name to the tea, such as something that evokes island living, an emotion, or a historical moment.

It's possible to blend teas at home, too. You might not have access to hundreds of teas, or the types of flavoring agents tea companies have (which are expensive and not available to anyone outside of manufacturers), but you can still play around with flavor using ingredients found in your kitchen, or after a quick trip to the grocery store. In the process, you'll probably learn a lot about the teas, because when they're matched with other teas or a certain dried fruit, new flavor notes emerge.

Cuppa Wisdom

When we sip tea, we are on our way to serenity.
—Alexandra Stoddard

History of Blending

Teas were first blended in seventeenth- and eighteenth-century Africa, and the ingredients for each were separately stored in glass jars before the blending process began. It was also common in England beginning in 1870 with Twinings.

Irish Breakfast, Earl Grey, and English Breakfast are good examples of teas for which the tea company was trying to get a reproducible flavor profile and wanting to stretch the most expensive leafs and use the less-expensive ones at the same time.

Field Notes _____

Twinings is credited for creating Earl Grey, a blend of tea flavored with oil of bergamot, a citrus fruit. Later, the tea company, owned by Thomas Twining, shifted gears and produced a variation of that tea.

Today, tea blending is intentional and carefully thought out, but not all teas started honestly on behalf of the tea merchant. Outside of flavor, stretching teas was important, and while that's not so applicable to home blenders, it's still good to know.

Getting Started

In some ways, creating a tea blend is just like matching up a romantic couple. You become acquainted with each and start to think how the two can coexist in harmony but also enhance each other.

Your ingredient options are nearly limitless. We suggest orange, lemon, vanilla, cinnamon, ginger, rose petals, lychee nuts, and honey. In some cases, you might be able to explore the differences between liquid and dry forms.

Hot Water _____

Large tea companies use liquid and dry forms of flavorings in their teas, but because the kitchen-grade products available to home consumers aren't the same quality as what manufacturers can get their hands on, adding a desirable flavor that doesn't disrupt the makeup of a leaf is very, very challenging. Feel free to experiment, but know that your best bet for blending might be to just blend the teas themselves, staying away from liquid forms of flavoring.

Field Notes _____

Tea manufacturers commonly use a stainless-steel table to blend teas, but we're guessing you don't have one in your kitchen. So just find a cool surface or large mixing bowl, and you'll be fine.

To blend, simply scoop all the ingredients together into one pile, making sure they're evenly distributed. We recommend you wait a day or two before tasting the blends, to give the flavors time to meld. The mixture continues to marry the flavors the longer it sits, so you might want to play around with the time factor.

How much tea should you purchase? We recommend a couple ounces (of each tea) for every time you blend. This gives you more than enough to work with. Begin by brewing a cup of each tea separately so you can become intimately aware of what those teas bring to the table, which flavors you want to pronounce, for instance. Take notes on the body, flavor, and any other remarkable qualities in the tea.

Blending Tips

When blending teas, your goal should be to build a blend in which the whole is greater than the sum of two parts, and to create a particular flavor profile. What you think may taste full-bodied and flavorful may in reality end up being weak and unmemorable. You really have to be patient until that first "right" tea blend comes along.

If you decide to blend for flavor, it's usually best not to include more than three teas. Otherwise, the tastes you have carefully selected can be muddied or masked.

Blending Considerations

Blending two completely different tea types together can be problematic. For example, a delicate white tea would require a lower water temperature, while a pu-erh needs boiling water. Bigger-leaf teas infuse their properties into water more slowly than do small particles. By tweaking your proportions, though, you can nip this problem in the bud.

To get around this, you can also blend two teas that are the same but grown in different regions, or two teas that come from the same region but not the same garden. Altitude, rainfall, and sunshine, as you read in previous chapters, have an effect on how a tea tastes. You might be surprised at the new sensations on your tongue when you blend some of these teas.

And don't forget about aesthetics. Black tea leaves become more vibrant with a simple sprinkling of blue cornflower or dried raspberry pieces. Orange blossoms make a tea of drab light-yellow buds really sparkle.

Blending for the sake of creating body in a tea is another tactic. After you've tasted teas individually, you should be able to pick out what teas have large bodies and can possibly support a tea with less depth.

> **Field Notes** _____
>
> You could combine two teas because of their contrasting tastes. For instance, Yunnan teas have a peppery taste, which might balance well with another black tea that's malty, like Assam.

Brewing—Bringing Out Tea's Best

Brewing a great cup of tea isn't too tough, but because each type of tea needs just a little different attention, it can be tricky all the same. Before getting into the details of brewing individual tea, however, let's take a look at some common considerations.

Putting Your Best Leaf Forward

Perhaps it should go without saying, but we'd be remiss if we didn't stress the importance of buying well-made specialty teas. Commodity-grade teas, which account for the majority of teas available and nearly all bagged teas, just haven't had the necessary care in their production to harness and highlight their potential. The result is tea that has a clipped or flat flavor profile that's lacking the intriguing complexities of well-prepared specialty tea.

It's true that bagged teas are typically made from lower grades of tea, but all is not lost if you're especially fond of the convenience of tea bags. More and more specialty tea purveyors are offering top-quality whole-leaf teas in teabags. Look for companies that make their bags on the roomy side so the tea has ample room to unfurl and properly infuse.

If you haven't tried whole-leaf teas, they're definitely worth exploring. Your taste buds will thank you. These teas really aren't much more trouble to brew than are bags, and you'll uncover types of tea that aren't available in bags. Whole-leaf teas are becoming more and more common in mainstream

> **Field Notes** _____
>
> To help you locate a supply of good tea, we've provided a list of tea companies in Appendix D, including a few that offer bagged teas.

markets, but in many cases, your best bet is to buy directly from importers whenever possible.

Now, what about freshness? Tea is more shelf-stable than coffee, somewhat reducing freshness concerns but not eliminating them. You'll almost always find fresher tea with more of its nuances intact if you get as close to the source as possible. Some of the most prized teas are seasonally harvested and are best consumed within a few months. Good purveyors buy the best of a season's harvest and only as much as they can sell in a reasonable time. And although it may be disappointing to occasionally find your favorite tea temporarily out of stock, it's better than buying an old tea only to learn it's permanently out of flavor.

> **Field Notes** _____
>
> Like the rest of us, every tea buyer has his or her own favorite types of tea, and these are the teas he or she most aggressively seeks out. It's often possible to pick up on these biases, and if you do, be sure to check out those selections, as they are likely to be of very good quality.

Try teas from several retailers until you find a company that stocks teas that are most pleasing to your palate. Good tea buyers sample teas tirelessly until they've located lots that excite them, so the trick is to find one whose preferences are akin to your own.

Storing Tea

Tea has a longer shelf life than does coffee, so it's easier to keep fresh longer. This is especially handy because it's possible to have several kinds of tea on hand—to suit your tastes at a whim—while still maintaining freshness. Teas aren't immortal, however, and do require proper storage to retain their delicate flavors for as long as possible.

> **Hot Water** _____
>
> When storing your teas, keep them away from strongly aromatic foods like spices—unless you want tea *thyme* at tea time.

Teas should be kept in a sealed container away from light and moisture. Glass jars are probably your best bet. Just store them in a cool place in your kitchen, maybe inside a cabinet or cupboard. Or you can store the teas in resealable plastic bags or light-proof storage containers. Whichever method you use, keep the teas out of sunlight if at all possible.

Under good conditions, you can expect your teas to last a few months, losing flavor gradually over time. Do keep in mind, however, that tea's freshness is best gauged from the time it was produced rather than when it was purchased, so buy in small quantities from reputable specialty tea sellers.

Field Notes _____

When you first encounter a $10 tin containing a couple ounces of a fancy-sounding oolong, you're likely to suffer sticker shock. A little tea goes a long way, though. We use about 5 grams for 8 ounces water when brewing, which yields roughly 6 brewings from 1 ounce. High-quality whole-leaf tea often provides multiple infusions while still retaining good flavor—in fact, many oolong connoisseurs relish the delicate nuances unlocked with each successive infusion. With about 18 cups worth of tea per 1 ounce, the cost of that tempting oolong is less than 30¢ per cup. Plenty of teas are even more affordable than this.

Using the Best Water

The water you brew with directly impacts the quality of your brewed tea, as it's responsible for extracting the goodness in tea and it makes up so much of the final product. Tea's delicate flavors can be negatively affected by the chlorine added to municipal water supplies, and well water may be too high in mineral content to properly extract tea. So it's worth the small investment of buying filtered water or using a filter to treat your tap water.

Hot Water _____

Avoid distilled water for making tea—just as you would for coffee—because it lacks the necessary mineral element for a flavorful infusion.

Selecting Brewing Equipment

The range of teapots and infusers available today is perhaps even more diverse than the leaves they're designed to brew. All that variety doesn't mean you'll have to learn a ton of ways to make tea, though, because most are really just a variation on a theme. Most provide you with a handy way of separating out the tea leaves when they've infused long enough. So whether you prefer a mug infuser or a teapot, chances are there's a tea brewer out there for you.

When you're shopping, keep a couple things in mind:

First and foremost, look for equipment that allows plenty of room for the tea to unfurl and expand; otherwise, you won't be able to get as much of the good from the tea because it won't be able to properly infuse. We've seen a number of infusers on the market that handicap their owners from the beginning with infusing baskets that are just too small for the amount of tea they brew. If it doesn't look like there'll be room for at least three times the amount of dry tea you'll use, keep looking for a better infuser.

Hot Water

There's a seemingly endless variety of infusers and pots for brewing tea, but not all afford the leaves enough room for brewing. These tools, like common tea balls and infusing spoons, often do not allow sufficient room for the teas to expand, which shortchanges you on flavor in the cup.

Heat retention is another consideration when shopping for a good teapot or infuser. If you typically brew green and white teas—which call for cooler water and short infusion times—you have a lot of leeway, because heat loss isn't as critical. However, to get the most out of long steepings, like when brewing blacks and pu-erhs, you'll want to be sure your infuser or teapot can properly maintain heat throughout the brewing cycle. Ceramics and cast iron do a good job of retaining heat, especially when preheated, so they make a good choice. We think it's usually a good idea to pass on plastic, though, as it's not good at retaining heat and has a tendency to take on odors and flavors.

A word of caution: while Yixing clay teapots make for some of the most beloved brew tools once the pot is seasoned, these pots need special care and handling and should be dedicated to brewing one kind of tea. Over time and with proper seasoning, these little pots pick up and retain tastes from the teas you brew in them and actually impart some of that flavor into every infusion. While this adds a new and interesting element of depth to the resulting tea, it does mean they aren't suitable as all-around teapots. (Yixing teapots need special care and handling. Follow the manufacturer's instructions to season them and avoid using soap to wash them, unless you like how soap marries with your favorite tea. See Chapter 20 for more on Yixing pots.)

Matching Water Temperature to Teas

To coax the most from tea but without overdoing it (and making a bitter cup), it's very important to use appropriate-temperature water. And because the ideal temperature varies by tea type, it's understandable that improper brewing temperature is one of the most common brewing mistakes.

Generally speaking, the more delicate the tea, the cooler the water needs to be. Sturdy teas, like most pu-erhs and almost all blacks, do best with near-boiling water, but most others need less heat. First-flush Darjeelings are known for their unique, delicate nuances and are a notable exception to the rule for blacks; for these teas, use water that's closer to 190°F.

Greens and whites do best with water that's roughly 180°F, although in cases of very tender types, you might have the best luck with water that's 10°F to 15°F cooler. The best temperature for oolongs depends on whether their character is more akin to greens or blacks. In most cases, 195°F water serves oolongs well, but you may want to use slightly cooler water when brewing lightly oxidized oolongs like pouchongs.

Given the importance of brewing temperatures and that most people don't carry a thermometer with them, it's fair to be a little concerned about achieving the correct temperature. It's not as difficult as it might sound, however. Water right off a boil is fine for most blacks, pu-erhs, and tisanes. Just-boiled water poured into a room-temperature mug tends to lose a minimum of 10°F almost instantly, so it's a good way to speed up the cooling process and prepare it for steeping oolongs. Simply allow the water to cool a minute or two before using it to infuse whites and greens. Exact results vary depending on your specific conditions, but this should get you close enough to allow your taste buds to guide you in tweaking the process.

> **Cuppa Wisdom**
>
> If there is magic on this planet, it is contained in water.
>
> —From *The Immense Journey* by Loren Eiseley

Infusing

When you have the correct-temperature water for the tea you're brewing, the actual process is very straightforward. Simply preheat your teapot or infuser with hot water, discard the preheat water, allow your tea to steep for a few minutes, and then remove the leaves. You can usually guess how long a tea needs to be steeped by looking at the size of the tea material; the smaller it is, the faster it infuses.

Short steepings of 2 or 3 minutes are usually best for greens and whites, although some prefer longer (7 minutes or more) infusions for white tea. If you want to try a longer steeping, it's usually best to use slightly cooler water (165° to 175°F). Oolongs do well with 3 to 4 minutes of infusion, and blacks and pu-erhs should be steeped for roughly 3 to 5 minutes. Some people enjoy very strong pu-erh infusions resulting from very long infusions (15 minutes or more), but that's not a taste for everyone.

> **Field Notes**
>
> For easy iced tea, make double-strength tea by using only half as much water as usual. Then, when you pour the hot tea over ice, it dilutes to the proper strength as well as chills it.

You can also try brewing with cold water for a unique, smooth taste. Use about as much tea to water you would normally use, but infuse with cold water and allow the tea to steep overnight in the refrigerator.

A Tea-Brewing Cheat Sheet

Water temperature? Infusion time? White, green, oolong? Whew! That's a lot to remember! If you're overwhelmed with all this tea-brewing information, relax. Here's a quick cheat sheet to brewing tea you can glance at when you need a refresher.

Tea	Amount	Brewing Temperature	Infusion Time
White	1 TB.	180°F	3 to 4 minutes
Green	1 tsp.	180°F	2 to 3 minutes
Oolong	1 TB.*	195°F	3 to 4 minutes
Black	1 TB.**	205°F	3 to 5 minutes
Darjeeling (first flush)	1 tsp.	190°F	3 minutes
Pu-erh	1 TB.***	205°F	3 to 5 minutes
Tisane	1 TB.	205°F	4 to 6 minutes

Use 1 teaspoon for pearl-shaped oolongs, as they are denser.
**Small-leaved blacks may only require 1 to 2 teaspoons.*
***Use a tablespoon-size piece of compressed cakes.*

The Least You Need to Know

◆ When blending a tea, it's usually best not to incorporate more than three types, because any more than that sacrifices some of the flavors and disguises certain qualities.

◆ Try to have one type of tea as the base to ensure all the components have similar brewing requirements.

◆ Teas require slightly different brewing conditions depending on how they were processed.

◆ The more delicate and less oxidized a tea is, the cooler the brewing temperature and the shorter the infusion time.

Chapter 20

Tea Culture and Rituals

In This Chapter

- A worldwide journey across cultures and tea ceremonies
- Tea ceremonies' place in the modern world
- Tea traditions all your own

You've probably seen movies, wandered around museum exhibits, or even read cartoons detailing how people in a particular culture take their tea. Some countries have a loose, casual approach; in other cultures, formal attire and manners are expected. In many cases, great attention is paid to costume, music, food, utensils, and the location of the ceremony.

In this chapter, you learn about the silent and laborious process Japanese tea ceremonies are known for, or the fancy edibles that accompany high tea for the Brits. When you ask for tea, what you get will vary and will depend on what country you're in when you ask.

In this chapter, we hope to demystify tea customs and practices around the world so you better understand them and would feel confident taking tea while on a trip or among members of a certain ethnic group. Or perhaps you'll want to replicate the other parts (recipes and ambiance) associated with a particular tradition, to bring a true cultural experience to your tea time.

Tea Around the World

In America we have no defining, structured principles as to how we drink tea; nor do we have any universally accepted tea rituals. Basically, we shop for the tea at the store (asking ourselves questions like *Peppermint or Earl Grey? Bagged or loose?*), go home, put on some hot water, and soon we have tea to sip. We might drink tea with friends, alone at night before bed, or in the morning with breakfast. Tea drinking for most is a very laissez-faire concept.

But this in no way implies we lack appreciation for tea. The drink is a staple on most restaurant menus, and few households do not have tea stored in the pantry. (Even so, America is the only country where, upon ordering tea in a restaurant, you will be asked, "Hot or iced?")

It's only in the last 10 years in the United States that tea shops appeared in mass numbers outside Chinatown neighborhoods (the largest being New York City and San Francisco) or inside fancy hotels in metropolitan areas. In cities such as San Francisco, New York City, and Washington, D.C., you'll find tea rooms with a modern twist—places where not only tea is served but also complementary cuisine. Light sandwiches are served if it's of British style, and noodle dishes and cookies if Asian is the theme for the tea. Also, many coffee shops now carry (and brew) a line of specialty teas, which speaks of a commitment to carrying fine quality.

Field Notes

In China, the art of preparing and drinking tea is called *cha dao*.

And while we're in this tea renaissance, it's a perfect opportunity to brush up on other cultures' customs. Sociologists have analyzed tea as a part of social custom and interactions among people, but even at its simplest, tea speaks volumes about a particular culture. Questions about what time of day the tea is drunk, the variety of tea offered, if milk or sugar is added to the tea, and what kind of food it's served with all vary depending on the country.

China: Birthplace of Tea

In part because China can lay claim to the fact that tea was first discovered there, when it comes to tea customs, China is one of the most diverse countries. How one takes tea—and the type of pot, brewing method, and tea itself—varies depending on the 17 different regions—so much so that if you traveled around the country, experiencing tea ceremonies, you would get quite an education along the way.

Yunnan, which is high in the mountains, produces aged pu-erh tea and high-grown black teas. Naturally, this is what the locals drink. Aged pu-erh tea, in fact, is well liked by people in Yunnan for its medicinal qualities. A "tea ceremony" in Yunnan might be as simple as sipping a glass while sitting on a bamboo stool. By contrast, in Hong Kong, the teahouses tend to be more upscale and often serve dim sum (a selection of small dishes served family-style) on fine china and in an equally decorative setting. This type of elegant gathering is called *ah cha* in Chinese.

Field Notes

Cha to (*chah toh*) is the name for China's traditional tea ceremony. Literally, it means "to drink tea."

Buzz Words

Yixing (*YEE-shing*) stoneware (made from purple clay) is from China's Jiangsu region and is commonly used for brewing tea. **Guywan,** a covered cup, is the type of infuser used at most Chinese tea ceremonies.

In most areas of China—in Yunnan and Hong Kong as well as the growing regions of Zhejiang, Hunan, Sichuan, Fujian, and other large cities—the kind of tea set used is a tiny teapot made of *Yixing* stoneware (from China's Jiangsu province) and equally tiny matching cups without handles. The stoneware is handmade of purple clay and is unglazed. Tea leaves are infused in a covered cup called a *guywan*, and a bamboo scoop (or even chopsticks or high-quality tweezers) is used to place the leaves in the cup. Porcelain teapots are also used in China to brew tea.

When the person serving tea is pouring the tea into cups, he or she does this in a circle, with only one long pour for each cup, creating a steady rhythm. Each cup is only filled halfway, out of a traditional belief that the rest of the cup contains friendship and affection.

If the event is not in a traditional teahouse, there aren't a lot of hard-and-fast rules for the type of ambiance to accompany tea drinking in China, but the host always tries to create a warm, relaxing environment and might even play soft music.

Teahouses in China are as common as pubs in England, and serve as gathering points for meeting friends, handling small-business affairs, or relaxing between home and work. Tea is also served at restaurants throughout China and is brought to diners' tables even before the meal begins because the tea is viewed as a refresher, and when the meal concludes, to aid digestion. If you've dined in a Chinatown restaurant in the United States, you were probably brought a steaming pot of tea even before you decided what you were having for dinner. Tea is considered a staple in the meal.

The Chinese are also devoted to their tea for medicinal purposes, and consume green tea more widely than they do white, oolong, or black tea. Aside from social customs, there's a great awareness among the Chinese of natural-healing properties, and many are able to prescribe a tea for a specific ailment.

Tea ceremonies are held in China when a couple marries, a man takes up a concubine, or some sort of life-changing, important occasion happens. The ceremony is formal and heavily influenced by how the elders and ancestors conducted the ceremony.

Egypt: Land of Red Tea

Karkady is the tea most Egyptians enjoy drinking daily, whether it's in a café or at home. The tea is most popular in southern Egypt but is by no means absent from the country's northern culture. Hibiscus, a 6-foot-tall cane that grows wild in Egypt, turns the tea red, which is quite beautiful when served in the traditional clear, tiny glass.

> **Buzz Words**
>
> **Karkady,** hibiscus flowers and sugar with hot water, is a popular tea in Egypt.

Like the British, Egyptians also enjoy an afternoon tea, most times adding lemon, milk, and sugar to a steaming cup. Often, after dinner, a dessert tea of dried mint mixed with tea leaves and brewed in hot water is served.

Great Britain: Flying High (or Low)?

When most people think of the term *taking tea*, the Brits come to mind, with their elaborate displays of finger sandwiches, scones, and cakes. But there's more than one type of tea in Britain.

Low tea is much more of a formal affair, with fine china, expensive linens, elaborate flatware, perhaps arrangements of flowers, the sound of music, and a doting wait staff (if the tea is taking place in a restaurant or café). High tea is a casual version, without all the fuss and frills and with more filling food than what's served at low tea.

> **Cuppa Wisdom**
>
> Tea to the English is really a picnic indoors.
> —Alice Walker

High, or afternoon, tea (served between 3 P.M. and 5 P.M.) was introduced as a partial solution to the problem of too much time between meals. Between morning breakfast and dinner (typically served at 8 P.M.) there's no substantial meal, and people are often hungry during the day or early evening and prone to snacking. At high tea, more-filling foods accompany the tea, perhaps replacing any later dinner. At low tea, a delicious spread of toasts, cucumber or watercress sandwiches, scones, and other light foods are served.

No one type of tea must be served for afternoon tea; any will do. Whether it's high or low tea, the tea is served alongside slices of lemon, sugar, cream, and milk. Expensive, elegant linens, flatware, and dishware are used for teatime, too.

The English truly enjoy their tea, drinking between three and four cups a day, at work, at home, and in casual settings, not necessarily at a formal tea.

India: Sugar and Spice

Chai is the Hindi word for "tea" in India—any tea, not just one kind. This can be confusing to Americans because we have adopted the Hindi word *chai* to describe how tea is prepared in India and to represent spicy teas. For people in India, though, that actually describes what they drink most often, but various forms of black and green tea are sometimes drunk, too.

Chai is a black tea sweetened with sugar and spices, such as cardamon, cinnamon, and ginger. Optional flavorings might include mint leaves or other herbal elements. Chai is thought to have healing properties for ailments like a common cold, but even without this belief, tea would still be as common as coffee, juice, or water for people in India.

India's availability of brewed chai is endless, and although tea isn't India's national drink, it's certainly the favored beverage. Disposable clay cups of chai are sold in train stations and on trains. Along busy streets, stalls and kiosks sell chai, prepared very strong and with lots of milk and sugar. If you invite someone to your home and don't prepare fresh tea, you are considered a rude host.

Many Indian households brew chai on their stovetop, making a lot all at once and then consuming it over a day or two throughout the days. Ceremony is not a big part of drinking

Buzz Words

Chai (rhymes with *sky*) is the Hindi word for any tea served in India. That said, however, the most common tea in India is usually black and sweetened with sugar and spices, such as cardamon, cinnamon, and ginger.

Field Notes

If you ask for chai in India, don't expect the type of chai latte (black tea, spices, and steamed milk) you get at an American coffee shop. In Hindi, *chai* simply means "tea." You'll probably get a black tea sweetened with sugar and spices.

the chai; instead, it's rather informal and no different from the way any other beverage is drunk in the home.

Japan: Green and Serene

The Japanese regard tea ceremonies, or *chanoyu*, as a form of spirituality, much as a church service or yoga practice in the United States might be a special, personal time for someone to connect more deeply with him- or herself. Japanese cultural centers and museums in the United States often host traditional Japanese tea ceremonies to introduce Americans to the custom, which is difficult to explain in a textbook or short description. The ceremony is so difficult to do properly, in fact, that schools around Japan train people in this disciplined ritual.

A full tea ceremony is a light meal and lasts 4 hours, and includes traditional Japanese sweets made with red beans and rice cake. If there's no meal, it's just 1 hour. Usually the host invites no more than a few people to participate, and during this time no words are exchanged while everyone watches the host prepare the tea. The way the host cleans and prepares each item is done with grace and precision, and each step seemingly flows into the next. If the host is a woman, she wears a kimono, a silk robe with beautiful embroidery. Before beginning to prepare the tea, the host gazes briefly into the water ladle, called *hishaku*, to ensure that his or her mind is free of distractions.

> **Buzz Words**
>
> Chanoyu (cha no you) is what the Japanese call the place where they hold a traditional tea ceremony. Translated, it means "hot water for tea." *Ocyakai* (oh kuh kye) is what they call the ceremony.

Several utensils are used to perform a traditional Japanese tea ceremony:

- *Hishaku*, a water ladle
- *Mizusashi*, a cold-water container
- *Chawan*, a tea bowl
- *Chakin*, a wiping napkin
- *Chasen*, a bamboo whisk
- *Chashaku*, a tea scoop
- *Chaki*, a tea container
- *Kensui*, a waste-water container

The ceremony is ideally held in a clean, uncluttered room where only a large teapot is set in a sunken alcove in a bed of flat rocks and charcoal to symbolize connections with nature. Flowers are arranged carefully and as an art form and displayed in an alcove area along with a scroll or other form of artwork. In some regions of Japan, a very small, private house designed solely for hosting tea ceremonies are used, but in many cases it's a room in someone's home. When each guest enters into the space, he or she must bow and then crouch to show respect for the host.

Matcha, a powder form of green tea, is mixed with boiling water in a shallow bowl with the help of a *chasen*, or bamboo whisk, until a head of froth forms. The host will, after whisking, pick up the *chawan*, place it in her left palm like a tray, and turn it twice away from her using her right hand. It must be turned 90 degrees each time, so the front of the bowl faces away from the host. If a meal is served, it's a variety of sweets (such as pickled vegetables and rice cakes) along with miso soup, cooked white rice, and raw fish (plain or pickled). But even before the tea is served, guests are offered a tray of *kashi* (sweets). No sugar, milk, or lemon is served with the matcha tea.

During the ceremony, guests are either seated on *tatami* mats (square straw mats used as floor coverings) or sitting back on their heels. Each time someone sips from the bowl of tea, he or she then makes sure the front of the bowl is facing the host.

Most Japanese homes contain a *tetsubin*, a traditional teapot made of cast iron with a decorative design. It is also used to warm the water at a traditional Japanese tea ceremony. Originally used as a way to add heat and humidity to homes, the *tetsubin* was put to use for making tea after Buddhist monks first brought the fragrant leaves back from China.

Buzz Words

A traditional teapot in a Japanese home is called a **tetsubin** (*set-SU-bin*) and made of cast iron. Intricate designs are etched into the pot's exterior.

If you're in Japan, not necessarily at a tea ceremony but at a place where you are ordering tea, expect variety in the types of green tea offered. To the Japanese, *tea* simply means green tea, and rarely are black, white, or tisanes served. But there are many shades of green.

Malaysia: Foamy Tea with Bubbles

In Malaysia, as well as neighboring Thailand, people drink tea as the Chinese do, except they may elect to add milk, sugar, or lemon, a taste acquired from Western influence. When pouring tea in Malaysia, it's from a teapot with a very small opening, and the teapot is lifted higher and higher, which Malaysians call "stretching the tea." This brings foam and bubbles to the tea, providing a smoother taste.

Morocco: Mint Is Nice

In Morocco, where spices are plentiful, the tea is just as rich. Mint tea is served in glasses and on a silver tray, and poured by the male head of the household. Sociologists and cultural critics, as well as historians, have stated for centuries that the teapot has phallic meaning as well—quite appropriate if the man is pouring. He uses a teapot with a long spout, holding the teapot high above each cup as he pours. A head of froth foams on top of the tea after it has been poured into the cups because of the increased air pressure.

Russia: From the Mouth of the Samovar

Tea in Russia is often brewed in a *samovar*, a decorated urn that's been used in many Russian households since the 1730s. It first came into use because at one time it was difficult to import fragile ceramic cups and pots from China, and the Russians needed another means for brewing tea. Originally coal-fired, now electric samovars are available.

> **Buzz Words**
>
> A **samovar** is a large metal urn used to brew tea, and has been used in Russia since the 1730s.

The idea is to create a tea concentrate, keep it hot, and then dilute it. The top portion of the urn holds tea leaves, while below it a water heater keeps the water hot, sometimes for many hours. Brewed tea is poured from a faucet on one side.

Sri Lanka: Sweet Ceylons

Most of the teas grown in Sri Lanka are black and have a beautiful amber hue when brewed. The tea is typically served with sugar and a little milk and offered at breakfast, lunch, and in the afternoon. A thick, crunchy toast topped with a fruity jam might accompany tea in the morning, and for lunch, a side of hoppers (a variation of pancakes or crepes made of rice flour, coconut milk, sugar, salt, and yeast, and sometimes dressed up with curry and a spice sauce) is often served. The food served at an afternoon tea is fairly light and not as elaborate as a British low tea. Curds containing buffalo milk and bun cakes that are clotted and deep-fried pair nicely with a pot of tea.

Tibet: Tea as Sacred Offering

In Tibet, the locals drink tea almost every day. And because the time taken to drink tea is considered sacred and special, a lot of care is taken in the preparation.

A traditional tea ceremony in Tibet is called *tsampa*. Su Yu Ch'a is the special, oily tea a host makes for very important guests. Its origin traces back to when a Chinese princess from the Tang dynasty married into a Tibetan royal family, and her native tea was promptly adapted to suit the locals. To make this tea, a brick of green tea is ground, boiled in hot water for a few minutes, and after straining is combined with salt and goat's milk or yak butter. Tea is very strong and has a distinct flavor. While making the tea, each movement's noise is very important to the ceremony overall.

If you are a guest at *tsampa*, it is considered impolite to drink all the tea in your cup. Instead, drink only half and leave the rest unfinished. This tells the server you would like more. And if after a few cups, you don't want any more tea, simply pour the rest on the floor. This might seem odd to us—to create a mess—but it is tradition and a form of respect in Tibet.

> **Cuppa Wisdom**
>
> There are few hours in life more agreeable than the hour dedicated to the ceremony known as afternoon tea.
>
> —Henry James

Turkey: Strong and Plentiful

Turkish coffee has great strength, so it's not surprising the tea commonly brewed in Turkey does, too. Tea is brewed strong and black and then strained into petite curvy glasses. Tea is considered an everyday beverage, as available as any other drink, and not necessarily restricted to any time of day or particular event. If you enter a Turkish household, you might find a pot of tea with fresh leaves on the stovetop, ready to add hot water at a moment's notice to brew fresh tea.

Tea is such an important part of life in Turkey that it's said mothers will ensure their future daughter-in-laws can prepare the tea properly for not only her husband, but all other family members. This continually passing down to the next generation has helped keep signature teas within family trees for years.

Uruguay: A Communal Drink

Yerba maté comes from a tall evergreen tree that grows wild in Uruguay and is a beloved beverage for people in that country. Drinking the grassy-tasting herbal beverage is not just a custom in Uruguay, however; Argentina, Paraguay, and Brazil also have prepared and served the drink for many, many years.

Leaves that are dried, chopped, and ground into a mulchlike mixture are placed into the bottom of a gourd, combined with hot or cold water, and sipped with a metal straw called a *bombilla*. The gourd comes from a calabash plant, and the bottom half is hollowed out and cured, creating a beautiful communal cup. Drinking yerba maté is usually done in a small group of people who pass around the gourd and take turns drinking from it.

Lost Traditions? Or Compassion for the Past?

Many teenagers and young people in the countries where tea has a deep, rich tradition may not have ever participated in a formal tea ceremony. That's not to say tea is completely absent from those cultures. Tokyo, Shanghai, and Mumbai all have teahouses, and they're not too difficult to find.

Many of China's traditional teahouses closed down during the 1920s and 1930s (when political leaders called tea drinking an "unproductive leisure activity"), but café-style places to have tea still exist; the same is true in Japan. Young people aren't often acquainted with traditional tea ceremonies, although they may witness them at weddings or other celebrations for family members.

What has really captured the interest of Asian teenagers today, though, are drinks like *bubble tea* (a Taiwanese drink invented in the 1980s) and anything else frozen, blended, or sweetened.

Buzz Words

Bubble tea is a chilled, blended drink of many flavors (ranging from papaya to green tea to mango) with pearls of tapioca on the bottom of the drink. These "bubbles" can be sucked up with a straw.

And although the Japanese as a whole rarely consume any teas that aren't green, a slow switch to black tea with hot milk is occurring. It's not replacing the green-tea custom, but it is enhancing the variety of teas sold in stores and offered on menus. This is still a pretty new trend, happening just in the past 15 years and prompted in part by Western-style tea rooms and coffee shops opening in the country, providing a different tea-drinking experience.

Establishing Your Own Tea Traditions

If you're set in your own tradition, in which you drink tea at the same time every night or morning, for weeks straight, and going so far as to select the same type of tea, we'd call that a ritual. Even though you may not be dragging out a *tatami* mat or getting married, we still consider it tradition. Personal traditions, although they may not be derived from ethnic culture, are still ritualistic in nature.

If you're a tea lover, you've probably come to rely on a certain time of day or even occasion (when friends come over, or to offer comfort and support to a sad or frustrated family member) to pull out the tea stash, brew some hot water, and settle in for a cup or two. Being mindful of tea's place in our culture, as well as for others worldwide, is the best way to appreciate tea.

The Least You Need to Know

◆ The British have two tea traditions, high tea and low tea. High tea is casual; low tea is more formal.

◆ Done properly, the Japanese tea ceremony is complex. A number of schools and instructors offer guidance and training on just how to do it correctly. But it is also a sacred part of family culture.

◆ Personal tea traditions are the little rituals or habits we develop around taking tea. They are both comforting and important.

Part 5

Coffee and Tea's Holistic Side

In Part 5, we take a look at a couple of hot topics related to the bigger pictures of coffee and tea. First, we explore relevant social and environmental causes, like fair trade–certified coffees and teas. Here you learn what the requirements are for some of the most common endorsements and what they mean for both consumers and producers. Then, we review some of the current science on the health effects of coffee and tea. Finally, we debunk some common myths and misunderstandings along the way, as well as take a look at some interesting health facts.

Chapter 21

The Humane Side of Coffee and Tea

In This Chapter

- Decode coffee and tea certifications
- Discover the history of the fair trade movement
- Relationship coffees and teas: what are they?
- Examples of environmental stewardship

There's an unselfish, altruistic side to coffee and tea that benefits the pocketbooks and lifestyles of tea and coffee farm workers, providing them with a healthier and better-paying job. You've probably noticed the labels, seals, and logos printed or stuck on certain coffee bags or tea tins/boxes. Pretty designs, catchy logos, sure, but what do they all mean? After all, you can't judge anything by its cover or packaging. You have to know the inside scoop when making your purchase.

Our goal with this chapter is to explain various certifications for coffee beans and tea leaves. You might find it interesting to realize how much you vote by how you spend your dollars.

Understanding the Labels

What should you look for when you're buying coffee and tea? And what do the labels mean, anyway? *Fair trade, certified organic, shade grown, bird friendly,* and *Rainforest Alliance–certified* are the labels available for coffee at the time of this writing. There is some crossover for tea; *fair trade* and *certified organic* are labels tea products are eligible to receive. *Biodynamic* is a farming term that comes with a certification, and both teas and coffees can apply for it.

> **Cuppa Wisdom**
>
> Where, after all, do universal human rights begin? In small places, close to home ... the factory, farm or office where he works ... unless those rights have meaning there, they have little meaning anywhere.
>
> —Eleanor Roosevelt

Before getting into the specifics of these terms, though, it's important to understand the reasons they were created, because they concern both social and environmental problems that were in desperate need of being resolved. Some of the problems have been eliminated due to positive change, but others remain, although they are constantly being studied for ways to improve.

Fair Trade: Ensuring a Living Wage

Historically, farmers at coffee plantations have been marginalized by the complicated commercial process of selling and purchasing coffee. They are forced to rely on swindlers, middlemen, and opportunists (called "coyotes" in Central America), whose sole role is to rip off the farmers and keep most of the export profits for themselves. And because the farmers were mainly in remote rural areas, poor, and without access to credit, transportation, or even information about fair market price, they accepted these coyotes' offers.

And so the problem continued. Coffee farmers weren't paid enough for their coffee and didn't receive access to quality health care, schools, and housing. According to data from the World Bank, 400,000 temporary and 200,000 permanent coffee workers lost their jobs in Central America in 2002 due to sinking coffee prices. Consequently, and not just in Central America, both the low prices and the presence of coyotes created a high level of job turnover, with workers forced to leave behind their family, friends, and hometowns for jobs in larger, metropolitan areas, simply because the pay was higher and the benefits more substantial. While this is certainly not the case for every plantation, it is quite common at many and serves as the reason why Fair Trade Certification standards were established.

TransFair USA, the official granter of Fair Trade Certification for products sold in the United States, is a third-party nonprofit certifier for not just coffee and tea, but also cocoa, rice, fruit, and sugar. The organization works with farmers in 60 countries, including Asia, Africa, and Latin America. With the arrival of the Fair Trade Certification, the situation for farmers is improving. The goal is to help small-scale farmers and their families in rural, impoverished areas earn a better income, help them hold onto their land, enroll kids in school, and invest in the quality of the beans they grow and sell.

> **Cuppa Wisdom**
>
> Trade justice for the developing world and for this generation is a truly significant way for the developed countries to show commitment to bringing about an end to global poverty.
>
> —Nelson Mandela

At the time of this writing, the minimum a coffee producer received for Fair Trade Certified™ coffee was $1.26 a pound ($1.41 if certified organic). In contrast, on the New York Board of Trade, the price for coffee fluctuates between 50¢ and 90¢. Since 1999, imports of fair trade coffee have grown an average of 70 percent per year.

Increasing the number of fair trade coffee cooperatives has helped tremendously, giving individual farmers a collective voice. There are currently 300 in 23 countries; on average, between 25 to 30 cooperatives are added each year. This provides an endless number of opportunities for the workers to express concerns about division of responsibilities and the environment in which they work.

When you purchase coffee that has a fair trade label, you know the cooperative, which is run democratically and transparently, has received the fair trade price. (By *transparent*, we mean there's not only a paper trail but a vision for how the additional monies will be spent.) Worker buy-in has been reached, and ongoing discussions about how to improve the farm are held—with all workers participating. There's no top tier of leadership like what's found at large farms—or even corporations—where only a small few make decisions on behalf of everyone else.

The fair trade standards, first implemented in 1999, also require that producer organizations practice sustainable farming methods and protect natural resources (like waterways and forests), prohibit harmful agrochemicals, and move toward organic production as soon as it's economically feasible.

> **Field Notes**
>
> Some examples of proper spending at a democratically run cooperative include a boost in the growers' income, an investment in social programs (like education or health services), or business infrastructure.

Fair Trade 'Round the World

TransFair USA's standards for fair trade coffee only apply for the United States; 19 organizations worldwide have different fair trade labeling strategies. Each country has established its own set of guidelines, with Europe being far ahead of the United States in its sophistication with not only a system but also consumer buy-in and support.

The first fair trade coffee label was issued in 1988 under the guidance of a nonprofit organization in the Netherlands called Max Havelaar. This was a quality seal for coffee in the Dutch market, which soon after expanded to Denmark. Aside from certifying coffee roasters, the foundation had made steps to certify companies offering chocolate, bananas, and tea, too. Max Havelaar still certifies these products.

Aside from TransFair USA, other organizations have similar missions. For example, in 1992, Fairtrade Labelling Organizations (FLO) International formed in Bonn, Germany, founded by European Fair Trade Association and Transfair Germany. Originally under the name Transfair International, FLO now certifies fair trade coffee, tea, cocoa, sugar, honey, rice, fresh fruit, juices, and sports balls. FLO is the worldwide certifying organization for more than 800,000 producers and their dependents in more than 40 countries. TransFair USA belongs to FLO as a national initiative member.

Fair Trade Federation, located in Washington, D.C., works to promote fair trade and educate consumers about issues that affect small producers. The organization, which works with wholesalers, retailers, and producers of not just coffee and tea but also handicrafts, teas, and clothing, is aggressive about researching and formally endorsing positions on pending global trade legislation. Fair Trade Federation's key mission is ensuring that farmers and artisans are not economically disadvantaged and can earn a living wage. But the difference between Fair Trade Federation and TransFair USA is that only TransFair USA is a certifier. However, Fair Trade Federation's logo (found on many products) means the company supports a commitment to fair trade products.

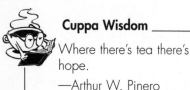

Cuppa Wisdom

Where there's tea there's hope.

—Arthur W. Pinero

Two other Fair Trade organizations are the International Federation of Alternative Trade (more than 70 organizations from 30 nations and based in the United Kingdom) and the European Fair Trade Association (EFTA). EFTA has 11 fair trade organizations (in 9 European countries) as members, and collectively these countries import from more than 550 producer groups in 44 countries. The goal of EFTA is to encourage cooperation between its members and also push for adoption of fair trade in Europe's commercial trading.

Tea Growers Earn a Better Life, Too

Fair trade isn't limited to coffee, but it wasn't until 2001 that teas sold in the United States earned TransFair USA's fair trade label. As with coffee, fair trade tea ensures that the workers who pick the tea leaves, process them, and package them earn a livable wage, have safe work conditions, and can provide health care, education, and housing for their families. But unlike coffee, fair trade teas are grown on estates and not cooperatives. Better socio-economic conditions are still sought after, but under a different model. The resulting income from fair trade sales is made not to the cooperative (as there isn't one) but to a worker-led joint body, which is comprised of a group of workers that accurately reflects the cultural and gender makeup of workers at the estate.

According to TransFair USA, the following conditions must be met on an estate before Fair Trade Certification is granted:

- Absence of forced or child labor

- Wages that meet or exceed legally established minimums

- Freedom to organize democratically

- Adherence to national and international labor protections

- Safe working conditions, including protection from exposure to harmful agrichemicals

Field Notes

Tea estates in Japan are not eligible for Fair Trade Certification, because as a fully developed nation, the workers are already paid a good wage.

Currently 70 fair trade–certified tea estates spread across 9 countries in Asia and Africa, home to some of the poorest tea-producing communities.

As with most other agricultural crops, estate tea fields are often layered with chemicals and artificial fertilizers designed to help the plants grow at a faster rate. Historically on tea farms, the workers themselves were responsible for such tasks as weeding and gathering cow manure (for use as a fertilizer). But beginning in the 1970s, chemical usage in agriculture peaked, as did technological advances, and workers were exposed to the chemicals more often than before.

According to TransFair USA, nearly 100 percent of fair trade teas sold in the United States also organic. A core focus of making conditions "fair" for the workers—according to the Fair Trade Certification—is ridding the fields of harmful chemicals, which the

Field Notes

Market research has also shown that consumers who buy fair trade teas are also interested in certified-organic teas, so tea companies have made a concerted effort to link the two labels into one product.

workers would be exposed to for many hours and days on end if there were no intervention. Creating sustainable farming conditions, essentially promoting better environmental health for the land and the people, is a win-win situation.

If a tea producer has Fair Trade Certification, a social premium (1 euro/kilo) is passed back to the estate to allow such things as hiring school teachers, building maternal-health clinics, and bringing electricity to villages. This premium is paid to a joint body (a democratically organized group of people) that ensures the money is spent accordingly.

Skepticism About Fair Trade

With all the positive change and movement for certifications, however, some voices are speaking out against the fair trade coffee and tea models. Opponents have expressed disappointment that the certification does not formally ensure that the coffee beans and tea leaves are of highest quality, because the main qualifiers are fair treatment of workers and not necessarily criteria for good coffee. (Fair trade proponents respond that if a coffee cooperative is concerned with getting a higher price for their beans, they will ensure a gourmet product, and likely advocate handcrafted beans and leaves.)

Skeptics also question TransFair USA's motives, because even as a third-party certifier, in some ways it runs like a company concerned with its bottom line. TransFair receives money from the cooperatives and estates it certifies, as well as the licensees in the United States that sell products featuring the TransFair USA label. A few critics have gone so far as to make the claim that even with a floor price for fair trade coffee and tea, the receiving party must then divide it among the farmers, which means they're not getting the full fair trade price all to themselves, but instead receive only a portion of it. One might assume it would all even out in the end, with each farmer earning the same amount of pay for the same amount of work, but there's the possibility for leadership at the cooperative that may create an imbalance of payment. (It's worth noting, however, that each cooperative is supposed to be democratically run per FLO's annual inspections, which check for this.)

Even so, fair trade coffee continues to be the highest-selling fair trade product in the United States. It accounts for $100 million of the $19 billion U.S. coffee market; and in 2002, 10.6 million pounds of coffee were sold—an increase of 54 percent from the previous year. Sales of fair trade tea have spiked, and the predictions from industry analysts as well as U.S. tea companies all point toward continued profits, in part because of an increased focus on the health benefits of tea.

Relationship Coffees and Teas

Relationship coffee or tea refers to an instance when the coffee roaster or tea buyer has a relationship with the farm or estate where the product is grown. There's a direct connection between the coffee roasters/tea buyers and the producers, meaning that no middleman, exporter, or importer is in charge of those transactions (although they may be involved for logistical reasons). It takes a few years for this type of relationship to develop, but when it does, the two parties can work together and exchange feedback about processing techniques, how the brewed beverage tastes in the country where it's exported, and any other matters that would better the product.

A coffee roaster or tea buyer often takes trips to meet with the producers and see where the coffee or tea is grown, often cupping the coffee or tea on-site. It's a strong grower-buyer relationship, unlike what occurs with most commercial beverage imports, where the coffee roaster may have never seen the farm where the coffee is grown. And in many cases, the coffee roaster doesn't even know what farm the coffee beans are from, as he or she purchases from an importer.

> **Buzz Words**
>
> **Relationship coffee or tea** is when tea and coffee buyers have a direct line to the grower. Sometimes the relationship evolves to the point that a tea buyer has exclusive availability to a portion of the crop.

There's no official label or seal for relationship coffee or tea, although you may read about it in a company's marketing materials. Many coffee roaster and tea company employees are engaging in the opportunity to get up close and personal with a coffee farm's operations, become intimate with its staff and processes, and work as partners to produce quality coffee.

These relationships address other topics as well, such as how to sustain the land and whether or not money can be donated for improvements to the farm's infrastructure. Technology upgrades may be necessary but not affordable to the farm owner. That's when a roaster or tea purveyor with deeper pockets might be able to assist with the cost, because the long-term result will be better, more consistent processing, which usually equates to a higher-quality drink. Plus, roasters or tea purveyors can offer an exclusive product they had a hand in shaping for its cup character.

Greener Beans and Leaves

While social responsibility by tea and coffee companies is indeed praised, so are the "green" habits that can be formed simply by educating ourselves. For example, you may already be doing your part by reusing a commuter mug when you visit your neighborhood coffeehouse. But the need to preserve the environment goes deeper than your personal sipping mug, of course.

Organic Coffee and Tea

The market for certified-organic coffee and tea has practically exploded, piggybacking on an organic-buying trend that includes organic-cotton T-shirts, pasta sauce, and chocolate, among other items. People are using their purchasing power by not supporting products that have been exposed to chemicals during production. Herbicides, pesticides, manufactured chemicals, and commercial fertilizers are commonly applied to coffee crops and tea fields using traditional farming methods. In fact, coffee is the third most-sprayed crop in the world, after cotton and tobacco.

The certification of organic coffee and tea is very important, not just for those of us who order a hot cup, but also because it protects the workers from long-term chemical exposure, which could (but not always) lead to disease and adverse health effects.

Standards authored by the National Organic Program, a division of the U.S. Department of Agriculture, certify products in the United States as organic. These rules were implemented in October 2002, replacing a system that independent third parties had handled before.

According to the Organic Trade Association, sales of organic food and beverages totaled $10.4 billion in 2003, and the industry has been experiencing a 17 to 20 percent annual growth rate. To put this into perspective, industry experts expect that by 2009, organic foods and beverages will be a $32 billion industry.

Organic coffee has become so popular that Starbucks, as well as the country's top specialty coffee roasters, carries at least a handful of organic coffees. It's not uncommon at all to have an organic coffee as one of the daily brews at a café these days, whereas 10 years ago it would have been considered unusual.

Field Notes

Today many coffeehouses offer a discount on tea, coffee, and espresso drinks if you bring in your own thermos. It's a great incentive on days when you have to dash off to work or someplace else and don't have time to enjoy your beverage in the café anyhow.

The same is true for organic teas. Very few specialty tea companies do not include a handful of organic teas in their product line, because they've seen that there's strong support for organic teas in the United States. With more and more awareness of the danger of exposure to chemicals in our own country, as consumers we're willing to support poorer nations battling that same health problem because it helps us and the growers.

Hot Water

Some food and beverage manufacturers label their product "all-natural" or "natural." Don't confuse this with "organic," which has to undergo a certification process to earn the label.

Shade-Grown Coffee

In some parts of the world, bird species and areas of forested lands are in danger when development occurs, whether for a luxury hotel resort or for a shopping center. Sometimes canopy trees are cut down so coffee plants can grow under full and constant sunlight.

Having a coffee farm under direct sun harms the environment, though. Chemical pesticides and fertilizers are sprayed, exposing the harmful chemicals to workers who handle the plants and also passing on those toxins to the consumer. When the trees disappear, birds are forced to find another nesting spot, which might result in their death due to the stress associated with this change or an inability to adapt to the new environment.

Certifying coffee as *bird friendly* (also referred to as "shade grown") is a big step toward making sure bird populations aren't wiped out and the climates' forests remain. The two go hand in hand, so it's a win-win situation.

Coffee farms need one of two types of shade to be certified bird friendly: rustic or planted. Under the philosophy of the more trees that are present, the more diverse the bird population will become, the guidelines require a minimum canopy cover of 40 percent and that there be no trimming of plants or vines present on the trees. Farm inspectors also ensure that the forest converted to coffee production does not have any legal protected status.

Buzz Words

Bird-friendly coffee, certified by the Smithsonian Migratory Bird Center of the National Zoo, requires one of two types of shade, either rustic or planted, thus providing a safe place for birds to nest.

Naturally occurring forest trees—along with crop trees like avocado, citrus, and hardwood—are commonly used to shade coffee plants. In Latin America (from Mexico south to Peru), a forestlike habitat provides a home for birds, as well as a haven for shade-grown coffee. With the bird-friendly certification on certain plantations the coffee is also guaranteed to be organic. This means no chemical pesticides whatsoever have come in contact with the land, as stipulated by the certification.

You may have seen the bird-friendly label on coffees—birds flying through a canopy of leaves and above coffee beans. When you buy coffee featuring this label, you're also directly assisting the bird populations. Companies that sell bird-friendly coffees contribute 25¢ per pound to support the Smithsonian Migratory Bird center's research and conservation programs.

Cuppa Wisdom

And of course there must be something wrong, in wanting to silence any song.

—Robert Frost

In the United States, many outlets, from independent coffeehouses and restaurants to retail café chains, sell roasted bird-friendly coffees. Not just for bird watchers, but also for the environmentally conscious consumer, bird-friendly coffees are, excuse the pun, soaring. People like that they can make a difference in strengthening bird populations worldwide just by the type of coffee they purchase.

Rainforest Alliance Certification

You may also have seen a label on coffee beans for Rainforest Alliance–certified coffee. This label ensures the coffee was grown on farms where forests are protected from development; rivers, soils, and wildlife conserved; and workers are treated with respect (much like the Fair Trade Certified™ standards demand). Treating workers kindly and fairly, per this certification, means they're paid a decent wage and given access to medical care and education.

The standards were created in 2001, and the certification program is managed by Sustainable Agriculture Network (a coalition of leading conservation groups in Belize, Brazil, Columbia, Costa Rica, Ecuador, El Salvador, Guatemala, Honduras, Mexico, and the United States). This network certifies farms in Mexico, Central America, Brazil, Columbia, and Peru. Aside from the United States, countries such as Canada, Europe, and Japan also use this certification.

How much acceptance have the standards received? A couple examples: in 2005, Caribou Coffee, at the time the nation's second-largest coffee retailer, made a commitment to—by 2008—have half of its green coffee be Rainforest Alliance certified. Why buy this type of coffee? Caribou Coffee stated it knew it would be receiving quality product and also made the employees "feel great about where they work."

In 2004, Millstone Coffee, owned by Procter and Gamble, announced that it would carry two Rainforest Alliance certified coffees under its Signature Collection label. It's expected that soon other coffee companies will follow.

Biodynamic Beans and Leaves

A relatively new eco-friendly type of coffee beans and tea leaves are grown using *biodynamic* methods, which basically takes organic farming to the next level. Biodynamic farming, which avoids chemicals and pushes for a deeper reliance on nature-based farming relying on the lunar calendar, is based on principles developed by Austrian philosopher Rudolf Steiner. Biodynamic farming of fruits and vegetables has become more popular among farming circles, although it's certainly far from mainstream.

The first biodynamically grown coffee was introduced in the United States in 1993, grown on a farm in Chiapas, Mexico (and roasted and sold by Café Altura). Since then, other examples have hit the marketplace, including a freeze-dried biodynamic coffee from Papua New Guinea and Kona coffee. Kodaikanal, India, is home to a cluster of biodynamic coffee plantations, and it's likely that in future years, there will be more examples of biodynamic coffee farming.

The first biodynamic tea estate in the world is Makaibari in the Darjeeling region of India. Established in 1859, it sits high in the Himalayas, protected on all sides by virgin forests and diverse wildlife. In the early 1990s, this estate earned its biodynamic certification. Others are in areas of Sri Lanka, as well as Darjeeling, where in 1999 a total of 10 had been certified as organic, and many were on their way to becoming biodynamic.

> **Buzz Words**
>
> **Biodynamic** farming abides by the principle that no chemicals should be used in production; rather, the process should rely on forces in nature (sun, moon, planets, and stars) to reach the plants. A lunar calendar is used as a guide.

> **Field Notes**
>
> Rudolf Steiner also created Waldorf Education, which seeks to provide a creative and artistic approach to learning. Montessori schools throughout the United States continue to teach the methodology of Waldorf. Before his death in 1925, Steiner left a lasting impression on both educators and farmers.

Ambootia Tea, an estate in Darjeeling, is a great example of farming working in cohesion with local residents, of which there are about 4,500. The estate consists of 2,500 acres, but only about 750 are used for cultivating tea, with the remaining preserved for uncultivated flora and fauna. A small office assists other farmers in the area with earning organic certification.

There's currently only one certification available for biodynamic farming: Demeter, by the Demeter Association, a third-party independent certifier. To be certified, a farm must be entirely converted to biodynamic, all organic manures are treated with compost, and there must be a GMO-free (genetically modified organisms) declaration for all at risk from genetic modification. There many other standards—too many to list here; these are just three examples of what biodynamic farmers must adhere to when applying for biodynamic certification.

Help for the Coffee Industry

In most coffee-producing regions of the world, the standard of living is very, very low, and despite all the hours and hard work required to grow and process coffee, many families still aren't living a good life. Topics such as health care for workers, good schools, and fair wages for coffee farmers are continually being addressed by professionals within the coffee industry—and not just in the standards described earlier.

Cuppa Wisdom

What is necessary to keep providing good care to nature has completely fallen into ignorance during the materialism era.

Field Notes

In poverty-stricken nations like Honduras, Costa Rica, and Nicaragua, trees from the rainforest are burned to dry beans using wood or diesel fire. As a solution, a handful of U.S.-based research teams and energy companies have installed stand-alone off-grid solar dryers in these areas.

Coffee Kids

One of the most established and well-known non-profit organizations supporting a renewal for the coffee industry is Coffee Kids. With a slogan of "the richest coffee comes from the poorest people," Coffee Kids provides funds to improve the locals' nutrition, education, and health care and create opportunities for alternative incomes to coffee.

When Disaster Strikes

Natural disasters have spurred goodwill on behalf of the coffee industry. The 9.0-magnitude quake that rocked the Indonesian island of Sumatra in December 2004, subsequently triggering a tsunami, killing 283,000 people and displacing 1,126,000, was labeled as one of the worst natural disasters in a century. Ten countries were affected, many of them coffee-producing regions, such as Sumatra. Coffee roasters in the United States—including Starbucks Coffee Company, Peet's Coffee & Tea, and Caribou Coffee—responded immediately. (There were of course many donations from other companies as well.) Several U.S. specialty coffee roasters also promoted a "tsunami relief" Sumatra coffee. A certain percentage of what consumers paid for a pound of coffee was donated to relief efforts.

In October 2005, heavy rains from Hurricane Stan had a disastrous effect on coffee crops in Guatemala and Chiapas, Mexico. A special coffee-relief fund was created to funnel money to coffee growers in those regions; in response, specialty-coffee roasters gave in earnest.

> **Cuppa Wisdom**
>
> Destroying rainforest for economic gain is like burning a Renaissance painting to cook a meal.
>
> —Edward O. Wilson

Help for Rwanda

Rwanda is a relatively new producer of specialty coffee, but it's quickly gaining recognition among coffee connoisseurs. This new export has allowed some economic recovery from the country's genocide in 1994, in which 800,000 people were massacred in just 3 months.

Natives aside, the country's Bwindi and mountain gorilla species are not at their optimum population quite yet either. The gorillas, labeled as endangered species because only about 703 remain in the world according to the African Wildlife Foundation, live in the rainforests and wild areas of Uganda, Rwanda, and the Democratic Republic of Congo. The good news is that the mountain gorilla population is rising, and despite an infant mortality rate of 30 percent, the number of gorillas is up 17 percent.

> **Field Notes**
>
> Dr. Dian Fossey, a gorilla researcher in Zaire and Rwanda since the 1960s, founded the not-for-profit Dian Fossey Gorilla Fund International group in 1971. During the previous year, she fostered the first friendly gorilla connection with humans when Peanut, an adult male gorilla, reached out and touched her hand. In 1985, she was murdered in her cabin in Rwanda, where she was working to save gorillas' lives from poachers.

Public campaigns against gorilla poaching (illegal hunting for gorilla meat) in Rwanda and Uganda have heightened security controls and also helped raise support for organizations like the Dian Fossey Gorilla Fund, which help monitor and protect the gorillas. The staff at the Karisoke Research Center study the local gorilla population and also introduce them to tourists. (More than 70 percent of the gorillas have been visited by tourists.)

Café Femenino

Café Femenino is a vehicle for women in Peru who have suffered abuse, are poor, and lack adequate job skills to enter the coffee industry. By participating in the program, they are taught how to harvest coffee crops. So far, 464 female coffee farmers have been involved with Café Femenino.

In Peru, because of local customs and traditions, it's extremely rare for women to sell the coffee or make any decisions on how the financial profits will be used. Café Femenino is working to change that mind-set and bring it into modern times.

Government Support for Coffee with a Conscience

The U.S. government (through U.S. Agency for International Development, or USAID) has committed to helping coffee workers in nations lacking in dollars to adequately fund their industry. From 2002 to 2004, USAID invested more than $57 million in coffee projects in 18 countries in Latin America, East Africa, and Asia. For example, by establishing a sustainable coffee system run by small, family farms rather than conglomerates, it provides income; employment; and social, environmental, and consumer benefits. At the same time, USAID supports small- and medium-size producers to properly process and grade their coffee to ensure the beans are of good quality. And with new market information systems, local producers are armed with critical tips on how to price coffee.

Here's just a snapshot of what USAID is doing to support some of the world's poorest coffee-growing regions:

◆ In Colombia, a 5-year, $9.8-million program assists 25 producer groups with bettering their coffee, providing de-pulping machines, drying patios, coffee-tree nursery supplies, plant material, or fertilizers. Producers are trained in coffee cupping and grading techniques, too, so they can self-assess their coffee periodically.

◆ A gift of 10 coffee-washing stations to Rwanda produced 1,000 tons of coffee in 2004. Farmers in that country are also taught to compete in markets for gourmet, specialty, and fair trade coffee.

◆ Southern Highlands farmers in Tanzania have taken advantage of new direct export procedures introduced by the Tanzania Coffee Board.

◆ USAID has funded programs for a cupping facility in Honduras and Nicaragua and provided access to credit services in Nicaragua.

There are many, many examples of this type of outreach to coffee producers—too many to detail here. Not only do they ensure our supply of high-quality specialty coffee, but they also ensure better lives for its producers. It's important to learn about these and other socially reactive measures the industry is taking to preserve coffee workers' rights and better their lifestyles. As consumers, you have power to buy into these initiatives, and it won't cost more than a cup of coffee.

The Least You Need to Know

◆ Fair Trade Certified™ coffee and tea ensures that co-ops are organized democratically and are paid a minimum price per pound of coffee (more if certified organic).

◆ In 1999, the Fair Trade Certification label became available for coffees sold in the United States. It was introduced for teas in 2001.

◆ Coffee is the third most-heavily sprayed crop in the world; coffees certified organic do not use chemical sprays or fertilizers.

◆ USAID is an international development project through the U.S. government that through financial and educational programs has significantly helped specialty coffee growers in developing nations such as Honduras, Nicaragua, Columbia, Tanzania, and Rwanda.

Chapter 22

To Your Health

In This Chapter

- ◆ Learn about caffeine's healthful and not-so-healthful impacts
- ◆ Untangle coffee's confusing health-related report card
- ◆ Discover how tea's healthful reputation holds up

Coffee and tea, the world's favorite brewed beverages, have long histories infused with claims and questions regarding their health effects and benefits. Tea has traditionally enjoyed a wide following explicitly for its claimed health benefits. From losing weight to kicking a hangover and from preventing cancer to managing menopause, drinking tea has been heralded as a very healthy habit. Coffee's reputation for healthfulness, on the other hand, has been much more mixed. It's been both blessed and cursed (literally) for its effects, and even modern medical science has accused it of causing certain health problems only to subsequently praise coffee for preventing the same condition.

The challenge for consumers is sorting out the hearsay and less-credible claims to get a realistic picture of the health effects associated with coffee and tea. That's where this chapter comes into play. We won't be dispensing any medical advice, but we do discuss and attempt to clarify the current health-related findings for coffee, tea, and their common chemical constituent, caffeine.

Caffeine: A Healthy Kick Start?

If you're like most Americans, caffeine—the chemical responsible for much of the "boost" gained from coffee and tea—needs little formal introduction. In fact, studies report that roughly 80 to 90 percent of people in the United States consume caffeine daily—in some amount and from one or more of various dietary sources. Many even feel they can't start their day until after they've secured a cup of their favorite caffeinated beverage. Caffeine is so much a part of daily life that many people forget it's a psychoactive drug and, therefore, sometimes fail to give it the respect it deserves.

Getting the Juices Flowing

Caffeine goes to work stimulating the central nervous system shortly after you consume it and reaches its peak blood level in less than an hour. The physical makeup of caffeine is such that it fools the body into thinking it's adenosine, an important body chemical that slows down neural activity and plays a role in causing drowsiness. Caffeine shortstops the sleepiness caused by adenosine by taking its place at receptor sites. So instead of neuron activity decreasing and blood vessels dilating due to natural adenosine release, the opposite occurs, and this increased flurry of activity alerts the pituitary gland. The master gland mistakes this for an emergency situation and releases hormones to produce epinephrine (also known as adrenaline), triggering the classic fight-or-flight physiological response. To ready itself for action, the body does several things, including the following:

- Redirects blood flow away from the body's surface and stomach to critical muscles

- Increases heart rate, blood flow, and blood pressure

- Releases glucose (a simple sugar) into the bloodstream for energy

- Tightens muscles

- Opens airways

- Dilates pupils

In this heightened state of arousal, people feel more alert and energetic. And in addition to invoking these reactions, caffeine also inhibits certain enzyme actions, thereby extending and intensifying the effects of epinephrine.

A Little Goes a Long Way

Caffeine has a half-life of approximately 6 hours but varies depending on an individual's body chemistry and other factors, such as concurrent medications. This means that every 6 hours, the body is able to remove half of the caffeine in its system. So if, for example, you drink a couple cups of coffee in the morning—approximately 270 milligrams caffeine combined—your body won't have finished removing it by the time you go to bed.

Recent research indicates that some people naturally process caffeine more quickly than others. Roughly half of the population contains a gene that expedites the elimination cycle. Initial studies suggest that possession of this gene may also impact how caffeine affects the individual's health. Not surprisingly, those who have the gene for speedy elimination tend to have a lower association with at least some of caffeine's long-term health effects. Unfortunately, there's currently little way to know if you carry the gene, as no commercial test exists and it cannot be easily predicted by your perceived reactions to caffeine.

Field Notes

As you consume caffeine throughout the day, your blood levels of caffeine can stack up pretty quickly.

Although genetics generally determine how fast a person metabolizes caffeine, its elimination can be altered significantly in certain circumstances. Most notably, oral contraceptives, pregnancy, and smoking affect how long caffeine stays in the body. Smoking cuts that time approximately in half, but oral contraceptives can double the duration. In pregnant and nursing mothers, caffeine's half-life can be extended for up to 18 hours. The same caffeine-consumption habits impact individuals quite differently.

Hot Water

Doctors currently tend to advise pregnant and nursing women to significantly reduce or eliminate their caffeine intake. Caffeine has been associated with fetal complications, including miscarriage. Because caffeine's half-life is extended to up to 18 hours, caffeine levels can easily pile up for these women. What's more, fetuses are even less able to process caffeine, with half-lives of up to 100 hours, depending on the stage of development. Talk to your doctor about your caffeine consumption if you are pregnant or breast-feeding.

Too Much of a Good Thing?

When the body has too much caffeine, it becomes overstimulated. Signs of this include agitation, restlessness, sleeplessness, concentration issues, headaches, and nausea. Symptoms vary by person but are generally dose-dependent, becoming more and more unpleasant as the amount ingested increases. In these cases, the best thing you can do is to not take in any more caffeine and allow your body the time it needs to clear the drug. To prevent repeating the experience, it's important to wait not only until you feel better before having more caffeine but until your body's had a chance to fully eliminate it.

Caffeinated Habits

Like with many stimulants, the body gets used to caffeine after a relatively short period of continued use. As a result, routine users develop both a tolerance to caffeine as well as a physical dependence on it, which accounts for the differences in effects for occasional and routine caffeine consumers. Occasional users (who aren't tolerant of caffeine) tend to see a marked elevation in their blood pressure readings, whereas regular caffeine users do not.

Here, too, genetics appears to play a role, especially in regard to how strong the dependence becomes, but there are several things you can count on if you're dependent on caffeine. One of the most commonly lodged complaints from caffeine-addicted people who don't get their usual supply is splitting headaches. Without its usual caffeine, the body's blood pressure drops significantly, causing excess blood to build up in the head. Another common issue is dogging sleepiness and trouble with mental focus and acuity as the body adjusts to not only less mental activity but to the increased reception of adenosine, which promotes sleepiness.

Hot Water

Caffeine has made its way into so many products, foods, and beverages, it's not hard to unwittingly consume too much. Prevent yourself from overdoing it by paying attention to your caffeine intake. Some of the most common caffeine hosts (other than coffee and tea) include over-the-counter medicine, soda, energy drinks, sport waters, chocolate, and many coffee-flavored frozen desserts.

Caffeine addiction and withdrawal symptoms vary by person, with some people reporting little or no trouble while others have considerable problems. In addition to fatigue and headaches, common issues for caffeine-deprived addicts include difficulty working or concentrating, anxiety, depressed mood, irritability, and even flulike symptoms (nausea, vomiting, and miscellaneous aches and pains). Severity of these symptoms tends to be directly related to the level of physiological addiction, so cutting back may reduce or eliminate some symptoms.

If you're addicted and want to lower or break your dependence on caffeine, the easiest route to do this is by slowly curbing your caffeine intake. Even small amounts of caffeine can alleviate some withdrawal symptoms, so self-weaning is usually successful at breaking the cycle. Not everyone's chemistry is alike, though, so if you experience troubles with caffeine dependence, consult a doctor.

> **Field Notes**
>
> Withdrawal symptoms subside after several days without caffeine or may be erased by ingesting more caffeinated food or drink, which most caffeine addicts quickly and happily do.

When Context Counts

It's easy to assume caffeine will affect you pretty much the same regardless of the food or beverage it's in, but it's often not that simple. Because drinking a cup of tea typically brings the body about half or less of the caffeine content found in a cup of coffee, it's easy to write off any differences as merely a matter of caffeine quantity.

Dedicated caffeine fans, however, can tell you that there is indeed a difference in caffeine's effects depending on the form it takes. Even when the caffeine doses are equivalent, brewed coffee tends to provide more raw energy and alertness, whereas tea is known for providing a gentler, less-dramatic boost. This difference even accounts for some people's preference of coffee over tea and vice versa.

The primary cause for the differences, though, might have more to do with the other compounds present in coffee and tea and how they work together. Coffee and tea have many compounds in common, although certainly not all, and tea contains, among others, two compounds in particular that coffee does not: theobromine and theophylline. In the same class of chemicals as caffeine, these two augment caffeine's effects by acting in a complementary manner but on different body systems. As many advocates for eating whole foods point out, chemicals, like caffeine, don't always have the same effects when isolated from their natural sources.

An example of this can be seen in the 2005 results from a very large longitudinal study that followed female nurses for up to 12 years. In analyzing the data regarding blood pressure, researchers noted that soda consumption, whether diet or regular, was associated with increased blood pressure, whereas drinking coffee was not. And while researchers haven't yet fully explained the cause for the differences, it's clear that making comparisons between caffeinated beverages can be tricky, even when caffeine is assumed to be the primary agent of effects.

How Much Caffeine Is in Your Cup?

It's fairly easy to find out how much caffeine is in manufactured products like sodas because the manufacturer adds it in specific quantities. However, natural products such as coffee and tea present more of a challenge. The specific cultivar, growing conditions, processing methods, and roasting (for coffee) influence how much caffeine is in the final product. Moreover, how it's brewed determines how much caffeine actually makes it in the cup. Factors that may influence this include brewing temperature, particle size, duration, and specific method. And because so many factors play a role, the amount of caffeine in your cup may vary quite a bit.

The following table gives you a good idea of how much caffeine your favorite beverages might contain. A good rule of thumb for teas is that the more oxidized the tea, the more the caffeine the brewed tea has. This is especially handy to keep in mind for oolongs because the degree of oxidation differs from oolong to oolong, with some being more akin to blacks and others to greens. Pu-erh teas added another element—age—that makes generalizing the nature of pu-erhs' caffeine content difficult; however, their caffeination level tends to fall between that of greens and oolongs.

Approximate Caffeine Content of Common Beverages

Beverage	Caffeine
Brewed coffee	135 mg/8 oz.
Decaffeinated coffee	5 mg/8 oz.
Espresso	125 mg/1.25 oz. (single shot)
White tea	15 mg/8 oz.
Green tea	20 mg/8 oz.
Oolong tea	45 mg/8 oz.
Black tea	70 mg/8 oz.
Decaffeinated tea	2 mg/8 oz.
Soda	35 to 55 mg/12 oz.

The Misunderstood Brew?

If you're a long-term coffee drinker and keep an eye on the news, you've probably seen and read some contradictory information regarding coffee and your health. A number of possible reasons exist for this, and a couple are worth bearing in mind.

Although not universally the case, early studies of coffee's health impact often suffered from confounding variables that weren't taken into consideration. For example, coffee drinkers who were also smokers were included in studies with nonsmokers. We now know that the interaction between nicotine and caffeine produces unique effects that can't necessarily be lumped together. In other cases, small preliminary research was followed up with more rigorous and larger studies.

Another and related issue that adds confusion is the complexity of coffee. Brewed coffee is loaded with hundreds and hundreds of compounds, so trying to isolate which ones are responsible for specific actions is tricky at best. And because these chemicals may behave somewhat differently alone than they do when combined with others, it can take years of research to ferret out even seemingly simple associations.

Coffee is subtly complex in other ways, too, which makes it difficult to easily assess and to generalize findings. The realm of coffee includes robusta beans as well as arabica and various methods of processing, roasting, and brewing, but medical research doesn't always clearly separate those factors. And while some experiments have explored this, more are needed. For example, our taste buds tell us that coffee brewed with water that's too cool (the case for most homemade drip-brewed coffee) fails to extract some of the delicious compounds from the bean; however, we don't know if what we're missing out on may help or hurt our health.

Brewing Methods

One area that has received some attention is that of the effect brewing methods have on coffee's relative healthfulness. Most of the focus has been on filtered coffee compared with unfiltered, as in the case of espresso and the French press.

It appears that cafestol and kahweol, fatlike compounds in coffee beans that have been shown to increase LDL (bad) cholesterol, make

Hot Water

Researchers aren't generally sounding an alarm at this point, but if you're concerned about your coffee consumption and cholesterol counts, talk to your doctor.

their way into the cup in unfiltered brew or those filtered only by metal screens. Interestingly, these compounds do not reach the cup in coffee filtered with paper. However, American researchers seem to be content that the majority of Americans drink drip-brewed coffee, which seems to have stalled more detailed analysis.

Decaffeinated Coffee: Healthy Choice?

Like its caffeinated cousin, decaffeinated coffee's reputation has taken a bit of a roller-coaster ride over the years. Most notably, decaf coffee has been the focus of fewer studies, which provides researchers less data to use as context for evaluating and comparing findings.

There are also several ways to decaffeinate coffee, and the impacts of each, as they relate to health matters, aren't fully understood at this time. There are two primary issues to explore here: the inherent safety of the methods and the impact the processes have on other compounds in coffee. Many experts feel that the modern solvents do not cause residual health issues because their presence is very low after the decaffeination process and they all evaporate at temperatures achieved during the roasting process. It's less clear, though, if important chemicals other than caffeine are lost or damaged in the process. Tasters can discern differences between the methods, so it's possible that changes in the chemical makeup important to the health effects of the coffee have occurred.

Even given the shortcomings in our current understanding of decaf's impact on health, several studies have shown decaffeinated coffee to have similar effects as regular coffee. In most instances, one can predict how congruent the effects of decaf and regular coffee will be by understanding the role caffeine plays in the scenario. Generally speaking, the less important caffeine is to the effect in question, the greater the likelihood that decaffeinated and regular coffee will cause similar effects.

Perhaps one of the most notable differences that current medical research shows between regular and decaf coffee is how they affect LDL cholesterol. Coffee filtered through paper, which accounts for most coffee drank in the United States, is not thought to raise blood levels of the so-called "bad cholesterol," but research indicates decaffeinated coffee might. A 2005 study found significant increases in blood concentrations of precursors for LDL cholesterol in participants who drank between 3 and 6 cups of decaffeinated coffee daily over the course of several months. Larger, longer studies will have to be conducted to verify, but until then, talk with a doctor if you are concerned about increased cholesterol as a result of your decaffeinated coffee consumption.

Antioxidants to the Rescue

In recent years, *antioxidants* found in foods and beverages have been the focus of a lot of healthful-eating discussions. They prevent cell damage due to oxidation by intercepting free radicals and have been credited with reducing the impact of such diseases as macular degeneration. Antioxidants occur naturally in many fruits and vegetables, including coffee.

In fact, coffee is a dense source of the beneficial compounds and packs more antioxidant punch than most fruits and vegetables, wines, juices, and tea. The University of Scranton released research findings in 2005 spotlighting the importance of coffee as a source of antioxidants in the American diet. The report pointed out that not only is coffee one of the richest dietary sources of antioxidants available, it also accounts for the lion's share of the antioxidants Americans consume.

As you might imagine, the exact amount of antioxidants in coffee depends on a variety of factors like varietal, processing, roasting, and brewing. It's thought that more lightly roasted beans maintain greater antioxidant levels than do darker roasts.

It's likely to be some time before scientists discern conclusively just to what degree antioxidants are responsible for the positive health effects attributed to coffee, but they are currently believed to play an integral role.

Buzz Words

Found naturally in many plants, fruits, and vegetables, **antioxidants** protect the body from damage caused by free radicals, which are produced as the body metabolizes food. Coffee is one of the highest dietary sources of antioxidants, and tea has high concentrations as well.

Field Notes

Milk proteins were once thought to interfere with the antioxidants in coffee, but current research has found that adding milk to coffee does no harm in this regard. So if you like a little milk with your brew, you don't have to worry about counteracting the body-protecting compounds in it.

Coffee: Cause or Cure?

While an exhaustive review of current medical science is beyond the scope of this book, let's take a quick look at some of the hot areas related to coffee and health.

Parkinson's Disease

There has been concern about a link between coffee and Parkinson's disease, and current research indicates a relationship does indeed exist—for the better. For example, a 30-year study tracked about 8,000 Japanese American men in Hawaii to assess the relationship between drinking coffee and Parkinson's. It uncovered significant decreases in the risk of developing the disease for those who regularly drank coffee, with those drinking more having less likelihood of developing the disease. Caffeine, it appears, may play a significant role in this association, as noncoffee caffeine consumption showed similar relationships.

Type 2 Diabetes

Several studies have cleared coffee as a risk factor for type 2 diabetes (formerly called adult-onset diabetes and accounting for 90 to 95 percent of diabetes cases). In fact, it appears regular coffee drinkers have a significantly lower incidence of the disease, with higher consumption levels linked to lower diabetes incidences. While the cause of the relationship is not yet fully understood, coffee's high level of vitamins, minerals, and antioxidants are thought to be behind the effects.

Cardiovascular Disease

Coffee's effects on the heart and related systems has long been questioned and explored, but such studies have often yielded contradictory and confusing results. As mentioned briefly earlier, a recent study has shone light on why this may be: genetics. The study, released in early 2006, examined the relationship between nonfatal heart attacks and coffee consumption in more than 4,000 Hispanic Americans living in Costa Rica. When adjusted for confounding variables, researchers found that the risk was directly related to the presence of a gene that provides for slow metabolism of caffeine. Those having the "slow" gene—slightly more than half of the participants—who drank 2 to 3 cups daily were found to have a 36 percent greater risk of having a nonfatal heart attack. When daily consumption increased to 4 or more cups, the associated risk jumped 64 percent.

Regular coffee drinkers with the "fast" gene had a decreased risk of nonfatal heart attacks: 22 percent for 2 to 3 cups and 1 percent for 4 or more cups. Moreover, age appeared to play a role in risk level, with those younger than 50 with the "slow" gene having twice the risk of those just 10 years or more older.

While the study is undoubtedly provocative, it's important to note that this kind of gene-related research is a young science and it's likely that future research will enhance our understanding and ability to practically use these data. For example, we may one day have commercially available tests to better help us assess our individual health-related risks and to make informed decisions as consumers. In the meantime, moderation is likely the best course of action.

Other research on the cardiovascular effects of coffee has effectively cleared coffee of connections to long-term rises in blood pressure. A link to fatal arrhythmias (irregular heartbeats) has also failed to be supported by clinical studies.

Osteoporosis

Calcium has been found in the urine of coffee drinkers, so researchers have been concerned about a possible connection between coffee consumption and osteoporosis. And although it appears that coffee consumption is indeed related to lower bone-mass densities, the effect has been shown to be offset by milk consumption. Women who regularly drank milk during most of their adult lives did not have lower bone densities associated with routine coffee drinking.

It's not clear whether vitamin supplements have the same impact, so be sure to consult with a physician if you are concerned about developing the disease.

Coffee and Cancer

With the prevalence of cancer today, researchers have been diligently trying to assess for risk factors and connections, and coffee is no exception. Although once thought to cause fibrocystic breast conditions and possibly breast cancer, experts haven't found support for the hypothesis. In fact, a study published in early 2006 found evidence of a protective effect from coffee drinking in premenopausal women (but not post-menopausal women). The link to pancreatic cancer also has been found to be weak to negligible.

But there may be more good news regarding cancer for coffee drinkers than simply a lack of bad news. Reports have found possible reduced risks of colon, liver, and bladder cancers associated with frequent coffee consumption. In one large study of Japanese men, liver cancer incidence dropped by about half in coffee drinkers. Another study found lower bladder cancer rates for heavy smokers who were also coffee drinkers. Some research tends to credit caffeine for these protective effects, while others point to coffee's high antioxidant concentration. And although coffee isn't being heralded as an anti-cancer wonder, evidence thus far does lift the dark cloud that once hung over it.

Tea: Healthful Wonder?

Tea has been heralded as a healthful beverage pretty much since its discovery, and over the years, it's been regarded as helpful in the prevention and treatment of scores of aliments. For the tea consumer interested in understanding the health effects of tea, a dilemma has emerged somewhat different from that for coffee drinkers.

Generally speaking, findings tend to be more congruent—at least in a big-picture manner—for tea than they are for coffee. Where coffee has suffered from a struggle to determine first if it's harmful or not to our bodies, it's fairly well accepted that tea is reasonably safe. What's more, considerable consensus exists that tea is indeed beneficial in a number of ways. The much-debated questions are more along the lines of investigating just how helpful it is, in what cases, and why.

One of the primary challenges for consumers exploring tea's health effects is discerning what results may be most realistic from those that, while interesting, aren't as applicable. And in so doing, a subsequent complication is quickly uncovered: the sheer volume of research conducted about tea is simply staggering. And although this makes it about as challenging to ferret out applicable information, at least we can rest at ease, as the confusion surrounds tea's degree of impact and not so much its very nature.

> **Cuppa Wisdom**
>
> Eat not to dullness; drink not to elevation.
>
> —Benjamin Franklin

Tea Packs a Healthy Punch

Research has found that tea is loaded with beneficial compounds. Like coffee, tea is a dense dietary source for vitamins, minerals, and body-protecting antioxidants. But unlike coffee, tea is rich in the bioactive chemicals known as catechins (pronounced *CAT-a-kins*) and polyphenols. While these compounds have antioxidant properties, it's currently thought that much of their benefit might be attributable to how they help cells manage common processes, such as cell growth and death. This may account for much of tea's impacts on the spread of cancers, which are characterized by uncontrolled spreading of abnormal cells.

The Power of Processing

As we discussed in Chapter 16, tea leaves and buds can be processed in a number of ways to produce the wide variety of teas available today. A key difference among the types of tea—white, green, oolong, black, and pu-erh—is the degree to which the enzymes in tea are allowed to oxidize, which affects the chemical makeup of the resulting tea. Therefore, while all teas contain roughly the same compounds, the relative amounts of the various subtypes of catechins and polyphenols are a bit different among classifications of tea.

Is it enough to alter the health effects between, say, green teas and black teas? Quite possibly—at least to a degree—but it's not well understood at this point. Studies have not conclusively found that one type is significantly more or less beneficial in practice. So while there are some differences, it's probably best not to worry too much about the "best" tea and simply to enjoy your favorite teas.

Tea and Medical Conditions

An analysis of all the current tea-related research would fill volumes, but let's take a look at a few important areas of study and what's been found.

Cavities

Tea is a natural source of fluoride, and tea brewed with unfluoridated water has about the same concentrations as treated water does. It's only natural then to wonder if tea might help thwart tooth decay and cavities. Laboratory studies generally support that it may; however, few studies have thoroughly explored whether regular tea use does indeed prevent cavities.

A large study on teens in the United Kingdom (where water is generally not treated with fluoride) found, though, that even those tea drinkers who sweetened their daily brew developed significantly fewer cavities.

Weight Loss

Dieters in Asian cultures have been using tea to help stay slim for decades. And although some animal studies have been supportive of the claim, controlled studies on people haven't conclusively shown a direct link. It's still possible, however, and because dieters are often reminded to keep their fluid intake up, there's no reason to toss tea from your diet plans at this point.

Cancer

Tea's possible anti-cancer properties have, understandably, stirred a lot of interest and subsequent study. So far, the most promising results have come from the lab, either as animal or in vitro (test tube) studies. These models have shown promising preventative actions against several types of cancer, including skin, breast, bladder, pancreas, colon, prostate, lung, mouth, esophagus, and stomach.

Expect to see future studies conducted on human subjects to try to more conclusively discern what the real-world anti-cancer effects of tea consumption are.

Heart Attacks

Several studies have found a link between regular tea consumption and a reduction in risk for heart attacks and other cardiovascular health concerns. And while it's too soon to call the evidence conclusive, a 2001 review of 10 studies found that, on average, a 3-cups-a-day tea habit was associated with an 11 percent decrease in risk for heart attacks. A large Dutch study also linked tea drinking—this time roughly 1.5 cups daily—to a marked drop in heart attack rates. The challenge in interpreting results from many of the studies done so far is that they have been relatively small and/or narrow in scope.

Interestingly, research in this area has been largely focused on black tea, and while it's likely that green tea confers similar benefits, it's not yet known for certain. Future research is needed both to clarify if all teas provide some benefit as well as to conclusively establish how much tea may be necessary to see protective effects.

The Hidden Health Risk

It's no secret that Americans are big-cup people and that much of the commercially available coffee drinks (and to a lesser degree, tea beverages) are served in large portions. While that may not hold a lot of inherent harm, it does potentially magnify some concerns.

Perhaps the most obvious issue is that of excessive caffeine intake. Someone drinking three 12-ounce coffees a day—a small to medium cup size at most cafés—is taking in more than 600 milligrams caffeine, which is far more than most medical practitioners recommend.

But for the countless Americans who enjoy added milk, flavorings, and sweeteners in their coffee and tea, the large portions elicit a different health concern: high empty-calorie intake. A glance at the nutritional data provided by large café chains like Caribou Coffee and Starbucks reveals menus full of drinks high in calories. Many large (20 ounces at most cafés) specialty espresso-based drinks, such as mochas and fla-vored lattes, are packed with several hundred calories. Consuming even a couple such drinks a day can quickly pack on the pounds and expand waistlines.

> **Field Notes**
>
> Skipping the whipped cream on top of your lattes or other espresso-based drinks can save you more than 100 calories. If you drink them regularly, exercis-ing the no-whip option even occa-sionally will help you avoid racking up unwanted calories.

And in addition to a lot of calories, these drinks often contain sodium, fat, and choles-terol levels sufficient to cause concern for regular consumers. Obviously, these added factors can open the door to many health-related issues in themselves, so it's impor-tant to watch your consumption of these large confections.

All Things in Moderation

Although it'll probably be some time before medical evidence is conclusive enough about the health effects of coffee and tea to recommend optimum consumption levels, all is certainly not lost. Most current medical research does support the conventional wisdom of moderation. Maintaining a healthy lifestyle, including a balanced diet and regular exercise, is still your best bet for warding off medical issues. Too much of any-thing can upset the balance, so embrace and enjoy your favorite coffees and teas—both for their health benefits and great taste—but simply do so in moderation.

The Least You Need to Know

- ◆ Caffeine provides increased energy by shortstopping the natural slowing of nerve-cell activity and by subsequently triggering a fight-or-flight type response in the body.

- ◆ Physiological dependence on caffeine occurs when the body gets used to regular caffeine intake and can lead to withdrawal symptoms, like headaches and fatigue, if the habit is not maintained.

- ◆ Genetics may play a role in determining how coffee affects your health.

◆ Coffee is by far the most significant source of antioxidants in Americans' diets due both to coffee's inherent density of the protective compounds and to the amount Americans consume.

◆ Coffee brewed using metal filters (espresso and French press, among others) appears to contain fatlike compounds that can increase LDL cholesterol levels; paper-filtered coffee does not.

◆ Tea, too, is rich in antioxidants, but also contains catechins, which may account for many of tea's health benefits.

Appendix  A

Glossary

antioxidants   Compounds that protect the body by neutralizing free radicals.

arabica   Refers to the *Coffea arabica* plant, which is used almost exclusively in specialty coffee for its fine flavor.

barista   The coffeehouse equivalent to a bartender.

biodynamic farming   Farming principles according to the lunar cycle.

bird-friendly coffee   Coffee carrying this label has been grown under a canopy of trees and is not disruptive to migratory bird patterns. The Smithsonian Migratory Bird Center issues the criteria for this seal.

blind cupping   When tasters don't know the coffees or teas being sampled.

bombilla   A metal straw with a strainer used to drink yerba maté.

bubble tea   A chilled beverage popular in Taiwan and now available in the United States that's blended tea and fruits with tapioca pearls on the bottom.

café au lait   A drink made of roughly equal portions steamed milk and strong coffee (cold-brewed works very well).

café noir   "Black coffee" in French. It's served with a carafe of water, a dark-chocolate square, and a sugar cube.

Camellia sinensis The plant from which all tea leaves come. The leaves are picked from the top of the plant.

cappuccino An espresso-based drink made with velvety, frothed milk.

cha dao The art of preparing and drinking tea in Chinese.

cha to The name for China's traditional tea ceremony.

chaff The papery skin released from coffee during roasting.

chai The Indian word for "tea." Commonly refers to black tea mixed with spices and milk.

chanoyu The traditional Japanese tea ceremony.

***choryesang* (or *daeryesang*)** The name for a traditional Korean wedding table setting.

cooperative A democratically organized group of farmers who work together to produce and market their coffee or tea.

crema The golden-red froth on top of a well-prepared espresso.

CTC Stands for the *cut-tear-curl* process of producing black teas.

cupping The systematic method of evaluating coffees and teas.

demitasse A small, 3-ounce cup used to serve espresso.

dispersion screen On an espresso machine, this is the screen directly above where the portafilter locks that helps ensure even wetting of the grounds.

doser A chamber on a coffee grinder with a horizontally positioned paddle wheel that's operated by the flick of a lever. Each pull of the lever causes the fins of the internal wheel to push out approximately the desired dose of grounds.

dry processing Refers to the coffee-processing method of preparing coffee where the fruit is dried with the fruit still intact. Also known as *unwashed* or *natural method*.

espresso Coffee made using pressurized water, typically $1\frac{1}{4}$ ounces to make 1 shot. The word is also used to refer to any coffee or coffee blend that's used to prepare espresso.

fair trade A system of trade that promotes the democratic organization of farmers as well as "fair" compensation for their produce.

finish Refers to the flavor notes at the end of a taste as well as to how long those notes linger.

first crack   The first wave of popping noises roasting coffee makes. It also marks the light end of the roasting spectrum.

flavor profile   The entirety of the taste of a beverage, including finish, body, and other flavor characteristics.

fluid-bed roasters   Coffee-roasting machines that utilize forced hot air to keep the coffee in perpetual motion while roasting.

flush   When new leaves and buds sprout on the tea plant.

group or grouphead   The area that the portafilter locks into on an espresso machine.

gustation   A culinary term for "taste."

guywan   A covered cup used as an infuser at most Chinese tea ceremonies.

karkady   A tea made with hibiscus flowers and sugar with hot water, popular in Egypt.

latte   An espresso-based drink combined with steamed milk.

lungo   A long shot of espresso that's between $1\frac{1}{2}$ and 2 ounces.

maracuya   A round fruit about the size of a lime and has a tart taste. It's also called a passionfruit.

microfoam   The fine, tightly packed bubbles that make up well-frothed milk.

olfaction   A culinary term for "smell."

orange pekoe   A grade of orthodox black tea.

orthodox teas   Traditionally processed loose-leaf teas.

parchment (also called pergamino)   The thin, papery covering on coffee beans that's removed before export.

peaberry   A small round coffee bean that occurs as a result of only one bean forming in the coffee fruit rather than the normal two.

portafilter   The handled device on an espresso machine that holds the metal filter basket and grounds.

pouchong tea   A very lightly oxidized oolong with characteristic qualities of green tea.

"pulling a shot"   Preparing espresso, so named because early espresso machines required the barista to pull down on a lever.

relationship coffee or tea   Coffee or tea grown under conditions where the coffee or tea buyer has a relationship with the farm that grows the coffee or tea.

ristretto   A short or restricted shot of espresso, usually ¾ to 1 ounce of fluid.

roasting   A process wherein raw, green coffee beans are heated to an internal bean temperature of 375° to 450°F, which prepares them for traditional brewing.

robusta   A type of coffee plant that's hardier and a heavier producer than *Caffe arabica* but without as fine a flavor. Sometimes used in espresso blends to promote crema production but otherwise not used in specialty coffees.

rosetta   A leaf design poured onto the top of a latte or cappuccino.

samovar   An urn used for brewing tea, typically with some sort of heat source. Commonly found in Russian culture and used to brew tea.

second crack   The second wave of popping during the coffee-roasting process. It also marks the gateway to a dark roast.

simpling   Experimenting with one herb at a time to make a tisane.

shower screen   *See* dispersion screen.

single-estate coffees   Coffees grown on one farm.

stretching   The initial phase of steaming milk that involves incorporating air into the milk, thus increasing its volume.

tamper   A heavy tool used to pack espresso grounds.

tetsubin   A cast-iron teapot used in Japanese culture and traditional tea ceremonies.

third place   Someplace, often a coffeehouse, many people go after work and or when they're not home.

tisanes (or herbal teas)   "Teas" considered nonteas because, instead of tea leaves, they consist of the flowers, leaves, and roots of other plants. Tisanes are typically caffeine-free.

tsampa   The traditional tea ceremony in Tibet.

wet processing   The method of processing coffee in which the beans are first separated from the fruit, fermented for a period of time to loosen the remaining fruit, and finally washed free of the remaining sticky fruit/pulp.

whole-leaf teas   Teas that contain leaves that are large and intact. To earn this grade, the tea leaves cannot be broken.

yerba maté   A grassy drink native to South America that's made from the yerba maté plant.

Yixing   Type of clay teapot native to the Jiangsu region of China.

Appendix B

Pairing Food with Coffee and Tea

Coffee and tea are often enjoyed with common foods such as muffins or sandwiches. But they don't have to be just drinks to wash down a bite of food. Good pairings of coffee and tea with food are synergistic. Every sip of tea or coffee encourages you to have another bite of that food, and each bite calls for another sip.

The Power of Pairing

A bold cup of coffee or pu-erh tea served with, say, a light, delicate dessert can create the equivalent of a bad, stormy relationship marked with bitterness and contempt—you may not like either of them. Call it a case of irreconcilable differences or a "blind date" gone bad. A proper pairing, however, unlocks a taste sensation that could not have been achieved otherwise.

You want to be mindful of pairings not only to achieve blissful matches but to stay away from unpleasant accidental couplings. For example, a light salad dressed with a vinaigrette, served with a delicate Panama Bouquet coffee or Silver Needle tea will likely neutralize the beverage's unique characteristics. (Vinegar easily pollutes a pairing.)

Drumming up effective pairings can present daunting challenges when you're attempting to zero in on the best ways to awaken your palate. While individual preferences vary, there are important principles in guiding the tongue to that wonderful experience a well-composed pairing presents.

Take Time to Smell the Roses

Aromas are critical when eating and drinking. The tongue only recognizes five different tastes (sweet, sour, salt, bitter, and umami—a savory taste akin to soy sauce) while the nose can discern thousands of smells.

When smelling coffee or tea and a single food item, many olfactory stimuli are introduced. Some aromas can mask, or neutralize, the others. But in some cases, sensory synergy occurs, a whole new sensory experience.

Pairing with a Purpose

Just as when you're blending teas and coffees, you have to first understand the flavors of the taste components and what you want to accent. It's the same way with a food and beverage pairing. There are several pairing considerations each for coffee/tea and food, including acidity, spice, aftertaste, and intensity. Choosing what aspects of the coffee or food you desire to focus on will help guide you to a pleasing pairing.

Harmony is the goal of culinary pairing. The obvious way to achieve this is to pair like flavors, but the opposite can be equally as effective. Chocolate and citrus may not be the same, but they mesh well on the tongue.

Even tricky pairings, like when you're trying to match a drink with spicy foods, can be navigated when you focus on complimenting specific elements of the food. For example, a heavy-bodied Java coffee that doesn't have any tongue-tingling acidity can not only stand up to spicy food but can actually augment it with a rich mouthfeel. One option for pairing tea with a spicy cuisine is to capitalize on the strong, smoky character of Lapsang Souchong tea. Not only can the tea hold up to the powerful spice notes, but the tea character creates a third dimension to the food's taste.

> **Hot Water**
>
> Watch out for flavors that pollute and cloud the desired tastes. Creamy, fatty foods coat one's palate and can make it difficult to detect other flavors.

Put Your Best Cup Forward

The most memorable pairings are those that involve high-quality specialty coffees and teas that are properly brewed and fresh. Let's say you're trying to pair coffee or tea for their fruity nuances. If the beverage is not well prepared, the fruit notes won't shine through.

Consider what would happen if you took a delicate white tea and brewed it as if it were black tea. The subtle and unique character you're looking for in white tea would be clipped by the poor brewing.

Tasty Trial and Error

The importance of trying, tasting, and testing a wide variety of combinations can hardly be overstated. How unfortunate, then, for those 35 percent of people who have an inability to sense certain smells! The range of missed sensations tends to be very minor though, and although these missed sensations don't typically interrupt your overall perception of food or drink's taste, they can influence the finer details.

Add to this individual preference, and you can see why it's important to taste and sip on your own brews and create pairings based on your palate. The more you explore the rainbow of coffee and tea flavors available, the more educated your palate will be, making you a capable pairing artist.

Appendix

Coffee Resources

We hope that by now you're fired up about great coffee and interested in continuing to build your knowledge base and in getting the goods. With that in mind, we've gathered a list of roasters, green coffee sellers, and educational and informational resources. Rather than viewing this as an afterthought, we spent a lot of time at the cupping table slurping samples and feel confident recommending the businesses listed here. That said, there are thousands of coffee purveyors in the United States, and absence from this list does not indicate a lack of quality. We wholeheartedly encourage you to try all the coffees you can and hope this list will serve as a starting point.

Coffee Roasters/Retailers

Allegro Handcrafted Coffee
Thornton, CO
303-444-4844 or 1-800-277-1107
www.allegrocoffee.com

Ancora Coffee Roasters
Madison, WI
608-255-2900
www.ancora-coffee.com

Barefoot Coffee Roasters
Santa Clara, CA
408-248-4500
www.barefootcoffeeroasters.com

Batdorf and Bronson Coffee Roasters
Olympia, WA
360-754-5282 or 1-800-955-5282
www.batdorf.com

Caffe Trieste
San Francisco, CA
415-550-1107
www.caffetrieste.com

Caribou Coffee Company Inc.
Minneapolis, MN
763-592-2200
www.cariboucoffee.com

The Coffee Bean & Tea Leaf
Los Angeles, CA
1-800-TEA-LEAF (1-800-832-5323)
www.coffeebean.com

Counter Culture Coffee
Durham, NC
919-361-5282
www.counterculturecoffee.com

Diedrich Coffee
Irvine, CA
949-260-1600
www.diedrich.com

Distant Lands Coffee Roasters
Tyler, TX
1-888-262-5282
www.dlcoffee.com

Espresso Vivace Roasteria
Seattle, WA
206-860-5869
www.espressovivace.com

Equal Exchange
Canton, MA
781-830-0303
www.equalexchange.com

Gillies Coffee Company
Brooklyn, NY
718-499-7766 or 1-800-344-5526
www.gilliescoffee.com

Green Mountain Coffee Roasters
Waterbury, VT
1-888-879-4627
www.greenmountaincoffee.com

Illycaffè
New York, NY
1-877-ILLY-DIR (1-877-455-9347)
www.illyusa.com

Intelligentsia Coffee and Tea
Chicago, IL
1-888-945-9786
www.intelligentsiacoffee.com

J. Martinez & Company
Atlanta, GA
404-231-5465 or 1-800-642-5282
www.martinezfinecoffees.com

Kauai Coffee Company
Kalaheo, HI
808-335-3440
www.kauaicoffee.com

Novo Coffee
Denver, CO
303-295-7678
www.novocoffee.com

Peet's Coffee and Tea
Berkeley, CA
1-800-999-2132
www.peets.com

The Roasterie
Kansas City, MO
816-931-4000
www.theroasterie.com

Sacred Grounds Organic Coffee Roasters
Arcata, CA
1-800-425-2532
www.sacredgroundscoffee.com

Starbucks Coffee Company
Seattle, WA
1-800-235-2883
www.starbucks.com

Stumptown Coffee Roasters
Portland, OR
503-230-7797
www.stumptowncoffee.com

Taylor Maid Farms
Sebastopol, CA
707-824-9110 or 1-888-688-7272
www.taylormaidfarms.com

Terroir Select Coffees
Acton, MA
1-866-444-5282
www.terroircoffee.com

Thanksgiving Coffee Company
Fort Bragg, CA
1-800-462-1999
www.thanksgivingcoffee.com

Tully's Coffee
Seattle, WA
206-233-2070
www.tullys.com

Zoka Coffee
Seattle, WA
206-217-5519
www.zokacoffee.com

Green Coffee

Sweet Maria's
Oakland, CA
1-888-876-5917
www.sweetmarias.com

Coffee-Related Organizations

Barista Guild of America
Long Beach, CA
www.baristaguildofamerica.org

Coffee Kids
Santa Fe, NM
505-820-1443 or 1-800-334-9099
www.coffeekids.org

International Coffee Organization
London, England
+44 (0)20 7580 8591
www.ico.org

Specialty Coffee Association of America
Long Beach, CA
562-624-4100
www.scaa.org

TransFair USA
Oakland, CA
510-663-5260
www.transfairusa.org

Coffee Publications and Websites

Barista Magazine
Portland, OR
971-221-9307
www.baristamagazine.com

Brewspot.com

Coffeegeek.com

Coffeereview.com

Fresh Cup Magazine
Portland, OR
503-236-2587
www.freshcup.com

Roast Magazine
Portland, OR
503-282-2399
www.roastmagazine.com

Tea and Coffee Trade Journal
New York, NY
212-391-2060
www.teaandcoffee.net

Coffee Education

American Barista and Coffee School
Portland, OR
1-800-655-3955
www.coffeeschool.org

Coffee School
Glebe, Australia
(02) 9552 6771
www.coffeeschool.com.au

Copenhagen Coffee Academy
Copenhagen, Denmark
+45 35 25 59 20
www.copenhagencoffeeacademy.com

London School of Coffee
+44(0) 208 439 7981
www.londonschoolofcoffee.com

Seattle Barista Academy
1-800-927-3286
www.seattlebaristaacademy.com

Tea Resources

We recognize that it's still difficult to find a selection of good-quality specialty teas throughout all regions of the United States, so we spent a lot of time slurping samples when compiling this appendix. While not exhaustive, this resource list is a good place to start when shopping for leaves for your next cup.

Your local tea room may carry any one of these brands (perhaps under a private label), so you may be able to find these teas closer to you than you might think.

If you're thirsting for more knowledge about tea, we've also included contact information for magazines and organizations that cover the tea industry.

Tea Retailers

Adagio Teas
Clifton, NJ
www.adagio.com

Celestial Seasonings
Boulder, CO
1-800-434-4246
www.hain-celestial.com

Choice Organic Teas
Seattle, WA
206-525-0051
www.choiceorganicteas.com

Equal Exchange
Canton, MA
781-830-0303
www.equalexchange.com

Gypsy Tea
Ojai, CA
805-646-1996
www.gypsytea.com

Guayakí
San Luis Obispo, CA
1-888-GUAYAKI (1-888-482-9254)
www.guayaki.com

Janam Tea Shop
Jersey City, NJ
201-432-4TEA (201-432-4832)
www.janamtea.com

Mighty Leaf
San Rafael, CA
415-491-2650
www.mightyleaf.com

Numi
Oakland, CA
510-534-6864
www.numitea.com

Oregon Chai
Portland, OR
1-888-874-2424
www.oregonchai.com

Pixie Maté
Boulder, CO
303-444-MATE (303-444-6283)
www.pixiemate.com

R.C. Bigelow Inc.
Fairfield, CT
1-888-BIGELOW (1-888-244-3569
www.bigelowtea.com

The Republic of Tea
Novato, CA
1-800-298-4832
www.republicoftea.com

Rishi Tea
Milwaukee, WI
414-747-4001
www.rishi-tea.com

SerendipiTea
New York, NY
1-888-TEA-LIFE (1-888-832-5433)
www.serendipitea.com

Shizuoka Green Tea
Walnut, CA
909-598-9255
www.shizuokatea.com

Tazo
Seattle, WA
503-736-9005 or 1-800-299-9445
www.tazo.com

TeaSource
St. Paul, MN
877-768-7233
www.teasource.com

Tea Publications and Websites

Brewspot.com

Fresh Cup Magazine
Portland, OR
503-236-2587
www.freshcup.com

Tea A Magazine
Scotland, CT
1-888-456-8651
www.teamag.com

Tea and Coffee Trade Journal
New York, NY
212-391-2060
www.teaandcoffee.net

Tea-Related Organizations

Specialty Tea Institute
212-986-0250
www.teausa.org

TransFair USA
Oakland, CA
510-663-5260
www.transfairusa.org

Tea Education

The Tea School
1-888-456-8651
www.teamag.com/school.htm

Index

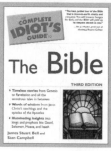

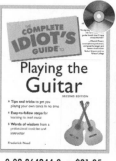